JEAN E. BROWN ◆ **ELAINE C. STEPHENS**
SAGINAW VALLEY STATE UNIVERSITY

Teaching Young Adult Literature
Sharing the Connection

Wadsworth Publishing Company
IⓉP™ An International Thomson Publishing Company

Belmont ◆ Albany ◆ Bo nn ◆ Boston ◆ Cincinnati ◆ Detroit ◆ London ◆ Madrid ◆ Melbourne
Mexico City ◆ New York ◆ Paris ◆ San Francisco ◆ Singapore ◆ Tokyo ◆ Toronto ◆ Washington

Education Editor: Sabra Horne

Editorial Assistants: Janet Hansen, Kate Peltier

Production Editor: Carol Carreon Lombardi

Designer: Andrew H. Ogus

Print Buyer: Diana Spence

Permissions Editor: Jeanne Bosschart

Copy Editor: Karie Youngdahl

Cover Illustrator: Jude Maceren

Technical Illustrator: Random Arts

Compositor: TBH Typecast, Inc.

Printer: Malloy Lithographing, Inc.

Wadsworth Publishing Company
10 Davis Drive
Belmont, California 94002, USA

International Thomson Publishing Europe
Berkshire House 168-173
High Holborn
London, WC1V 7AA, England

Thomas Nelson Australia
102 Dodds Street
South Melbourne 3205
Victoria, Australia

Nelson Canada
1120 Birchmount Road
Scarborough, Ontario
Canada M1K 5G4

International Thomson Editores
Campos Eliseos 385, Piso 7
Col. Polanco
11560 México D.F. México

International Thomson Publishing GmbH
Königswinterer Strasse 418
53227 Bonn, Germany

International Thomson Publishing Asia
221 Henderson Road
#05-10 Henderson Building
Singapore 0315

International Thomson Publishing Japan
Hirakawacho Kyowa Building, 3F
2-2-1 Hirakawacho
Chiyoda-ku, Tokyo 102, Japan

Library of Congress Cataloging-in-Publication Data
Brown, Jean E.,
    Teaching young adult literature : sharing the connection / Jean E. Brown, Elaine C. Stephens.
      p.   cm.
    Includes bibliographical references and index.
    ISBN 0-534-19938-0
    1. Young adult literature, American—Study and teaching.   2. Young adults—United States—
Books and reading.   I. Stephens, Elaine C.,.   II. Title.
PS490.B76   1995
809'.89283—dc20

94-35183

To my sister, Mary, who enriched my childhood by helping
to open the world of books for me; and to Jeremy, who enriched
my life for the last seventeen years.

    JEB

To my mother, Opal Walkington Amon, who is forever
young at heart.

    ECS

Contents

CHAPTER 4

Connecting Young Adult Literature with Students   65

PART TWO

Establishing the Connections with Young Adult Literature   89

CHAPTER 5

The Literature Curriculum: Involving the Young Adult Reader   91

CHAPTER 6

Implementing the Young Adult Reader Involvement Model   112

CHAPTER 7

Teacher Roles for Teaching Young Adult Literature   134

CHAPTER 8

Selecting Young Adult Literature   158

PART THREE

Making the Young Adult Literature Classroom Work 189

CHAPTER 9

Creating an Environment for Young Adult Literature 191

CHAPTER 10

Improving Classroom Interaction: Making Discussion and Writing Real 210

CHAPTER 11

More Strategies for Using Young Adult Literature   235

Preface

We have written *Teaching Young Adult Literature: Sharing the Connection* for anyone who wants to learn about and teach young adult literature. It can be used in either undergraduate or graduate courses in young adult literature. It can also be a valuable addition to an English methods course, because the pedagogy developed and explored in this text can be generalized and applied to literature study in general.

This book is designed to be a companion to reading and responding to young adult literature. By providing a combination of theory and practical ideas that can be implemented in any classroom, *Teaching Young Adult Literature* will complement the rich variety of books available to youthful readers. In most chapters, we discuss several books in detail and make reference to numerous others. We urge you to read extensively from the books we suggest or others recommended by your instructor while studying about the field of young adult literature. Based on an understanding of the role of writing in responding to literature, we also recommend that you keep a journal to reflect upon your readings.

Organization of the Text

The text is arranged in eleven chapters that combine both theory and practice about using young adult literature in the classroom. It is divided into three sections: Part One: Setting the Stage for Young Adult Literature; Part Two: Establishing the Connections with Young Adult Literature; and Part Three: Making the Young Adult Literature Classroom Work.

Features to Enhance Involvement

Each chapter begins with a quotation either from or about young adult literature and a journal-writing prompt (discussed in more detail below). Other features include the following:

Sharing the Connection, actual responses from teachers and students writing about books they believe are too good to miss. These entries are authentic comments that have not been edited.

Bridging, in which we show the potential connections between a work of young adult fiction and one or more other literary works.

Literature Involvement Strategy, which provides a specific teaching/learning strategy that can be used in the classroom.

Talking with . . . , beginning in Chapter 3, are in-depth interviews with authors of young adult literature.

Summary and Suggested Activities appear at the end of each chapter to reinforce and personalize the concepts presented.

Appendices A through G provide useful lists of books, awards, organizations, and resources.

Journal Writing in This Text

We recommend that you keep a journal while reading young adult literature and this text. The journal prompt at the beginning of each chapter and suggested writing and discussion activities at the end of each chapter will help you. These are only beginning points, however, and we encourage you to experiment with your own methods. In Chapter 1 we present another type of journal writing experience, the Dialogue Journal, in which students respond to each other's responses. Additionally, if you are currently teaching, we urge you to implement journal writing in response to literature in your own classroom.

The Evolving Field of Young Adult Literature

Because the field of young adult literature is an evolving one, misconceptions abound. We, therefore, list the premises upon which this text was developed and which serve as the framework for our exploration of using literature with young adults.

An effective literature curriculum reflects a balance among traditional works, the classics, and works of young adult literature. We believe that traditional works of literature provide a vital contribution to the aesthetic, intellectual, and social development of readers. The literature curriculum, however, should be a dynamic one that is inclusive rather than limited to the canon. As Purves et al. (1990) discuss, the range of "literature" has increased in recent years. As the variety of literature expands, it increasingly reflects the interests, the experiences, the aspirations, and the activities of readers at every phase of their lives.

Reading literature can be a process of self-discovery.   Adolescence is a time of exploration and seeking in which self-discovery is a natural outgrowth of the changes young adults experience. We believe that reading a variety of quality literature is a facilitating and nurturing process that provides students with insights not only about themselves but also about their society and their world. Literature provides new perspectives for readers and brings with it the potential for seeing, recognizing, and more important, accepting diversity among people and cultures. By helping students develop a multicultural perspective, literature can help students acknowledge, appreciate, and value the diversity of society.

Students will read if they have an opportunity to read material that is interesting and relevant to their lives.
The amount of reading done by many young people seems to decrease during the adolescent years, but this trend can be slowed by thoughtful selection of reading material. Teachers who accept and foster a wide range of reading selections are more likely to meet both student needs and interests. And the more students read, the better readers they will become.

Decisions about what students read, how and when they read, and what we hope to have them learn from their reading necessitate a reconceptualization of the roles of teachers.   It requires that teachers know a broad repertoire of traditional as well as young adult literature. It also requires that teachers demonstrate an understanding of the reading process, the developmental stages of the adolescent reader, and the methodological skills both to teach literature and to help students to become better readers. For teachers who seek to involve today's students with literature, we identify these roles: the Teacher as Reader, the Teacher as Expert Guide/Reading Coach, and the Teacher as Researcher. In this text, we explore these roles and their classroom implications as well as present a framework for instruction and a number of literature teaching strategies.

Suggestions for Using this Text

For instructors who are using this text in their courses, we suggest you consider using some or all of the instructional formats described in Chapter 9 to facilitate your students' involvement with young adult literature. Additionally, you may find the information on journal writing in Chapter 10 useful.

Acknowledgments

There are many people who helped to make this book possible. We are especially grateful to the nine authors who are featured in the *Talking with . . .* sections in Chapters 3–11: Joan Bauer, Marion Dane Bauer, Chris Crutcher, Russell Freedman, Joyce Hansen, Monica Hughes, Graham Salisbury, Virginia Euwer Wolff, and Laurence Yep. They generously shared their time and insights about their work and writing for young people. We also thank their editors and publishers: Catherine Balkin of HarperCollins, Lori Benton of William Morrow & Company, Wendy Lamb of Bantam Doubleday Dell, Gina Maolucci of Henry Holt, Marjorie Naughton of Clarion Books, and Christie Smith of Simon & Schuster. We send a special bouquet of thanks to Marjorie Naughton of Clarion Books for her ongoing interest and support.

This book reflects the influences of our students throughout the years. We especially appreciate the assistance and interest of Deb Gleissner, Melissa Kazmarek, Randy Kreger, Michelle Kulas, Pat Otterbacher, and Sandy Payne.

We would like to thank the reviewers who offered valuable suggestions during the development of this text: Hugh Agee, University of Georgia; Sandra Bone, Arkansas State University; Mark Christiansen, University of Tennessee, Knoxville; Brenda Dales, Miami University; Jean Dummer, College of St. Catherine; Mark Faust, University of Georgia; Timothy Shanahan, University of Illinois, Chicago; John Stansell, Texas A&M. Louise Garcia Harrison and Sharon Hunter, teachers at Heritage High School, Saginaw (Michigan) Township also read and critiqued the manuscript. We are grateful for their time and perceptive insights.

We thank the editorial staff at Wadsworth for their constant professionalism, including education editor Sabra Horne, and we thank Trish Schumacher, advertising specialist, for her marketing plans for the book. Thanks to Kate Peltier who, as editorial assistant, juggled dozens of details for us with patience and humor. We have been particularly lucky to have worked again with two consummate professionals: Carol Carreon Lombardi, our production editor, and Andrew Ogus, our designer. Carol is always a delight to work with, unfailingly helpful and supportive. We appreciate Andrew, whose wry wit is surpassed only by his creativity and vision. Any project is enhanced by Carol's and Andrew's contributions. A special thanks to Andrew and Sabra for finding and selecting Jude Maceren to do the cover for this book. We also thank Suzanna Brabant, who first signed this project, and who has always provided us with support and sage advice.

About the Authors

Jean E. Brown (*right*) (Ed.D., Utah State University) is professor of teacher education at Saginaw Valley State University. Active in the National Council of Teachers of English, she is past president of the Michigan Council of Teachers of English. She is author of numerous publications, including a textbook on content-writing instruction, *Toward Literacy* (Wadsworth, 1993). She is also contributing editor of *Preserving Intellectual Freedom: Fighting Censorship in Our Schools* from The National Council of Teachers of English. Dr. Brown has received many awards, including the C. C. Fries Award for leadership and contributions to the field of English education and the Earl Warrick Award for Excellence in Research.

Elaine C. Stephens (*left*) (Ph.D., Michigan State University) is professor of teacher education at Saginaw Valley State University. She works extensively with classroom teachers and is in demand for professional development activities. She is also director of the Greater Saginaw Valley Regional Center for Professional Development. She is author of numerous publications, including a textbook on content-writing instruction, *Toward Literacy* (Wadsworth, 1993). Dr. Stephens has received many awards, including the Franc L. Landee Award for Excellence in Teaching and Michigan Association of Governing Boards of State University Award for outstanding contributions to education.

PART ONE

Setting the Stage

Part 1 of this text provides a foundation for using young adult literature in the classroom. In Chapter 1, What Is Young Adult Literature?, we discuss the nature of young adult literature and examine some of the works that are currently being read. Additionally, we present the benefits of using young adult literature in the middle school or secondary curriculum. Three ongoing features of the book are introduced in Chapter 1.

Chapter 2, Exploring Books and Authors, is designed to introduce readers to the wealth of young adult books that are available for classroom and leisure reading. In this chapter we also explore various types of literature by presenting books that exemplify the types, from realistic fiction to picture books, that are appropriate for young adults. We conclude the chapter by introducing four frequently read authors of young adult books: M. E. Kerr, Norma Fox Mazer, Gary Paulsen, and Richard Peck.

The nature and stages of development of today's youth are presented in Chapter 3, Learning About the Young Adult in Young Adult Literature. The characteristics of youth are illustrated by characters and situations from young adult literature. This chapter also begins the first of a series of interviews with leading authors of young adult literature. This feature is called "Talking with. . . ." In this chapter we talk with Chris Crutcher.

Chapter 4, Connecting Young Adult Literature with Students, presents the value of using young adult literature to facilitate students' knowledge of themselves, others, and the world. Additionally, we explore strategies for involving students with their reading. In this chapter we feature a conversation with Joyce Hansen, whose historical fiction received the Coretta Scott King Honor Book Award.

CHAPTER 1

What Is Young Adult Literature?

The broad appeal of adolescent literature lies in part in its treatment of universal themes and in part in its high quality. Its writers write well. They tell good stories, inhabit them with memorable characters, place them in well-described settings, and do it with prose that causes readers to linger now and again for a second reading, a moment of appreciation for the well-turned phrase or the artistic metaphor.

Ted Hipple

Journal Writing: Responding

Describe any experiences you have had with young adult literature. What do you think of when you hear this term?

_____

The field of young adult literature is unique because its significant evolution has occurred within the past two generations. Its growth in popularity with young people, its increase in acceptability with teachers, and its improvement in quality are indicative of the genre's coming of age. It is rapidly becoming a part of the entire literature experience for young people; indeed, it is the frequent choice of readers from pre-teen to high school years. It is increasingly an accepted part of many English courses in secondary and middle schools to supplement, enrich, and extend basic text material in content-area courses.

The National Council of Teachers of English (NCTE), in its *Guidelines for the Preparation of Teachers of English Language Arts*, recommends that "secondary English teachers must be widely read in literature for adolescents, as well as in standard and classic works" (1986, p. 9). This is one standard used by NCTE to determine whether middle-school and secondary English teacher education programs are in compliance for national accreditation. The acknowledgment that young adult literature is a valuable part of our literary heritage has helped create a greater awareness of the genre and establish its legitimacy and credibility.

Why Read Young Adult Literature?

We believe young adult literature is a genre to be read, experienced, and enjoyed along with other literary genres. Literature for young adults is a vital addition to the school curriculum. It has the potential to integrate and to unify learning in all content areas by celebrating the uniqueness of different cultures and their people while reaffirming the universal traits that define our humanity. Exploring literature not only helps readers in their quest for self but also helps them to see themselves in the broader context of their society, their culture, and their world. More effectively than probably any other vehicle for learning, literature invites students to explore and discover both the "little picture"—self-understanding—and the "big picture"—an understanding of how students can fit in and relate to their world. Aleksandr Solzhenitsyn, in his 1972 Nobel acceptance speech, discusses the inherent value of literature:

> It can overcome man's unfortunate trait of learning only through his own experience . . . recreating in the flesh what another has experienced, and allowing it to be acquired as one's own.

The concept of vicarious experiences is a powerful notion. Literature should transport readers to unknown places and help them understand what others experience. Literature provides a powerful means by which we can "walk in another's shoes" and begin to understand what another experiences. For this reason, we feel that the study of literature for young adults enhances the discovery not only of the self but also discovery of the social context. We view literature as a framework for a broad understanding of the self, of individuals, of society, and of cultures. In support of this type of inclusive cultural perspective, Sasse (1988) cites the *Guidelines for the Preparation of Teachers of English Language Arts* (1986) from the National Council of Teachers of English in the belief that teachers and prospective English teachers need

> "an extensive body of literature and literary types in English and in translation;" that is, literature "by people of many racial and ethnic groups, and by authors from many countries and cultures" (p. 9). They must also be able to "use a variety of effective instructional strategies appropriate to diverse cultural groups and individual learning styles." Specifically, teachers are to "be aware that learning styles and ethnic backgrounds, for example, influence students' language experiences and development" and to "become knowledgeable about the various cultural backgrounds and cognitive characteristics of their students" (p. 11). Finally, the guidelines stress teacher attitudes, specifically "a desire to use the English language arts curriculum for helping students become familiar with diverse peoples and cultures." In a multicultural society, teachers must be able to help students achieve cross-cultural understanding and appreciation. Teachers must be willing to seek and to use materials which represent linguistic and artistic achievements from a variety of ethnic and cultural perspectives. In such diverse cultural contexts, students explore their own perceptions and values. (p. 14)

Bridging

*Bridging
a YA Novel
with a Classic*

Michael in A. C. LeMieux's
<u>The TV Guidance Coun-
selor</u> is having a difficult
time. Comparisons be-
tween Michael and
Holden Caulfield provide
an initial bridge to J. D.
Salinger's classic <u>The
Catcher in the Rye</u>.

As Crawford (1993) states: "Literature is an excellent resource for learning to understand how other people live and think. It provides the opportunity to talk about how people are alike as well as different. . . . Literature provides us the opportunity to explore cultural and ethnic differences . . . [it] helps us teach democratic values for working together" (p. 25).

What Is Young Adult Literature?

In the past twenty-five years, literature written specifically for and about young people, ages eleven to eighteen, has emerged as a significant literary field. In simple terms, young adult literature may be defined as books written specifically for and about youth. It is a body of literature written for an adolescent audience that is, in turn, about the lives, experiences, aspirations, and problems of young people. In other words, the term *young adult literature* describes the primary audience for these works as well as the subject matter they explore. Young adult literature, therefore, focuses upon youthful characters and explores their sense of identity, their adventures, their dreams, and their trials. For example, Kate, in Zibby Oneal's *In Summer Light,* struggles to establish herself in the shadow of her successful and famous father; Tengo, in *Waiting for the Rain* by Sheila Gordon, struggles for a more equitable life in spite of apartheid in South Africa; and Janie searches for her true identity in *The Face on the Milk Carton* by Caroline Cooney. As these youthful characters face challenges and difficulties, they grow and develop. Because adolescence is a time of significant development, young adult literature appropriately reflects the range of changes that adolescents may go through.

In a 1992 address to the annual fall ALAN (Assembly on Literature for Adolescents) Conference at the National Council of Teachers of English convention, noted author of young adult literature Walter Dean Myers said, "Literature gives strategies for living." While this is a significant notion for examining literature of any sort, we feel that it is particularly powerful as we look at literature written for a young readership. No group is as actively seeking answers as adolescents; they need and search for "strategies for living." Author Sandy Asher supports this notion of the search that adolescents experience as they read. Asher (1992) explores the interrelationship between youth and their experiences as readers: "Generally, adults choose books that reflect and reinforce attitudes they already hold. Young adult readers, on the other hand, are actively searching for ideas, information, and values to incorporate into their personalities and into their lives. The books they read become a very real part of them" (p. 79).

Readers of young adult literature have opportunities to identify with powerful role models like Allegra (Virginia Euwer Wolff's *The Mozart Season*), Louie Banks (Chris Crutcher's *Running Loose*), and Otter (Laurence Yep's *Dragon's Gate*). They encounter memorable young people like Adam Farmer (Robert Cormier's *I Am the Cheese*), Cassie Logan (Mildred Taylor's *Roll of Thunder, Hear My Cry, Let the Circle Be Unbroken,* and *The Road to Memphis*), Brian (Gary Paulsen's *Hatchet*), and Laura and Howie (Brock Cole's *The Goats*). These encounters have the potential to change readers' lives and perspectives. Rosenblatt (1983) examines the experiences of the readers:

> For them the formal elements of the work—style and structure, rhythmic flow—function only as a part of the total literary experience. The reader seeks to participate in another's vision—to reap knowledge of the world, to fathom the resources of the human spirit, to gain insights that will make his own life more comprehensible. Teachers of adolescents, in high school or in college, know to what a heightened degree they share this personal approach to literature. (p. 7)

The youthful protagonists in young adult fiction provide models with whom readers may identify. As teachers, we encourage and seek to foster this identification with characters, their circumstances, and their challenges because we know this type of involvement hooks students on reading.

To gain a perspective about the range of books written for adolescents, we have chosen five quality young adult books—three fiction and two nonfiction—to explore in some depth. These books are significantly different from each other in the audience they attract, level of sophistication, character development, and other literary elements. The books are *Waiting for the Rain* by Sheila Gordon, *The Goats* by Brock Cole, *The True Confessions of Charlotte Doyle* by Avi, *Malcolm X: By Any Means Necessary* by Walter Dean Myers, and *The Boys' War: Confederate and Union Soldiers Talk About the Civil War* by Jim Murphy.

One of the major premises of this book is that young adult literature provides opportunities for reader exploration. While this exploration encompasses heightened self-knowledge and personal understanding, it also has the potential to provide readers with understanding in two other significant ways. Literature broadens and enhances readers' sense of their world while it helps them to expand their knowledge of events, situations, and human interactions.

Certainly, in *Waiting for the Rain,* a book appropriate for use with high school students and winner of the Jane Addams Peace Award, Gordon provides readers with opportunities for exploration in these three areas.

Waiting for the Rain, set in contemporary South Africa, is the story of the friendship between two young boys. Frikkie is the nephew of a Dutch farmer, and Tengo is an African whose father works on the farm. Frikkie spends each vacation with his aunt and uncle and longs for the day when he can work and live at the farm all year. Tengo longs for a chance to learn and to live in the world beyond the farm. The friendship of the boys is one of childhood, of play, and of carefree oblivion to the society in which they live. As they grow older, the differences between the boys increase, and Tengo is keenly aware of these differences. For example, Frikkie thinks school is a waste of his time. His future is secure because he is his uncle's heir and will inherit the farm. Tengo longs for as much education as he can get. His aunt works in Johannesburg for a wealthy, liberal white family who send their old textbooks to the farm for Tengo to study. Tengo cannot get enough of them; they simply whet his desire to learn more. For Tengo, whose life is uncertain, education provides a new path. For Frikkie, whose future is already determined, schooling seems simply to delay his progress.

A turning point in the book occurs during a party at the farm. Tengo and several others, including Ezekiel, an old and respected African man, have been asked to help with the serving and cleaning up. Frikkie has broken some dishes:

> "Oh, it doesn't matter—" the other cousin said. She was a thin, freckled girl of twelve, with a mass of red, frizzy hair. "The boy can clean it up." She turned to old Ezekiel. "Hey, boy—Jim—what's-your-name, come over here and wipe this mess up off the floor."
>
> Tengo found that he had got from the pantry door to the middle of the kitchen without being aware he had moved. The shock of the girl's words had propelled him across the room as if he had been catapulted. He found himself standing in front of her, shaking with an intensity of hot rage that for a moment choked him and made it impossible for him to speak. He could not believe what his ears had heard—a strange girl addressing the respected old Ezekiel as if he were one of the stray farm dogs.
>
> In a tight, low, terrible voice, Tengo spoke the words that came to him then. *"Don't you call that old man boy."* He took a step toward her. *"You have no respect!"* His voice rose as he felt pure anger surge through him. "Can't you see! He is one of the elders of our tribe—he is older than the oubaas—he is from the chief's family! *Who says you can talk to him like that*—" He lifted his hand as though to strike her, and his voice dropped as

he hissed at her through clenched teeth. "Don't you ever call an old man *boy* again." (pp. 62–63)

A gulf develops between the boys the day after this incident. Frikkie has persuaded his cousin and sister not to make trouble for Tengo even though he has spoken out. Frikkie goes to say good-bye to his friend because his vacation is over and he must return to school. He also wants to reassure Tengo that there will be no problem about the previous day's incident. Tengo has chosen not to be there to say good-bye. "Frikkie liked things orderly and unchanging. It troubled him that he would have to leave without saying good-bye to Tengo" (p. 68).

Although Frikkie ignores the changes in Tengo and in their relationship because they are too puzzling for him to understand, Tengo recognizes them and has no desire for things to be as they were. The changes in their lives continue until the two meet again as adults, when they must confront their differences and the differences in their cultures.

Waiting for the Rain is at one level about the traditional theme of friendship between two boys. More than this, though, it transports readers to the world of apartheid and the bitter struggle for equality in South Africa. Reading the book encourages students to reflect on their attitudes and beliefs about discrimination and inequality. They gain a perspective of life in South Africa, but they may also gain insights about the racial history of the United States. This understanding can be heightened by matching *Waiting for the Rain* with books that examine race relations in this country such as *To Kill a Mockingbird* by Harper Lee. *Waiting for the Rain* has the power to awaken students to a different culture, a different region of the world, and a different perspective.

The Goats by Brock Cole, winner of several awards including ALA Best Book for Young Adults, School Library Journal Best Book of the Year, and Booklist Best Book of the 80s, explores the survival, personal growth, and subsequent development of a friendship between a thirteen-year-old boy and girl. They experience a painful rejection by their peers and then demonstrate increasing independence through a number of adventures. Laura and Howie, who are strangers at the book's beginning, are at nearby boys' and girls' summer camps. A camp ritual is to identify a "goat," or someone who is gawky and doesn't fit in with the others. Laura and Howie, the designated goats, are tricked to take off their clothes to go swimming. The other kids steal their clothes and leave them naked and stranded alone on an island. Rather than be humiliated and rejected by their peers, Howie and Laura escape and live by their wits, joining forces to prove that they are winners.

The initial bond between the two is forged by necessity. They are determined to escape from the island and get away from the possibility of an embarrassing return to the camp. As they make their escape, a rescue party of counselors from the camp returns to the island, but Laura and Howie have no desire to be rescued. They find a closed-up cottage and break in; they also take clothes and some canned food. Thus prepared, their journey begins. It is a journey in the archetypal sense as both of the characters mature and gain self-awareness. They also develop a friendship that evolves as one of necessity to one of mutual caring and respect.

One of their adventures takes place when they get on a bus transporting young people to a different camp, one for African Americans. In the time that they spend with these campers, they find acceptance and friendship. The following is the narrator's description of Laura's reaction to the experience:

> The girl didn't know why she felt like crying. She didn't feel nervous and scared anymore. Maybe it was because they were nice to her. Nice to a goat. She'd almost forgotten that she was supposed to be a goat. No, not forgotten. She wouldn't forget, and she wouldn't forgive, either. But it didn't seem important in the same way. It was as if it had all happened to some other, littler kid. She was crying a bit for that kid, too. It wasn't the same as feeling sorry for herself, because she wasn't quite the same person. But she still felt bad about what had happened to that little kid. (pp. 93–94)

The Goats provides a valuable reading experience for early adolescents because they are at a developmental stage when the peer group becomes increasingly important. The victory that Howie and Laura achieve over their initial rejection by their fellow campers assuages one of the greatest fears of many young adults. Furthermore, their ability to operate successfully and independently, without adult support, demonstrates to readers struggling with similar issues that they can achieve such autonomy. The theme of a friendship between a female and male is also used in Katherine Paterson's *The Bridge to Terabithia* and Richard Peck's *Remembering the Good Times*.

Avi's award-winning historical fiction, *The True Confessions of Charlotte Doyle,* is set in 1832. It is a first-person account of a young woman's adventures and struggles as the only female on a ship taking her from a sheltered, upper-class school environment in England to her wealthy family in America. A "well-bred" young lady, Charlotte, through some mysterious circumstances, finds herself unchaperoned on this rough sea voyage. Caught in a series of confusing and dangerous conflicts between the demented, autocratic captain and his mutinous crew, Charlotte must not only decide whom to trust but also face the serious consequences of misplaced loyalties based on class distinctions.

Subsequently, Charlotte learns to think for herself as well as to take actions unheard of for a young lady of her station and era.

> Sobbing in absolute misery, I threw myself onto my bed. I wept for Zachariah, for Cranick, even for Captain Jaggery. But most of all I wept for myself. There was no way to avoid the truth that all the horror I'd witnessed had been brought about by me.
>
> As the ghastly scenes repeated themselves in my mind, I realized too that there was no way of denying what the captain had done. Captain Jaggery, my friend, my guardian—my father's employee—had been unspeakably cruel. Not only had he killed Cranick—who was, I knew, threatening him—he had clearly meant to kill Zachariah for no reason other than that he was helpless! He singled him out *because* he was the oldest and weakest. Or was it because he was black? Or was it, I asked myself suddenly, because he was *my* friend?
>
> Just the thought made me shiver convulsively. Tears of regret and guilt redoubled.
>
> My weeping lasted for the better part of an hour. Aside from reliving the fearsome events, I was trying desperately to decide what to *do*. As I grasped the situation, the crew would have nothing but loathing for me who had so betrayed them. And they were right. After their kindliness and acceptance I *had* betrayed them. (pp. 103–4)

The True Confessions of Charlotte Doyle is notable not only for its well-crafted plot of suspense and intrigue that appeals to both males and females, but also for its superb character development and its exploration of important moral issues. Charlotte's journey from England to America can be viewed as symbolic of the journey that adolescents must make from childhood to adulthood, as they learn to accept responsibility for their own behavior and make choices involving complex questions of authority, friendship, and good versus evil. Charlotte is a significant female role model in young adult literature as she defies convention, initially to right a wrong and ultimately to be true to herself.

Avi's work is also a valuable contribution to the field of historical fiction for young people. Increasingly, history and social studies teachers are using young adult literature to help students develop a better understanding of a time period, its people, and effects of economic conditions and social conventions on them. *The True Confessions of Charlotte Doyle* will appeal to the student who hates history, teach the novice about sailing ships and the seas, and delight the history buff. It is the winner of several awards, including ALA Best Book for Young Adults and School Library Journal Best Book of 1990.

We have looked at three outstanding novels as exemplifying good reading for young adults; however, we would be shortsighted if we did not also

Sharing the Connection

The True Confessions of Charlotte Doyle
Avi

I liked this book because it was a great thriller to read. It left me so intense at times I could not put it down until I read that Charlotte was OK! The best part of the whole book was when Charlotte was put on trial by the crew for murder! The book made me think of how a young woman of 16 could go through so much. It also made me think women do just as good as men. I think this book would be very inspiring for women who don't have a lot of courage in themselves. This book also made me feel very strong and excited. Because Charlotte is so strong, the next day I felt like I could do anything! I was so excited when I read this book because of all the adventure it has. I would recommend it to anyone!

Vanessa Fick, student

acknowledge the significant role of nonfiction in reading for students. One current example is Walter Dean Myers's timely biography, *Malcolm X: By Any Means Necessary.* Published within a few months of the release of Spike Lee's film, *Malcolm X,* the Myers biography is an appropriate response to heightened interest about the African American leader, making the story of Malcolm's life accessible to youthful readers. Myers focuses on the events that influenced the evolutionary changes in Malcolm's life.

> The twenty-year-old Malcolm was put into prison with people who had stolen, who had killed, who were career criminals. To escape this dehumanizing process, to remain an alert, vital person, Malcolm needed to separate himself from the bulk of the prison population. To do this he relied on the fact that he was bright. He began to read as much as he could and also began taking a correspondence course in English.
>
> Malcolm had heard about an experimental prison reform plan in Massachusetts. The program was being conducted at an institution in Norfolk, Massachusetts. The program at Norfolk provided the prisoners with considerably more freedom than was available at either Charlestown or Concord Reformatory. Malcolm appealed to the Massachusetts prison authorities on a number of occasions to transfer him there. Usually the program was considered good for those prisoners with the best chance of rehabilitation, and eventually Malcolm was accepted.
>
> What the Norfolk institution offered primarily, besides the ability to individualize one's life, was an excellent library. Malcolm began to upgrade his reading. It was here that Malcolm learned about the great religions of the world, including that of Islam. (p. 62)

Popular interest in Malcolm provides an opportunity for readers to explore the issues of equality and race relations in this country from the time of Malcolm's release from prison in 1952 until his death in 1965. Other books about

Malcolm include Arnold Adoff's biography for children, *Malcolm X,* illustrated by John Wilson; and *The Autobiography of Malcolm X* written with Alex Haley, the most widely read adult book on this subject.

Another nonfiction work to consider is *The Boys' War: Confederate and Union Soldiers Talk About the Civil War* by Jim Murphy, winner of the ALA Best Book for Young Adults and the Golden Kite Award Book for Nonfiction. It is an informational account of boys under sixteen years of age who served in the Civil War. Based on diaries, journals, letters, and war records, it contains 50 photographs, often haunting, that greatly enhance the text. The book tells the stories of the many young boys, some as young as eleven or twelve, who left what they considered to be the boring drudgery of rural or small-town life for the anticipated glories of the battlefield. The following passage is typical of their experiences:

> Suddenly, the war that had been a romantic dream was all around them like angry bees. Elisha Stockwell found himself facedown on the ground, shells exploding all around and soldiers screaming for help: "I want to say, as we lay there and the shells were flying over us, my thoughts went back to my home, and I thought what a foolish boy I was to run away and get into such a mess as I was in. I would have been glad to have seen my father coming after me." (p. 33)

Although both sides prohibited boys under eighteen from joining and fighting, it is estimated that ten to twenty percent of the soldiers were underage when they joined. Recruitment fever ran high, and young boys, who were strong and well developed from hours of farm labor, lied easily about their ages—sometimes with their parents' knowledge. Officially, underage boys were allowed to join "nonfighting" units, such as the drumming corps, that placed them in the thick of the battles. Drumming was an essential means of communication in the Civil War, and many drummers were injured or killed. They also engaged in fighting.

The book provides a realistic description of the hardships the young boys endured and the brutalities of war. It also describes the day-to-day life of soldiers, the food they ate, the games they played to relieve the monotony, and the loneliness and homesickness they experienced. *The Boys' War* is an excellent addition to a history or social studies class studying the Civil War. It also is a good companion to other young adult literature such as Irene Hunt's *Across Five Aprils* and Ann Rinaldi's *The Last Silk Dress.*

The five books described here do not represent the entire range of young adult literature. The range of young adult literature is constrained only by the broad interests and concerns of its readers. The term *young adult literature*

Bridging

Bridging a Poem with YA Novels

Alice Walker's poem "Women" examines the multifaceted heritage that mothers provide their daughters. Two recent young adult novels—Carolyn Coman's <u>Tell Me Everything</u> and Kyoko Mori's <u>Shizuko's Daughter</u>—examine the complex and at times painful relationships between mothers and daughters.

describes the primary audience for these works as well as the broad subject matter they explore. We believe that as the field of young adult literature evolves, it becomes more similar to literature written for adults. One area in which the similarities become obvious is in literary themes, the overriding, unifying concepts that provide the framework for a book. Among the major themes in fiction for young adults are rites of passage, search for identity, familial relationships, need for independence, and interpersonal relationships. Each of these themes is also commonly found throughout all literature.

Although a thematic designation is more difficult to achieve in looking at nonfiction, there is consistency in the topics that appeal to young people and adults when they read nonfiction. Major types of nonfiction include biography, autobiography, and informational (how-to, travel, factual, craft, hobby, and cooking), among others. All of these types are read and enjoyed by both youths and adults. In Chapter 2, we describe the various types of young adult literature and provide examples of each type.

What Are the Current Developments in Young Adult Literature?

To understand the changing nature of young adult literature, we must examine how the genre has evolved. The development of contemporary, realistic young adult novels can be traced to the 1967 publication of *The Outsiders* by S. E. Hinton. Susan Hinton's first novel, written when the author was seventeen, marks the initial step toward a significant change in young adult literature. Abandoning the tradition of books about girls who were primarily concerned with getting a date for the next school dance, Hinton describes a gang of boys who live on their own. The book's narrator is the fourteen-year-old Ponyboy, who lives with his two older brothers after his parents' death. Ponyboy's gang is always at odds with another group, the Socs. Within the first few pages of the book, a confrontation occurs between Ponyboy and Socs. Ponyboy is rescued by his brother and the members of his gang, and the stage is set for ongoing encounters between the two groups.

As an early example of young adult fiction, *The Outsiders* describes adolescence as a time of rebellion. The absence of positive adult role models in the

book reflects an "us-against-them" mentality. Although *The Outsiders* can be
seen as reflective of its times—the late 1960s—its theme of the classic struggle
between social cliques is still relevant for today's students. Indeed, the role of
the peer group is a major motif in young adult literature.

> I was trembling. A pain was growing in my throat and I wanted to cry, but
> greasers don't cry in front of strangers. Some of us never cry at all. Like
> Dally and Two-Bit and Tim Shepard—they forgot how at an early age.
> (p. 91)

Young adult novels written in the 1990s describe conflicts similar to those
in Hinton's groundbreaking novel. Virginia Hamilton's *Plain City* (1993) is
representative of the evolution of the genre. Hamilton's protagonist, thirteen-
year-old biracial Buhlaire, is an outsider in her world. Her classmates shun her
and call her "a Water House kid" because her family lives in a house on stilts
along the river. Buhlaire's mother is an entertainer, a singer, and a fan dancer,
viewed by some as the town celebrity and by others as the town outcast.
Buhlaire is cared for by an extended family of aunts and uncles because her
mother is frequently on the road. Buhlaire knows little of her heritage except
what her mother has told her. She believes that her father is missing in action
in Vietnam, until she realizes, with the help of her school's principal, that the
war ended several years before she was born. This knowledge prompts Buhlaire to begin a quest to find out about herself and her family. The following
excerpt describes her reunion with her father.

> *What was he called?* "You're Junior. Junior Sims," she said. *My* dad!
>   "Yeah, that's me," he said. "I'm your daddy!" He laughed loudly. It
> began to snow on them again.
>   Buhlaire felt weak and deeply tired. "I'm so sleepy, all a-sudden," she said.
>   "Freezing yourself out here," Junior, her dad, said. "Even your tears
> are frozen." He laughed again. It sounded empty. "Need to get y'all outta
> the cold."
>   Something strange, yet sweet-sounding, about him, she thought. His
> voice was slow and easy, full of summer sun. *Daddy* . . . She'd waited so
> long. But now, for some reason, she felt let down. And if she could just lie
> still, she could figure out why she didn't care so much about her dad being
> with her right now. She just didn't.
>   She felt cozy, all wrapped up deep inside herself. Like snow, the thought
> *this is how you freeze* came drifting down on her. She was too tired. She
> couldn't feel anything much. Not even the cold now. (p. 107)

An important distinction between early realistic young adult novels and more recent ones lies in how they depict the role of the family. Relationships with parents and their impact, both positive and negative, are significant current concerns; in earlier works, family played little or no role. In general, the role of adults is more positive and complex in recent works.

In 1981, G. Robert Carlson, one of the major forces in bringing young adult literature into the classroom, provided this definition of the genre:

> Young-adult literature is literature wherein the protagonist is either a teenager or one who approaches problems from a teenage perspective. Such novels are generally of moderate length and told from the first person. Typically, they describe initiation into the adult world, or the surmounting of a contemporary problem forced upon the protagonist(s) by the adult world. Though generally written for a teenage reader, such novels—like all fine literature—address the entire spectrum of life. (p. 27)

While Carlson's definition describes young adult literature in the early 1980s, it also reflects how the field has evolved. Although current young adult literature still describes the experiences and lives of adolescents, it is no longer told predominantly from a first-person point of view. Point of view in young adult literature is now widely varied. In some cases, point of view is sophisticated and employs multiple narrators and shifts in point of view. (See Chapter 8 on the use of point of view and other literary devices.) Another change in the field is the expansion of the genre to include many types of writing, such as historical fiction, fantasy, mystery, biography and autobiography, information, drama, and poetry.

Realistic young adult literature is often mistakenly labeled as adolescent "problem" novels because the books depict traditionally taboo topics, such as divorce, suicide, substance abuse, child abuse, and teenage sexuality. This label, however, is far too simplistic. The first-person confessional approach is no longer as common as it once was, and the theme of initiation is only one of many themes that are ongoing throughout the genre. The following developments in young adult literature speak to the breadth and diversity of the field since the 1960s:

- Earlier young adult literature focused primarily on disturbed and highly rebellious youth, but contemporary novels also discuss the needs, problems, and interests of affluent, suburban youths.

- In the 1960s, rebellion in young adult literature was directed against authority figures and the establishment, but contemporary novels show rebellion in the context of seeking identity.

- The influence of the family is more pronounced, with a balanced portrayal of the role of parents and the influence of the extended family.

- The ethnic and cultural diversity of our society is receiving increased emphasis.

Increasingly, books for young adults do, as Carlson suggests, describe the whole human experience, especially as well-written books with credible plots, fully developed characters, and significant themes break old patterns. Additionally, current books provide readers with a variety of sophisticated reading experiences. For example, Lois Lowry's *The Giver* is a futuristic novel that can be read as a religious allegory; Ann Rinaldi's *Time Enough for Drums* is a historical novel examining the conflict and turmoil that the Revolutionary War created within families; *Staying Fat for Sarah Byrnes* is Chris Crutcher's novel of two youths, one injured psychologically by his father's rejection and the other injured physically and psychologically by an abusive parent; and Janet Bode's *New Kids in Town, Stories of Immigrant Youths* includes the nonfiction accounts of young people whose families have moved to this country. Young adult literature now embraces a variety of types of literature that reflect the rich range of adolescent experiences and lifestyles. As the problem novels of the late 1960s and 1970s, including such works as Judith Guest's *Ordinary People, One Fat Summer* by Robert Lipsyte, and Richard Peck's *Father Figure,* reflect the period in which they were written, so do current books, such as Carolyn Coman's *Tell Me Everything* and Will Hobbs's *Down River.* A strength of literature written for young adults is that it presents a timely response to the needs of its readers.

Young adult literature, like all good literature, creates that rare balance between dealing with timeless truths of humanity and reflecting the times and the nature of the society in which it was written. A significant element in the evolution of the young adult novel is the role and portrayal of adults. For example, in early works of realistic fiction such as those by Hinton and Zindel, there are no positive adult role models; however, many recent works tend to present a more multidimensional portrayal of adults. Chris Crutcher (personal interview, 1993) says that in all of his books there is an interpretive adult character who helps the adolescent characters to understand what is happening to them. The complete text of the interview with Crutcher in Chapter 3 provides more insights about the role of adults in contemporary young adult literature. Additionally, in Chapter 7 we present an overview of the history of literature for young readers.

Bridging

Bridging Works of Fiction

Sue Ellen Bridgers's <u>Notes for Another Life</u> examines difficult family problems that are reminiscent of Judith Guest's <u>Ordinary People</u>.

Is It Young Adult Literature or Not?

In a number of cases, a book with a youthful protagonist is sold and promoted as a book for youth on the basis of a marketing decision. For example, Cormier initially wrote *The Chocolate War* as an adult novel, but it was published as part of a juvenile collection. His reputation was established as a major author of young adult literature on the basis of this subjective categorization. It is far too simplistic, however, to assume that any work with an adolescent protagonist is written for adolescents. Although these books may appeal to youthful readers, they are often written as adult reflections on youth. For example, in *A Separate Peace* by John Knowles, the protagonist is an adult who goes back to his prep school to reflect on his youth and to put in perspective an accident that occurred there. Although this book is often used in high schools, it was not written specifically for a youthful audience.

Books like *A Separate Peace, A Portrait of the Artist as a Young Man* by James Joyce, *The Heart Is a Lonely Hunter* by Carson McCullers, *The Catcher in the Rye* by J. D. Salinger, and *Look Homeward, Angel* by Thomas Wolfe are representative of the literary tradition of the apprenticeship novel. An apprenticeship novel recounts the struggle of the protagonist to come of age and gain awareness of the world. The significant difference between young adult novels and adult novels about adolescents is perspective. In an apprenticeship novel, the point of view is often that of an adult reflecting on youthful experiences. The young adult novel, however, more often represents the perspective of youthful characters as they explore their world.

A number of adult books are popular for classroom use because they capture experiences familiar to youths and with which they can identify. Among these books are *Cold Sassy Tree* by Olive Burns, *To Kill a Mockingbird* by Harper Lee, *I Know Why the Caged Bird Sings* by Maya Angelou, *Ordinary People* by Judith Guest, and *The Adventures of Huckleberry Finn* by Mark Twain. Because these

---

Literature Involvement Strategy

Dialogue Journals

A variation of the Literature Response Journal is the Dialogue Journal, in which pairs of students conduct written conversations with each other about what they are reading. Initially, it is more effective to have students respond to each other's journals when they are reading the same book. Once students have had experience responding to each other about the same book, they can respond to reactions to books that they have not read. A variation on this is to have the teacher respond to the students' entries. The obvious difficulty in this approach is limitations on the teachers' time. Teachers might respond to the dialogue journals on an alternating basis, one class at a time.

books are popular among teachers and students, we will refer throughout this text to these and other adult books that are used in middle school and secondary classrooms.

Sue Ellen Bridgers, an acclaimed novelist of young adult literature, defines young adult literature in this way:

> Any book that holds a young person's interest, that portrays the human condition with care and is well crafted, could and should be a young adult novel. The categories of books are more a marketing device than a limit to the appeal a book might have. If the characters and situations in a novel are relevant and meaningful to the teenager, that's the book he or she will read. The book without the reader has no life; it is static without the imagination and experience of another mind, the hand eagerly turning the page, the receiving heart. (1992, p. 70)

Summary

Young adult literature focuses on the lives, experiences, problems, and aspirations of young people. It is a vital addition to the literature curriculum and should be read, experienced, and enjoyed along with other literary genres. Young adult literature provides role models for young people to identify with and has the potential to help them expand their knowledge and understanding of themselves, others, and the world.

Suggested Activities

1. In your journal, begin to develop a rationale for using young adult literature. Expand on it as you read each chapter in this text.

2. How would you define young adult literature to someone who is unaware of its existence?

Sharing the Connection

A Day No Pigs Would Die
Robert Newton Peck

I liked this book because it had to do with a boy, about my own age, who is becoming a man. The boy lives on a farm with his family. His dad kills pigs for a living. There's a very strong love between Rob and his dad that grows ever stronger. The work they do together is for their family. This story made me think of my dad and how we share a strong love and trust between us. It also gave me a new perspective on Life. It made me think that maybe the "simple life" that I hear people talk about isn't such a bad life to live after all. This is a story of an eldest son who labors with his father, who eventually has to give up a precious possession for the sake of the family; who after his dad dies, carries on his father's work and place in the family. His labor is a true labor of love.

Aaron M. Jamrog, student

3. What selections from young adult literature are you currently reading? What common elements do you see in them? Compare these selections with other literature you are familiar with, such as adult or children's literature.

4. Use the Dialogue Journal format described in this chapter's Literature Involvement Strategy to share what you are reading with a colleague, friend, or family member.

CHAPTER 2

Exploring Books and Authors

The "idea," more often than not, is something discovered by the reader while the writer continues, through her books, to try to find the truth from which ideas spring.

Paula Fox

Journal Writing: Responding

Identify a book or an author that you particularly enjoy. What qualities of the book or the author's work appeal most to you?

A classroom teacher recently described to us the frustration she felt when her students in a racially diverse urban high school repeatedly failed to read the assigned selections in their literature anthology. Her students complained that the selections were either too difficult or too boring. They asked why they couldn't read something else. She was frustrated, not knowing what else to have them read. Her principal agreed to purchase class sets of books that the teacher recommended, but she was uncertain of which authors and titles to select. We suggested that she look at some of the outstanding works of young adult literature. Furthermore, we recommended that she begin her curriculum revision by exploring Walter Dean Myers's *Fallen Angels,* a compelling novel of a young African American's experiences in Vietnam and by reading one of Gary Soto's gentle books, such as his short story collection, *Baseball in April and Other Stories,* and his novels, *The Skirt, Taking Sides,* and *Pacific Crossing,* about the Mexican-American experience. We also suggested she look at powerful nonfiction, such as Janet Bode's *Beating the Odds: Stories of Unexpected Achievers* and Susan Kuklin's *Speaking Out: Teenagers Take on Race, Sex, and Identity.*

In another conversation, a teacher from an affluent suburban middle school revealed his limited knowledge of the breadth of young adult literature and his misconceptions about its quality. He mistakenly believed that young adult literature includes primarily easy selections for at-risk readers and contains little of value for his college-bound students. We recommended that he begin by having students read Gary Paulsen's *The Island,* a contemplative work that might prove an appropriate bridge to Henry David Thoreau's *Walden* or *Blue Skin of the Sea,* an intricately crafted first novel by Graham Salisbury. Additionally, we suggested he explore the writings of Sue Ellen Bridgers, Virginia Hamilton, Richard Peck, and Cynthia Voigt.

After these conversations, we wondered how many teachers were in the same position. We informally asked a number of experienced teachers about their familiarity with young adult literature. Only a few teachers who had taken a course in the field or were self-taught were knowledgeable about books and authors for young adults. We heard from many teachers who indicated interest but had no idea where to begin to integrate young adult literature into their classes. Peck (1989) speaks to this problem:

> One of the reasons teachers do not recommend books may be that they do not know them. The average high school English teacher who has been teaching for some years may not be aware of all the books that are available for adolescents to read, particularly all the young adult novels. YA books have only been around for some 20 years, and many teachers may not be familiar with them, while others may have a negative, traditionalist prejudice about this kind of literature. A number of YA novels are excellent and worthy of literary study. . . . A novel like Cormier's *The Chocolate War,* to take but one obvious example, has all the literary elements of any serious adult novel: its structure, characterization, and literary style are complete and yield to the same kind of critical reading we could make of an older novel—*The Catcher in the Rye,* for example. More important, YA novels have been written for teenagers; they have subjects and themes that are relevant to that population of readers. (p. xviii)

As a result of these needs, we decided to address the question: "Where do I begin?" as the focal point for this chapter. We examined the results of Ted Hipple's survey (see Figure 2.1) about books and Don Gallo's survey about the most influential young adult authors. Additionally, we reviewed the yearly American Library Association's Best Books for Young Adults and the annual International Reading Association's Young Adult Choices listing. Beyond those sources we looked at our personal reading journals containing our reactions to the young adult literature we read. We also reviewed the reactions of our graduate and undergraduate students to their required and optional reading lists.

In this chapter, therefore, we seek to examine individual books and the collected works of authors that we believe make a significant contribution to the field. Obviously, a list of this sort is constantly changing. In a field that is

1. *The Chocolate War* by Robert Cormier
2. *The Outsiders* by S. E. Hinton
   The Pigman by Paul Zindel
3. *Home Before Dark* by Sue Ellen Bridgers
   A Day No Pigs Would Die by Robert Newton Peck
4. *All Together Now* by Sue Ellen Bridgers
   The Moves Make the Man by Bruce Brooks
   Jacob Have I Loved by Katherine Paterson
5. *Words by Heart* by Ouida Sebestyen
   Dicey's Song by Cynthia Voigt
6. *Summer of My German Soldier* by Bette Greene
   The Contender by Robert Lipsyte
   Bridge to Terabithia by Katherine Paterson
7. *After the First Death* by Robert Cormier
   I Am the Cheese by Robert Cormier
   Fallen Angels by Walter Dean Myers
   Roll of Thunder, Hear My Cry by Mildred Taylor

Figure 2.1   Important Young Adult Novels

growing as quickly as young adult literature, there cannot be a definitive list. We are always discovering books or authors whose work we had not previously known. It is this process of discovery that we want students to experience. Our list is neither static nor comprehensive; it is like a photograph that captures a particular moment rather than an unchanging scene.

Hipple (1989) reported the responses of teachers, librarians, publishers, and others to a survey asking what young adult novels they would like English teachers to know about. His results are listed in Figure 2.1.

In the spring 1989 issue of *The ALAN Review,* Don Gallo published the results of a 1988 survey of forty-one educators, all of whom had served as officers of the Assembly on Literature for Adolescents (ALAN) of the National Council of Teachers of English. He supplied them with a list of 169 authors of young adult books and asked them to determine the 100 most important authors. Thirty-three surveys were returned. The respondents first circled the names of those authors whom they believed to be the most important; then they underlined a second tier of authors. If the respondents did not identify 100 authors after two passes, they went through the list a third time, checking off names of a third level of authors. Listed in Figure 2.2 are the results of the weighted scores. The weightings were determined by giving three points every time a name was circled, two points every time a name was underlined, and one point every time a name was checked. The total number of points was added and the authors were then listed in rank order. While the results are more interesting than scientifically significant, they provide an overview of

1. S. E. Hinton; Paul Zindel
2. Richard Peck
3. Robert Cormier; M. E. Kerr;
   Katherine Paterson
4. Judy Blume
5. Sue Ellen Bridgers; Virginia
   Hamilton; Madeline L'Engle
6. Robert Newton Peck
7. Robert Lipsyte; Norma Klein
8. Scott O'Dell
9. Paula Danziger; Norma Fox Mazer
10. Paula Fox; Zibby Oneal
11. Maureen Daly; Ouida Sebestyen
12. Lloyd Alexander; Lois Duncan;
    Ursula K. LeGuin
13. Rosa Guy; William Sleator
14. Bette Greene; Jane Yolen
15. Harry Mazer
16. Robin F. Brancato; Mary Stolz
17. Laurence Yep
18. Isabelle Holland
19. Nat Hentoff
20. Vera (and Bill) Cleaver
21. Frank Bonham
22. John Neufield; Mildred D. Taylor;
    Todd Strasser
23. Cynthia Voigt; Sandra Scoppettone
24. Alice Childress
25. Walter Dean Myers
26. Anne McCaffrey
27. Jay Bennett; Christopher Collier
28. Joan Lowery Nixon; Kin Platt
29. Jean Craighead George
30. Joan Aiken
31. James Lincoln Collier
32. Eve Bunting; Ellen Conford; Phyllis
    A. Whitney
33. Lynn Hall; R. R. Knudson
34. Gloria D. Miklowitz; Rosemary
    Sutcliff
35. Susan Cooper; John Rowe
    Townsend; Jill Paton Walsh
36. Judy Angel/Fran Arrick; Hila
    Colman; Barbara Wersba
37. Joyce Carol Thomas
38. Lee Bennet Hopkins
39. H. M. Hoover
40. Bruce Brooks; Norma Johnson
41. Sandy Asher; Alan Garner; Sharon
    Bell Mathis
42. Jerry Spinelli
43. Gordon Korman; Katie Letcher Lyle;
    Julian F. Thompson
44. Kevin Major; Robin McKinley; Zoa
    Sherburne; Rosemary Wells
45. Larry Bograd; Leon Garfield
46. Avi; Barbara Girion; Susan Beth
    Pfeffer
47. T. Ernesto Bethancourt
48. Alice Bach; Zylpha Keatley Snyder
49. Katheryn Lasky; Nicholasa Mohr;
    Daniel Pinkwater
50. Hadley lrwin; Stella Pevsner
51. Robbie Branscum
52. John Donovan; Constance C.
    Greene; Myron Levoy, Marilyn Sachs
53. Chris Crutcher; Julius Lester; Gary
    Paulsen

Figure 2.2 The 100 Most Important Authors of Novels for Young Adults
(as ranked in the *ALAN Review* survey)

major writers of young adult literature. Were the survey to be run again today, major differences in the results undoubtedly would appear as a reflection of the works that have been written since 1988.

Although Gallo, in his listing of important authors, and Hipple, in his listing of important works, gathered their data from small, highly selective samples, their findings are interesting and useful as we establish a knowledge base for teachers to explore young adult literature. Throughout this text, we discuss books and authors representing the range of experiences that can be enjoyed through reading young adult literature. In the remainder of this chapter we will focus on two areas: first, an examination of types of books written for youthful audiences, and second, a description of several major authors of young adult literature.

Types of Literature

In this section, we define the major types of fiction and nonfiction written for young adult readers and provide examples of each. Under fiction, we examine realistic fiction, humor, mystery, fantasy, science fiction, and historical fiction. Figure 2.3 shows a schematic way of understanding the various fiction types. (Humor and mystery are not included in Figure 2.3 because they have a unique relationship with other types of fiction, which is discussed later.) Under nonfiction, we examine biography, autobiography, and informational books. Additionally, we discuss poetry, short stories, drama, and picture books for young adult readers.

Realistic Fiction

The major category of fiction for young adults encompasses books that reflect the contemporary world. Realistic books present a believable plot, lifelike characters with whom the readers can sympathize and empathize, and familiar settings such as school, neighborhood hangouts, the mall, and so on. Realism in literature does not imply an exact replica of life; rather, it reflects the writer's perspective in creating characters and situations as if they existed. In a realistic novel, authors avoid sentimentalism and sensationalism as they seek fully to develop characters with reasonable and believable conflicts. A type of realistic fiction for young adults that has been successful over the years is the problem novel—or what Donalson and Nilsen (1989, p. 83) call "the new realism." As early as 1977, Rinsky and Schweiker characterized the new realism as a style that

> invites close study of character and problem—a kind of case study the reader cannot for very human reasons give his own life but can objectively give to another's. It is not unreasonable to expect that the vicarious experiencing of fictional problems might aid the young reader to control the acts and scenes of his own life. (p. 472)

As we discussed previously, the term *problem novel* is misleading. Every novel must have a problem or conflict on which the action focuses. New realism in young adult literature refers to novels in which the characters encounter and must deal with significant challenges.

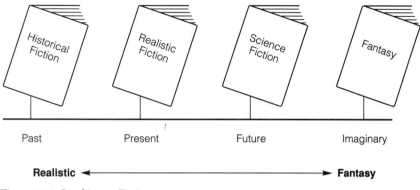

Past   Present   Future   Imaginary

Realistic ◄————————————————————► **Fantasy**

Figure 2.3   Looking at Fiction

The single most important aspect of the realistic young adult novel is the effectiveness of characters. Characters must be fully developed, believable people who function and respond either as the readers would or as people they know would. Part of the credibility of characters is their fallibility; they may make poor decisions or they may take foolish actions, but they learn from their mistakes. This learning process is the impetus for growth and change. Among the themes that are often explored in realistic fiction are alienation, search for a sense of identity, the importance of friendship, dealing and accepting change, and the changing role of the family, all of which provide opportunities for characters to learn and grow.

The following books are examples of the rich variety, breadth, and quality of realistic novels. They are Robert Cormier's *The Chocolate War,* Walter Dean Myers's *Fallen Angels* and Virginia Euwer Wolff's *The Mozart Season.*

The Chocolate War   Probably no young adult novel illustrates the power structure that can occur in schools as graphically as Robert Cormier's *The Chocolate War.* The novel depicts a power struggle between a malevolent administrator, Brother Leon, and a student named Archie, who is the leader of the most powerful students' group, the Vigils. Archie and Brother are locked in a psychological chess game of power, manipulation, and control with one another. Part of Archie's power comes from the "assignments" that the Vigils make—giving other students tasks to complete that range from simple pranks to risky challenges. Jerry Renault, a new student who is unable to get beyond being an outsider, becomes a perfect target for the Vigils. Jerry is vulnerable and alienated from his father, and grieving for his mother who recently died. He is powerless when given the assignment from the Vigils to refuse to participate in the school's fund-raising chocolate sale. The assignment makes Jerry a pawn in the power struggle between Archie and Brother Leon. For ten days Jerry goes along with the assignment, but on the eleventh day he takes charge of himself and his actions. The book provides an intriguing perspective on the concepts of power and corruption through the juxtaposition of Archie and Brother Leon and their manipulations of one another. Tragically, Jerry gets caught in the power struggle.

Fallen Angels In this novel by Walter Dean Myers, Richie Perry, after graduating from high school, is unable to afford college and fulfill his dream of becoming a writer like James Baldwin. He joins the army in part to earn money so his mother can keep his younger brother in school and in part to escape from the streets. When his medical profile verifying him not fit for combat duty doesn't get processed in time, he is sent to Vietnam by mistake. Filled with naive, romantic notions of war, Perry discovers its horrible reality when a new recruit steps on a mine less than a hundred yards from camp.

Walter Dean Myers wrote *Fallen Angels* in memory of his brother who died in Vietnam in 1968. Gripping and haunting, it is an action-filled account of the Vietnam experience seen through the eyes of a young African American soldier whose experiences mirror those of many others of his generation. It is also a powerful coming-of-age story as Perry struggles to survive—both physically and emotionally—and to achieve adulthood. He learns about the value of friendship and the senselessness of war. *Fallen Angels* is frequently compared with Stephen Crane's *The Red Badge of Courage* and is viewed by many as one of the most significant pieces of young adult literature in the last decade.

The Mozart Season As softball season and the school year fade into summer, twelve-year-old Allegra Shapiro learns that she has been selected as one of ten finalists for a Mozart competition for young violinists to be held on Labor Day. Softball had shaped the spring; the Fourth Violin Concerto would shape the summer. Her music teacher tells her that she will need to look within so that she will be able "to release the music inside of her." She struggles until her grandmother sends her a gift of her heritage. She begins anew with the concerto, finding not only the music within her but also her connection with her past as she plays both for herself and for her great-grandmother, who perished at Treblinka.

Virginia Euwer Wolff has created such a believable character in Allegra that the reader empathizes with her as she prepares for the competition. This book seems to be a simple story of a nice, talented girl; this, however, is a deceptive assumption. Although the book does not focus on a major conflict or problem, it presents a realistic picture of an introspective, thoughtful girl who is trying to make sense of her life and her history. Moreover, Wolff creates multidimensional secondary characters. Allegra's parents and brother play appropriate and believable roles in her summer of growth.

Humor

Among the most successful works of fiction for youthful readers are realistic works that include humorous elements. The works of Paula Danzinger, Ellen Cornford, Jerry Spinelli, Anne Fine, and Gordon Korman often present realistic characters who look at their world with a sense of humor. One of Gordon Korman's books, *Don't Care High,* is partially based on his own experiences in high school and reflects his philosophy that humor exists in every situation; it is the role of the writer to point it out. Joan Bauer's first book for young adults, *SQUASHED,* tells the story of sixteen-year-old Ellie Morgan's determination to win a giant pumpkin contest with Max, her beloved pumpkin. This book is much more than a funny story about growing pumpkins. Ellie and her father learn to understand and accept each other and to cope with the triumphs and tragedies of life.

Humor is not confined to realistic fiction. Writers of any type of fiction can use humor as a device to create situations to challenge and to develop characters. For example, fantasy writer Patricia C. Wrede uses humorous variations on traditional conventions of fantasy. In *Searching for Dragons,* the second book in the Enchanted Forest Chronicles, Princess Cimorene isn't a damsel in distress waiting for a knight to save her. She saves herself, Kazul, the dragon, and even the Enchanted Forest. Mel Gilden uses humor in his science fiction book, *The Planet of Amazement,* in which Rodney has zany adventures as he explores the universe. David Gale has edited a collection of original humorous short stories written by major young adult authors. The collection, entitled *Funny You Should Ask: The Delacorte Book of Original Humorous Short Stories,* includes stories by Gary Soto, Walter Dean Myers, and M. E. Kerr, among others.

Mystery (Suspense, Supernatural, and Horror)

While most works for young adults depend primarily on believable characters who react and interact in credible ways, mysteries depend upon carefully crafted plots filled with surprises, twists and turns, and clues, which must strike a balance between being too obscure and being too obvious. A mystery

**Figure 2.4   Relationship of Mystery to Other
              Types of Fiction**

can be set in any time; it could be a historical fiction, science fiction, or fantasy. See Figure 2.4

Mysteries share the following characteristics: fast-moving and suspenseful plots, realistic dialogue, and incidents that are perplexing for the characters and the reader. With the background of a station on the underground railroad, Virginia Hamilton's *The House of Dies Drear* is a mystery filled with mysterious figures, secret passageways, a hidden treasure, and a hint of the supernatural. *Dead Man in Indian Creek* by Mary Dowling Hahn is a typical mystery: a dead body, an unlikable suspect, and two youthful would-be detectives.

In Lois Duncan's *Daughters of Eve,* Tammy has a fearful premonition in one of the opening scenes. As time passes, however, she discounts it. Thus the reader is initially alerted to the danger and then is lulled into a false sense of safety, as is Tammy. Later, the reader and Tammy realize that her first impression was well founded. Although this book reflects the interest students have in the supernatural, it is not unduly emphasized.

The most popular books among many youthful readers are horror stories. Some critics speculate that their charm is that readers experience a sense of relief when they finish a gruesome horror book. They realize that their own lives are not so bad compared with the characters in the book. Books in this category range from the gentle ghost story *A Taste of Smoke* by Marion Dane Bauer to the supernatural tales and vampire stories of Caroline Cooney. Patricia Windsor, respected author of books such as *The Sandman's Eyes* (winner of the Edgar Allan Poe Award for the Best Juvenile Mystery of the Year) and *The Christmas Killer,* writes books she describes as dark fantasy. Their emphasis is on what the reader feels, and they do not have the violence, blood, and gore of typical horror books. Christopher Pike and R. L. Stine are the two widely read authors of horror books. Although their books seem superficial and predictable to adult readers, they have an enormous appeal to youthful readers. In *Remember Me,* Pike kills his main character in what is labeled a suicide in the first few chapters. He spends the next two hundred pages having her prove that she was murdered and finding the murderer from beyond the grave. Perhaps part of the popularity of these works is that they have a great deal in common with made-for-television movies.

Fantasy

Fantasies combine elements of realistic fiction with the realm of make-believe. A wide range of literature falls within this category. Some

> **Bridging**
>
> *Connecting Suspense Stories*
>
> Since the work of Edgar Allan Poe is often included in literature anthologies, the bridge between the stories of Poe and the novel <u>The Man Who Was Poe</u> by Avi is a natural one for students who enjoy suspense and mysteries.

works combine a basic sense of believability with a well-constructed plot, well-developed characters, and a setting from which characters may logically move into the imaginary world. Others are more closely related to mythology and involve imaginary creatures such as dragons and hobbits. Such books are known as high fantasy.

Fantasy epitomizes the concept of "fight the good fight" as it frequently pits a hero against a villain and involves the quest for truth and classic confrontations with strange, imaginary beasts. Among the classic fantasies for youthful readers are C. S. Lewis's seven-part series, *The Chronicles of Narnia,* which begins with *The Lion, the Witch, and the Wardrobe.* In these allegories, he presents a traditional theme of fantasies—the conflict between good and evil. The examination of such dualities is often the basis for the conflict in fantasy: light versus dark, strength versus weakness, innocence versus guilt, and life versus death.

In a more contemporary fantasy and ghost story, Marion Dane Bauer's *A Taste of Smoke,* a boy killed in a fire one hundred years before appears to thirteen-year-old Caitlin when she and her older sister, Pam, go camping. Caitlin is deeply moved by his story. Her concern creates a bond between her and the dead boy, who then reaches out to her for help.

Dealing with Dragons by Patricia C. Wrede tells the story of a beautiful princess, Cimorene, who is bored with the behavior expected of princesses. This liberated princess wants to do more exciting things than embroidery, dancing, and painting; she definitely does not want to be rescued by and marry a prince, especially since she is smarter than most of them. Cimorene goes to live with the dragons and has a number of adventures. This book is the first in a series, and, in fact, many high fantasies are written as series.

Science Fiction

William Sleator defines science fiction as "literature about something that hasn't happened yet but might be possible some day" (1992, p. 4). Science fiction combines characters and their relationships with plausible accounts of science, technology, and futurism. For example, *House of Stairs* by Sleator presents five young people being tested and conditioned in a behaviorist experiment gone awry. Science fiction may also present the reader with moral and ethical dilemmas to explore. These dilemmas frequently involve the effects of technology on human beings, conflicts between competing interests, and the consequences of decisions that fail to take into account ecological considerations.

Science fiction is always set in the future and frequently presents characters as pioneers exploring new worlds. Because of the futuristic perspective, science fiction depends on well-developed characters to involve readers. Science fiction also depends on logical, plausible explanations for its scientific details and inventions.

One significant theme in science fiction is the creation of utopian communities. For example, Lois Lowry's award-winning book, *The Giver,* is a powerful story of a futuristic society in which members have no memories of the past and no true feelings, because memories and feelings create pain. One member of the community, the Receiver of Memory, is designated to hold the collective memories of past generations. When decisions requiring wisdom must be made by the community, the Receiver calls upon the memories to provide guidance. When the young person selected to be the next Receiver-in-training begins questioning the value of life without memories and feelings of love, serious cracks appear in this utopian society.

Another ongoing theme of science fiction examines the threats to the existence of our planet. Robert C. O'Brien's *Z for Zachariah* remains popular with high school students even though it was published in 1974. In this book, the world as we know it has been destroyed by nuclear war. In the valley where she grew up, only Ann has survived until a stranger arrives. She nurses him back to health after he becomes ill with radiation poisoning. Then Ann must choose between succumbing to his harsh tyranny or leaving the valley to seek the possibility of other survivors.

Science fiction, whether we look at the works of the major authors for adults such as Arthur C. Clarke, Isaac Asimov, and Ray Bradbury, or the authors for young adults such as Monica Hughes, William Sleator, and Madeleine L'Engle, presents adventure, excitement, entertainment, conflict, and a look at what the future might bring. It is popular among youthful readers and frequently includes series or sequels such as Monica Hughes's stories of people from Earth who have gone to live on the planet Isis, *Keeper of the Isis Light, Guardian of Isis,* and *Isis Pedlar.*

Historical Fiction

Historical fiction, like science fiction, draws on a separate reality as its basis and for many of its ideas. Historical fiction provides a factual framework for an author to build a story upon. The characteristics of these books include the following:

- Authenticity of detail about the period, which reflects careful research

- Presentation of historical figures in a manner consistent with their documented actions and words

- Accuracy of chronology of events

- Characters who are believable

- Relevance of the story to current times, attitudes, and beliefs as well as to the historical period

- A vivid and accurate sense of history

Norton (1983, p. 76) discusses the process of creating a historical novel: "Authors of historical fiction whose books are noted for authentic backgrounds reveal that hundreds of hours are spent researching county courthouse records, letters, old newspapers, and history books, conducting personal interviews, and visiting museums and historic locations before the story is written." In the author's note that serves as a preface to *Wolf by the Ears,* Ann Rinaldi (1991) speaks about the process she used in preparing to write the book:

> It is important that the reader know that I have portrayed Jefferson's character as faithfully as I found it to be, after intensive study. Many of his quotes and sentiments are taken from his letters. I do not wish to distort or to improve upon American history. I wish to interpret it through my fiction, to make it more interesting so my readers, once their interest is quickened, will pursue it further. (p. ix)

Bridging

Utopia

In <u>Invitation to the Game</u> by Monica Hughes, a group of young people are compelled to begin a new society. The social ramifications of this book provide an appropriate bridging experience for students to read about popular utopian communities or to read <u>The Blithedale Romance</u> by Nathaniel Hawthorne, which was based upon the utopian community of Brook Farm.

Historian Christopher Collier (1982), who writes historical fiction with his brother James, articulated his perspective of historical fiction:

> The books I write with my brother are written with a didactic purpose—to teach about ideals and values that have been important in shaping the course of American history. This is in no way intended to denigrate the importance of the dramatic and literary elements of historical novels. Nothing will be taught, and certainly nothing will be learned, if no one reads the books. (p. 32)

Frequently, historical fiction presents characters confronting themselves or characters confronting their society. These types of conflict provide the reader with opportunities to reflect upon the values, problems, moral dilemmas and issues of the novel's time. In the Colliers' *My Brother Sam Is Dead,* Tim feels torn between his love for his father and his brother, Sam, because they are on opposite sides of the war. Tim spends a great deal of time wondering what and whom he should believe. All people, young and old, experience such emotions at some time during their lives. This book also demonstrates the injustice of war. Sam, who has faithfully fought for the patriots against his father's wishes, is executed by a patriot general as a example for the other soldiers for leaving his post and stealing his own cows.

In Avi's *The Fighting Ground,* young Jonathan must confront the discrepancy between his image of war and the reality of battle. His perspective is altered when he is taken prisoner by three Hessian soldiers who, although they are the enemy, are not cruel men. Conversely, the American corporal who recruited him for battle is cruel and enjoys "killing too much." He has little understanding or compassion for his men.

Joyce Hansen's books *Which Way Freedom?,* a Coretta Scott King Honor Book, and *Out from This Place* realistically portray the role of African Americans during the Civil War and the period immediately following it. Although both books are fiction, they are based on actual events and provide the reader with another point of view of this turbulent period in our nation's history.

Elizabeth Howard's *America as Story: Historical Fiction for Secondary Schools* from the American Library Association is a useful source for teachers seeking information on books to incorporate into their curriculum.

Nonfiction

Although nonfiction has a number of definitions, we will focus upon those books that are factually based rather than based on the author's creation. Traditionally the English curriculum has equated literature almost exclusively with fiction. When many students have a choice, however, they read from the

large selection of quality nonfiction. Nonfiction's popularity
among youth is being recognized more frequently now and is
included in the curriculum. Works of nonfiction inform,
challenge, intrigue, and entertain. Many students read nonfiction exclusively. Carter and Abrahamson (1990) report in
Nonfiction for Young Adults: From Delight to Wisdom that
various research studies indicate that adolescent males show
a far greater preference for nonfiction than females do. They
define the field of nonfiction as all books that are neither
novels nor short stories, according to the designation of the
Dewey Decimal System. Among the most frequently read
works of nonfiction are informational books that cover a
broad variety of topics. Any teacher seeking to use nonfiction
will be greatly helped by reading Carter and Abrahamson's
book.

Biography and Autobiography   Biographies are the nonfiction
accounts of the lives of individuals. Biographies reveal the
vital relationship between an individual and the time period
in which he or she lives by offering insights into the period

> **Bridging**
> *The Reality of War*
>
> The main characters in the classic <u>The Red Badge of Courage</u> by Stephen Crane and in <u>The Fighting Ground</u> by Avi are young men with romantic ideas about war. In this bridging experience, readers see how each confronts the reality of war and even more importantly, how each deals with himself in a battle situation.

and into the character of its subject. Since authenticity is one of the major criteria for examining biographies, the portrayal of the times and their events
must support the portrayal of character. Another element of biography is the
frequent presentation of conflicts that the major character must overcome.
This element is engaging for students because it allows them to relate empathetically to the character attempting to resolve conflict. For instance, *Amos
Fortune, Free Man* by Elizabeth Yates chronicles the life of a man who was
captured in Africa and taken to New England as a slave. Through his sense of
honor and hard work, he gains his freedom after many years and overcomes
prejudice. The book also provides a vital picture of colonial America.

Some of the most successful recent biographies for youth are written by
Russell Freedman. In *Lincoln, A Photobiography,* the 1988 Newbery Medal
winner, Freedman provides photographs, political cartoons, and drawings to
accompany his text revealing Lincoln's life. He uses the same approach in his
other popular biographies, *Franklin Delano Roosevelt* (1990) and *Eleanor Roosevelt: A Life of Discovery* (1993), a Newbery Honor Book. *The Wright Brothers: How They Invented the Airplane* (1991) is also a Newbery Honor book.

Another approach to biographical writing is the autobiographical memoir,
such as the one M. E. Kerr, highly regarded author of young adult literature,
wrote of her youth and the people she knew growing up. By her own account,
Kerr wrote *Me Me Me Me Me Not a Novel* to show her readers where her

inspiration for both characters and events came from. Also in this category is *Starting from Home,* in which Milton Meltzer, a noted author of informational books for young adults, chronicles his early years.

A popular series of critical biographies of authors is Twayne's United States Author Series, Young Adult Authors, *Presenting. . . .* Focusing on the works of major authors for young adults, these books provide readers with insights into how the authors work and the role that significant events in their lives play in their works. The series includes the following authors, with other titles added on a regular basis:

Presenting Robert Cormier by Patricia Campbell

Presenting William Sleator by James E. Davis and Hazel Davis

Presenting Walter Dean Myers by Rudine Sims Bishop

Presenting Zibby Oneal by Susan Bloom and Cathryn Mercier

Presenting S. E. Hinton by Jay Daly

Presenting Judy Blume by Maryann Weidt

Presenting M. E. Kerr by Aileen Nilsen

Presenting Sue Ellen Bridgers by Ted Hipple

Presenting Norma Fox Mazer by Sally Holtze

Presenting Norma Klein by Allene Phy

Presenting Rosa Guy by Jerrie Norris

Presenting Paul Zindel by Jack Forman

Presenting Richard Peck by Donald Gallo

Presenting Lois Duncan by Cosette Kies

Presenting Madeleine L'Engle by Donald Hettinga

Informational Books   In their study of nonfiction readers, Carter and Abrahamson identified two primary reasons for reading informational books: to gain the satisfaction of learning new information and to experience the satisfaction of reaffirming what is already known.

Informational books are written on virtually every topic and can make a significant contribution in content classes. For example, in social studies or science classes informational books can serve as useful supplements to course content. *The Boys' War* by Jim Murphy could serve as an effective supplement to text material on the Civil War because it introduces multiple perspectives as it presents the first-person accounts of young boys who served during the war. Milton Meltzer's *Rescue: The Story of How Gentiles Saved Jews in the Holocaust* provides youthful readers with an awareness that humanity did not totally go awry during the Second World War. Each chapter describes the heroics of people such as King Christian X of Denmark and Raoul Wallenberg. This work provides different perspectives than those that are presented in history textbooks.

Books that provide students with information about directions they may take in their lives are valuable. Of particular interest to adolescents are books that explore careers. One book that appeals to young people is *Working: People Talk About What They Do All Day and How They Feel About What They Do* by Studs Terkel. It provides a realistic perspective about the work different people have chosen. For college-bound students, a number of guidebooks provide information about higher education. Books about hobbies, computers, and travel are also widely available. Many students are more likely to read if teachers make a variety of informational books available.

Other Types of Literature

The most frequently read genre of young adult literature is realistic fiction; however, poetry, short stories, drama, and picture books also have a definite place in the middle school and secondary school curriculum. Certainly, reading from a variety of literary genres will help students to recognize the breadth of literature and to find literature that appeals to them.

Poetry Perhaps no literary genre evokes a stronger (and too often negative) reaction from most adolescent students than poetry. Elementary students often have wonderful experiences with listening to poetry and participating in choral readings. They are captivated by the sounds of words, by the flow of the rhythm, and by the joy of rhyming. Something happens after these early experiences with poetry that results in the negative reactions of many middle school and high school students. Perhaps that difference is that younger children usually hear and experience poetry, whereas, in the middle schools and high schools, students are assigned to read and to interpret poetry. Too often the process of interpretation asks that students read a two-hundred-year-old poem from their literature anthology and decide what the teacher thinks the poem means. The vitality of the oral experiences the student has had in elementary school gives way to a dry, difficult, and often obscure academic exercise. It is no wonder that many adolescent students groan when they hear the word *poem.* Fortunately, some poets and anthologists have recognized the young adult readers' problems with poetry and have done something to change the situation.

In 1966, Stephen Dunning and two colleagues published a collection of contemporary poetry called *Reflections on the Gift of Watermelon Pickle;* three years later they followed it with a second collection entitled *Some Haystacks*

Don't Have Any Needles. These were groundbreaking books because Dunning brought together poems that were accessible to students—poems they could understand, experience, and enjoy. These collections were joined in 1970 by Arnold Adoff's powerful collection of African American poetry, *I Am the Darker Brother.* These books provide the foundation for later collections such as editor Richard Peck's *Sounds and Silences: Poetry for Now* and *Mindscapes: Poems for the Real World.*

Perhaps the most influential poets for young adult readers are two contemporary poets who also happen to be teachers. The first is Paul Janeczko, a high school teacher from Maine, who edits poetry collections and writes poetry. His books include *Postcard Poems: A Collection of Poetry for Sharing, Don't Forget to Fly, Strings: A Gathering of Family Poems, The Place My Words Are Looking For,* and *Poetspeak: In Their Work, About Their Work.* The second poet is Mel Glenn, who writes for and about high school students. His works include *Class Dismissed: High School Poems, Class Dismissed II: More High School Poems, Back to Class,* and *My Friend's Got This Problem, Mr. Chandler.*

Among recent collections of poetry for young people are *Poems That Sing to You,* selected by Michael R. Strickland, and Naomi Shihab Nye's *This Same Sky: A Collection of Poems from Around the World.* Nye's collection is a celebration of diversity. Nye is an accomplished poet who has published *Different Ways to Pray, Hugging the Jukebox,* and *Yellow Glove.*

Making poetry accessible to young adult readers is often simply a matter of looking to contemporary authors and compilers. Poetry can be about any subject and can be in any number of formats. The traditional ideas of poetry need to be revised so that poetry can take its place in the middle school and high school classroom.

Short Stories   While most high school anthologies feature short stories, traditionally they have not been stories written for young adults; therefore, they are often not stories that youthful readers relate to easily. In 1984, Don Gallo edited a collection entitled *Sixteen Short Stories by Outstanding Writers for Young Adults.* Gallo, in the introduction, talks about the book's uniqueness: "First, there has never before been a collection of short stories written specifically for teen-agers by authors who specialize in writing books for young people. Second, none of these stories has appeared in print before, except for one that appeared in a now defunct magazine in a slightly different form." In this collection, Gallo organizes the stories into five sections: Friendships, Turmoils, Loves, Decisions, and Families, each section relevant to the interests and concerns of young adults. Gallo has followed this collection with several others: *Visions: Nineteen Short Stories by Outstanding Writers for Young Adults* (1988), *Connection: Short Stories by Outstanding Writers for Young Adults* (1989),

Short Circuits: Thirteen Shocking Stories by Outstanding Writers for Young Adults (1992), *Within Reach* (1993), and *Join In: Multiethnic Short Stories by Outstanding Writers for Young Adults* (1993). These collections include stories by authors such as Joan Aiken, Robin Brancato, Sue Ellen Bridgers, Robert Cormier, Chris Crutcher, M. E. Kerr, Gordon Korman, Walter Dean Myers, Harry Mazer, Norma Fox Mazer, Robert Lipsyte, Richard Peck, Ouida Sebestyen, Todd Strasser, Robert Westfall, and Patricia Windsor, among other well-known young adult authors.

Other collections of short stories include Joyce Carol Thomas's multi-cultural anthology *A Gathering of Flowers: Stories About Being Young in America.* These stories reveal the diverse nature of our society and are by such authors as Ana Castillo, Gerald Haslam, Jeanne Wakatsuki Houston, Maxine Hong Kingston, Kevin Kyung, Lois Lowry, Gary Soto, Joyce Carol Thomas, Gerald Vizenor, Rick Wernli, and Al Young.

Some young adult authors have written their own collections of stories. Robert Cormier's *8 Plus 1* provides readers with insights about his life growing up in New England. Norma Fox Mazer has published two collections, *Dear Bill, Remember Me? and Other Stories* and *Summer Girls, Love Boys, and Other Stories.* Chris Crutcher revisits some characters from his novels in the six short stories in *Athletic Shorts.* Canadian author Martha Brooks has a collection of stories called *Paradise Cafe and Other Stories.* Gary Soto has two collections of stories that capture the experience of growing up Mexican American—*Baseball in April and Other Stories* and *Local News.*

The short story is a popular form of fiction for young people. Quality short stories will continue to be increasingly available for young adults.

Drama Probably the most neglected field for young adults is drama. Few playwrights have written for youthful audiences. Paul Zindel's *The Effects of Gamma Rays on Man-in-the-Moon Marigolds* was the first. For years, it was the primary dramatic effort by an author of young adult literature. One source of plays that may be appropriate in the classroom are the annual collections of prize-winning plays from the Young Playwright Festival, edited by Wendy Lamb. The award-winning playwrights are from ten to eighteen years of age. Among the books in this series are:

Meeting the Winter Bike Rider and Other Prize-winning Plays from the 1983–84 Young Playwrights Festival

The Ground Zero Club and Other Prize-winning Plays from the 1985–86 Young Playwrights Festival

Sparks in the Park and Other Prize-winning Plays from the 1987–88 Young Playwrights Festival

Hey Little Walter and Other Prize-winning Plays from the 1989–90 Young Playwrights Festival

A collection of one-act plays, *Center Stage,* edited by Don Gallo, is an effort to bring drama to a young adult audience. The authors represented in this volume are Sandy Asher, Robin Brancato, Alden R. Carter, Cin Forshay-Lunsford, Dallin Malmgren, Walter Dean Myers, Lensey Namioka, Jean Davies Okimoto, Susan Beth Pfeffer, and Ouida Sebestyen.

Picture Books   Until recently, teachers and students alike thought that picture books were just for young readers; however, a number of picture books can be used effectively with older students. Picture books have a strong visual content, and, indeed, their success is dependent on the artistic value of the illustrations and a well-written text. Picture books may cover any topic or concern. For example, some picture books address social problems, such as Eve Bunting's *Fly Away Home.* This book visually presents the story of a father and his son who are homeless and live at an airport. Sherry Garland, writer, and Tatsuro Kiuchi, illustrator, portray the lives of a Vietnamese family as its members face change and war in *The Lotus Seed.* Diane Stanley and Peter Vennema write and illustrate picture-book biographies. One of the biographies is *Bard of Avon: The Story of William Shakespeare,* which captures the man and his times in words and illustrations. A variation is the wordless picture book. These books, as the name implies, tell a story entirely in pictures. Jeannie Baker's *Window* presents a powerful ecological message in its view of the changing environment from a window.

Major Authors

Another approach to becoming acquainted with young adult literature is to explore a few of the major writers in the field. Students in a survey we conducted of reading preferences (Brown, 1992b) indicate that the author of a book has an influence on their choice of reading materials. The author was the third most frequently listed influence of female students, grades 9–12, and the sixth most frequently listed influence of male students, grades 9–12. Students frequently find an author whom they enjoy and then read everything that author writes.

Several sources of information about authors are helpful to readers. Among the most useful are two books edited by Donald R. Gallo for the National Council of Teachers of English: *Speaking for Ourselves* and *Speaking for Ourselves, Too.* Additionally, the About the Author series provides information about authors and their works. In this section, we highlight four authors for those of you new to the field of young adult literature and those wanting to expand your reading. The authors are M. E. Kerr, Norma Fox Mazer, Gary Paulsen, and Richard Peck.

M. E. Kerr

Author of many award-winning books, M. E. Kerr always wanted to be a writer. Raised in a small town in New York, she writes:

> I was very much formed by books when I was young. I was a bookworm and a poetry lover. I think of myself, and what I would have liked to have found in books those many years ago. I remember being depressed by all the neatly tied-up, happy-ending stories, the abundance of winners, the themes of winning, solving, finding—when around me it didn't seem that easy. So I write with a different feeling when I write for young adults. I guess I write for myself at that age. (1991, p. 1)

> Whether M. E. Kerr's books deal with difficult social issues such as a brother dying of AIDS in *Night Kites,* describe a complex relationship with a cultured grandfather who turns out to be a notorious Nazi war criminal in *Gentlehands*, or solve mysteries in the popular Fell series, they all are compelling stories with strong characterization, wry humor, and social and moral dilemmas. Kerr writes that "The stories that compel me are about differences in people: understanding them, and understanding those who can't accept them . . . surviving, with humor, others' and your own slings and arrows . . . trying to make some sense of it all, never losing sight of the power love lends" (1990, p. 108). A representative sample of her books is found in Appendix A.

Norma Fox Mazer

Lively and witty, Norma Fox Mazer, who has been writing since the age of thirteen, describes her own adolescence: "I laughed and cried and shivered and trembled through my adolescence: tremendous upheavals of feelings, yet all the time the eyes were there, the observer was there, watching, noting, remembering. . . . I thought I was the only one who felt different, apprehensive, vulnerable" (1990, pp. 8–9). Mazer's books speak honestly and convincingly of the emotions, changes, and challenges young people experience. Drawing on her own memories, she states that

> working-class towns, working-class families are important to me. They are the fabric against which my life was drawn. . . . Work and the need for work was a constant thread in our lives. And my parents sitting around and gabbing about the past, their relatives, and friends was another constant. I didn't recognize it then as storytelling. Today, with hindsight, I suppose that my insistent need to write, to tell stories, is directly related to those past moments." (1990, p. 140)

Norma Fox Mazer's most acclaimed book, *After the Rain,* is the story of Rachel and the loving relationship she develops with her gruff and distant grandfather who is terminally ill. Themes in this book occur in many of her other works: searching for self-acceptance, gaining independence from overly protective parents, and learning to deal with a first love and the self-doubts accompanying that relationship. Mazer's artistic skill at telling a good story and expressing a wide range of emotions makes her books compelling reading for young adults and adults. A representative sample of her books is found in Appendix A.

Gary Paulsen

Gary Paulsen, in a speech he gave in 1991, describes his junior high school experiences: "I was a nerd, a geek, whatever they call it now. I was the last kid chosen or not chosen at all and I didn't have many friends at all either." He failed ninth grade and had to repeat it. By his own admission, he barely graduated from high school. In the subsequent years, he tried several careers before becoming a writer at age twenty-six. His numerous books reflect his varied experiences. For nine years he ran dog sleds and participated twice in the Iditarod, the trans-Alaska dog race. Of his experiences in the frozen world of dog racing, he has said: "The beauty is staggering. . . . It's just incredible. Once you've done that, it's hard to get excited about a mall. It changes your whole life and that change is permanent" (1991). Although he never won a dog sled race, he feels that the experience was more important than winning: "To me, the race is the maximum expression of a person and a dog team. The best you can do is to win, but just to make it is something" (1991). His 1990 book *Woodsong* is dedicated to Cookie, his lead dog whom he kept as a house dog until her death. In the book he discusses his real-life racing experiences and describes the bond that develops with the dogs in the team.

Paulsen's books frequently explore the theme of survival in the wilderness, and he often explores rural life. Three of his books, *Dogsong, Hatchet*, and *The Winter Room,* are Newbery Honor Books. He wrote a screenplay for an adaptation of *Hatchet* and was 1991 recipient of the ALAN Award from the National Council of Teachers of English for his contributions to the field of young adult literature. His books have received a number of other awards. A representative sample of his books is found in Appendix A.

Richard Peck

A former junior and senior high school English teacher, Richard Peck writes: "Being a teacher made a writer out of me. After all teaching is the craft of communicating with strangers in a language you can find. It's the craft of meeting absolute deadlines. It's the craft of trying to give time a shape. These are the needs of the novelist" (1992a, p. 87). Other quotations from his text illustrates Peck's commitment to his craft and audience: "I exited the classroom to see if I could turn Life into novels instead of lesson plans" (p. 83); "The people I wanted to write for were my students. We'd spent years together, and from the first working day I'd learned things about them their parents dare never know" (p. 78).

Peck writes novels for mainstream young people that explore their issues, struggles, and anxieties. His books, without becoming morbid or hopeless, deal with serious realities such as suicide in *Remembering the Good Times,* peer-group pressures in *Princess Ashley,* and family problems. Peck writes

> We've given our mainstream readers a literature of nonconformity which they've accepted too calmly. We need a new one to question their provincial pieties without belittling the problems or telling them they don't have any. We need a literature that holds out hope to the children of parents who have become so successful in worldly ways that they seem impossible acts to follow. (1992, p. 76)

He asks, "How do we make role models of and for the conventional children of privilege and permissiveness?" (1992, p. 73).

Peck is considered one of the finest writers of young adult literature, and in 1990 he received the School Library Journal/Young

---

Sharing the Connection

Hachet
Gary Paulsen

If I were to choose a book that is a must to read, I would select Hatchet by Gary Paulsen. The reason for this choice is that every page of every chapter held my attention. This is the only book I have ever read that had a continual intensity in the story. Usually at some point in a book there is a section that adds little or nothing to the overall story. In Hatchet, the intensity seems to keep growing. When I finished it, I realized that this may have been the first time I read a book cover to cover without putting it down, not counting picture books. I would recommend anyone to read this book. I believe it is appropriate for a variety of audiences.

Joe Colombo, student

Literature Involvement Strategy

Sentence Collecting

Sentence collecting, as described by Richard Speaker, Jr., and Penelope Speaker (1991), is designed to foster aesthetic appreciation of literature, develop higher-level thinking skills such as analysis and evaluation, and promote student enjoyment of literature and language. The strategy is simple: as they read, students find sentences that appeal to them for one reason or another. They record these sentences, with title, author, and page number, on strips of paper or chart paper and display them in the classroom. The sentences then become the focal point for discussion. Teachers may want to begin the process of sentence collecting by sharing some of their own favorite sentences and modeling what criteria they used to select them. The following are a few of ours:

"Loving is truly the biggest risk a person can take, and the one that's the most worth it" (All Together Now by Sue Ellen Bridgers, p. 57).

"Small islands of sanity in a darkling plain where ignorant armies clash by night" (Celine by Brock Cole, p. 127).

"I played on against the wind, the movement of the ship and my own self-disgust, and finally the slaves began to lift their feet, the chains attached to the shackles around their ankles forming an iron dirge,

below the trills of my tune" (The Slave Dancer by Paula Fox, p. 67).

'"When somebody can look at you and insult you because you're old, or because you're young, or because you're black, or because you're . . . you're whatever you are, it's all the same. And what it's not is funny!'" (Won't Know Till I Get There by Walter Dean Myers, p. 148).

Some teachers and students collect phrases or many sentences, whereas others collect sentences that illustrate a particular type of writing or literary element such as imagery or metaphor. Some use the sentences as starting points for book talks, prompts for writing, or springboards for creative projects.

Sentence collecting can be used effectively with all four of the instructional formats we describe in Chapter 9. It can also be a part of a literature response journal or literature portfolio. A double-entry format is sometimes used, in which students record the quote on one side of the page and their response to it on the other side.

Sentence collecting is a highly effective strategy for involving students in literature and helping them to make connections between what they read and their own lives.

Adult Services Division Author Achievement Award from the American Library Association. His novels have received numerous awards and three of them, *The Ghost Belonged to Me, Are You in the House Alone?,* and *Father Figure,* were made into feature-length films. A representative sample of his books appears in Appendix A.

We have only begun to present an introduction to the field of young adult literature and some of its important authors in this chapter. Throughout the remaining chapters of this book, we will continue to discuss other books and authors. In Appendix B, we have included lists of the recipients of the major awards for young adult literature.

Summary

Major contributions to the field of young adult literature are a starting point for learning about works written for young people. The genre of young adult literature comprises a range of types of works. Teachers—in-service and pre-service—need to continue to explore the field and to read widely so that they can incorporate young adult literature into their curriculum to meet their students' needs.

Suggested Activities

1. In your journal, discuss what type of literature you enjoy the most and why.

2. Begin a list of young adult books and authors that you want to read.

3. Refer to Appendix B and select an award-winning book to read. After completing it, describe why you think the book received its award.

4. Use the Sentence Collecting idea described in this chapter's Literature Involvement Strategy with one of the young adult literature selections you are reading. If you are currently teaching, use this strategy with your students.

CHAPTER 3

Learning About the Young Adult in Young Adult Literature

Stories can help teenagers look at their feelings, or come to emotional resolution, from a safe distance. If, as an author, I can make an emotional connection with my reader, I have already started to help him or her heal. I have never met a depressed person, or an anxious person, or a fearful person who was not encouraged by the knowledge that others feel the same way they do. I am not alone is powerful medicine. If others feel this way, and they have survived, then I can survive too.

Chris Crutcher

Journal Writing: Responding

Reflect upon your own experiences in middle school or high school as a reader. What book do you remember as having a strong impact on you? How did it affect or influence you?

"The more I know about them, the less I truly understand them," remarked a friend of ours, the mother of five, who was describing her youngest child's latest teenage antics. Volumes have been written about adolescence, yet this time is, in our culture, one of the most perplexing and complex stages of development, both for the youths going through it and the adults accompanying them on this journey. Although there are many different ways to examine adolescent development, the perspective we take in this chapter and the next is to focus on what educators need to know to promote adolescents as readers and the role that young adult literature plays in their development. In order to select and use young adult literature effectively, teachers must understand adolescents, their needs, and their interests. We explore the characteristics of adolescents and current societal influences in this chapter within the context of using young adult literature in the classroom.

Adolescence as a concept is relatively new. It was first recognized as a separate developmental stage by G. Stanley Hall in his 1905 publication *Adolescence: Its Psychology and Its Relations to Physiology, Anthropology, Sociology, Sex, Crime, Religion and Education*. Among the societal changes that contributed to this new concept of young people were the evolution of the United States from an agrarian society to an industrial society, improved child labor laws designed to eliminate abusive sweatshop conditions, and the accessibility of secondary education to all students. More students stayed in schools longer and delayed entering the work force and marrying. These conditions created a whole new social group. Many young people, who in other times or other places would have been viewed as adults—working, living independently, and raising their own families—were, at the turn of the century, still living with their parents and going to school. In other words, their entry into adult society, with its inherent privileges and responsibilities, was deferred. Adolescence became an in-between period marked by confusion and frustration.

Characteristics and Developmental Tasks of Adolescents

Nearly a hundred years later, the definitional characteristics of adolescence remain remarkably similar:

> Some of the most complex transitions of life occur during adolescence, as the body changes from a child's to an adult's, relationships with others take on new meanings and levels of intricacy, and individuals become increasingly independent. For most, adolescence is, or at least should be, a time of expanding horizons and self-discovery as skills are acquired for establishing adult roles. (Elliott and Feldman, 1990, p. 1)

Yet for today's youth, adolescence is an even more complex time with increased expectations and greater possibilities and also increased risks and greater dangers. Some of the changes in our society affecting adolescents include

- Great variations in the family structure
- Major changes in roles, expectations, and opportunities for females
- Increased ethnic and cultural diversity
- A high school diploma as a minimum expectation and post-secondary education accessible to many
- Powerful influence of mass media and popular culture, and influences outside of the home
- Increased consumerism, often accompanied by more young people in the work place, usually in low-paying service jobs
- More forms and increased availability of entertainment and leisure activities
- Easier access to and increased use of alcohol and other drugs

- Changing sexual mores and increased dangers from sexually transmitted diseases

- The information and technology explosion that changes faster than much of the school curriculum

Chris Crutcher, child and family therapist and award-winning young adult novelist, provides a poignant picture of adolescence:

> One of the most ferocious enemies of any teenager is powerlessness. Developmentally they are in a time of separation getting ready to become adults. However, this culture draws that process out for as many as eight years. As a teenager, I am expected to pretend I am an adult, to be polite, to hide my feelings, though I am accorded few privileges that go with adulthood. I'm caught. My parents need to have power over me to keep me from doing incredibly ridiculous things that could damage me for life. My teachers need to keep me under control because they have twenty-five to thirty-five students before them, any one of whom would be more than happy to send the room spinning into total chaos. I may be studying things I'm not interested in, and am often told how important those things will be in my life, when I know that isn't true. Nothing seems under my control. Sexually I'm exploding like desert flowers following a flash flood, at the same time I'm being told only to keep it under control, not how to keep it under control. I don't know whether it excites me or terrifies me more.
>
> My separation, likely as not, appears in the form of rebellion. I am surrounded by people who are afraid that rebellion will get out of hand, and I can't talk about the fact that I'm afraid because my psyche is far too fragile to take that chance. I don't ask good questions and I don't get good answers. Because of the beliefs of many adults around me, I have confused respect with fear; sex or dependence or addiction or guilt, with love. I have been told I need to be less selfish, when, in truth, I need to be exactly as selfish as I am. I am told to think of others before I think of myself, which is a developmental impossibility. I have been told that some of my best traits, ones that include my as yet unpolished senses of humor and creativity, are unacceptable. In other words, many of the traits that will take me far in later life may be seen as threats to the people who are trying to help me become "responsible." (1992, p. 36)

Sue Ellen Bridgers talks about her reactions to adolescents:

> Young people energize me. I like the intensity with which many of them live. Their lives seem more exciting, more on the edge than those of adults.

But many middle class young people seem sad to me, too. If they are aware of world events, they have reason to be concerned, and I am appreciative of the positive outlets many have found to let their voices be heard about social and political issues such as the students in Colorado who succeeded in having tuna banned in their school cafeteria. Surely they will use that experience to tackle other environmental issues in the future.

But frequently teenagers' worries are turned inward, and they grapple with their problems alone. Too many of them don't seem to have appropriate skills or information to cope successfully. Then there are the kids in jail, on drugs, truant; there are children having children or suffering abuse many of us didn't know existed a few years ago. Kids who go to school hungry and sleep in abandoned automobiles, vacant buildings, boxes. Then there are the students who seem to be sleepwalking through school, their major interest their after-school jobs which provide car payments and gas. Their most urgent cause is getting an "open campus" lunch policy. Even those students intrigue me. What is going on behind their sleepy eyes? What motivates the teenage athlete? What kind of home life does the perfect student have? How will the decisions they make today affect their adult lives? What are they thinking, feeling, longing for? (1992, p. 66)

Although the majority of young people (and their parents and teachers) successfully survive this period, statistics from the Children's Defense Fund (Adolescent and Young Adult Factbook, 1991) present a troubling picture only too familiar to many teachers struggling to make a connection with today's youth.

Every day, teenagers give birth to 1,336 babies and teens younger than 15 give birth to 29 babies.

Every day of the school year, 2,478 teenagers drop out of school.

Every day, 4,901 teenagers and 2,976 young adults are the victims of violent crime.

454,000 junior and senior high school students are weekly binge drinkers.
8 million junior and senior high school students drink alcohol weekly.

Even with major societal changes, the significant characteristics of adolescent development have remained constant for many years. Feldman and Elliott (1990) articulate these core developmental tasks of adolescents:

becoming emotionally and behaviorally autonomous

dealing with emerging sexuality

acquiring interpersonal skills for dealing with members of the opposite sex and preparing for mate selection

acquiring education and other experiences needed for adult work roles

and resolving issues of identity and values (p.12)

While cultural changes in our society are causing some researchers and theorists to question the applicability of this developmental model for all young people today, Stover and Tway (1992) list "some of the common concerns of adolescents which seem to transcend cultural boundaries":

the need to define oneself outside the realm of the family

the need to come to terms with new visions of one's parents as "less than perfect"

the need to determine an individual set of moral, ethical, religious, or political principles

the need to come to terms with a developing sexuality and with the physiological changes brought on by puberty

the need to begin to develop positive relationships with the opposite sex

the need to begin to think about the future, about career options and job possibilities, about whether to marry or remain single

the need to forge a niche in the larger society (p. 140)

Young adult literature can play a significant role in helping adolescents understand and accept their ethnic and cultural similarities and differences. Giving youngsters of diverse backgrounds the opportunity to read literature that is reflective of their own experiences provides powerful affirmation of their identity and worth. At the same time, all young people, regardless of their background, benefit from learning about others and gaining a more comprehensive and balanced world view. Kathryn H. Au, in her 1993 book, *Literacy Instruction in Multicultural Settings,* describes a 1990 study by Linda Spears-Bunton (1990) of the responses of African American and European American students when African American literature was added to the traditional curriculum in an eleventh-grade English class.

This study by Spears-Bunton demonstrates the benefits of having students read culturally conscious multiethnic literature. Reynolds [the teacher] took a brave step forward when she decided to have her class read African American Literature and set the stage for the students to come to grips with the challenging issues of ethnicity, gender, and social class. Tensions and negative attitudes had to be confronted. Then, later, as they became immersed in reading *The House of Dies Drear* [by Virginia Hamilton], students were able to deal openly and honestly with issues of ethnicity and the relationships between African and European Americans, both past and present. Students, even those who had previously performed poorly in class, became committed to doing well on classroom assignments and tests related to their reading. (p. 184)

A public school colleague of ours, Louise Garcia Harrison, had a similar experience when she directed her urban class to explore their ethnic and racial heritage. Her students read works, as whole class activities, by Asian-American, African-American, and Hispanic authors, looking at both the literature and language, as the springboard for their own explorations. They then conducted individual study, learning about their own family and linguistic histories. Harrison felt that this was one of the most successful experiences that students had that year. Her students talked about gaining a sense of identity with their traditions that they had never had before. Among the other benefits was the sharing they did with one another and the appreciation and understanding they gained about each others' background.

We believe that young adult literature has the potential to be a unifying force in an increasingly diverse society. Virginia Hamilton (1990) speaks to the role of a good story in helping people to understand their commonalities:

Race, too, is an important element in my books, though I don't sit down at my typewriter determined to write a Black story. It just happens that I know Black people better than I know any other kind of people because I am Black and I am comfortable writing about the people I know best. But more than anything, I write about emotions and themes which are common to all people: family unity, friendships, the importance of individual freedom, and the influence of our past heritage on the present. My aim is always to tell a good story. (pp. 90–91)

Going to the Source: Looking at Characters in Young Adult Literature

One reason that youths read young adult literature is that they are able to see themselves in these books. In the previous section we looked at characteristics of adolescents and the changing conditions they face today. We will discuss these lists and synthesize that information with books and characters who exemplify the characteristic or who experience the conditions. This correlation shows the connection between today's youths and the literature that is being written for them. In our discussion we will first examine the characteristics of adolescents by identifying characters from different books, then we will do a more in-depth exploration of how each of the characteristics is exemplified in Chris Crutcher's *Stotan!*

Dealing with Issues of Identity

If we had to identify one overriding characteristic of adolescence, it would probably be that of seeking and articulating, in a number of ways, a sense of self-identity. These are the transitional years in which most young people struggle to search for an answer to the question, Who am I? Each of the several books in this discussion about identity presents a different facet of dealing with issues of identity.

In Laurence Yep's *Child of the Owl,* twelve-year-old Casey has floated around with her father, a compulsive gambler who is unable to hold a job. She has no connection with her family and she is removed from her Chinese American heritage. After her father is hospitalized, Casey goes to stay with her maternal grandmother who lives in Chinatown. At this time, Casey begins to ask about her own mother and to learn about her heritage. Her grandmother begins to share with Casey family stories. For the first time, Casey begins to get a sense of family and of her own identity.

In her historical novel *Wolf by the Ears,* Ann Rinaldi demonstrates that a search for identity is not just a twentieth-century concern. In this book, she creates and develops the character of Harriet Hemmings, the alleged daughter of Thomas Jefferson and Sally Hemmings. Harriet must decide whether or not to leave Monticello and furthermore decide whether or not to pass as white. She must choose between two worlds and decide how she will make an identity in the world she chooses.

Sharing the Connection

Number the Stars
Lois Lowry

I really liked this book because it was on a topic that I really am interested in. The story is about a girl and her best friend growing up in a very hard time. The time period of World War II really interests me. I like suspenseful stories, and there is a lot of suspense in the stories about this time. This story really made me think. I liked hearing about all the secret things that went on. I thought that the Resistance was so neat that I wanted to find some more books just like this one. I thought this book was terrific from the first page. The story was so believable and real that it made me get sad and happy at the same times that they were in the story. This is probably my favorite book and will be until I find another one as thrilling as this.

Emily Light, student

In the Australian novel *Peter,* Kate Walker presents a different type of search for identity. She sensitively depicts the struggle that fifteen-year-old Peter experiences when he fears that he may be gay because he is attracted to his older brother's friend who is gay.

Seeking a Sense of Independence

Zibby Oneal presents a complex character in Kate, the daughter of a famous artist, in *In Summer Light.* Kate has abandoned her own painting because of her relationship with her father, but then a case of mono keeps her at the family home for the summer when she is seventeen. This becomes a summer of self-discovery when Kate learns to believe in herself and her talent.

In Laurence Yep's *Dragon's Gate,* Otter is restless in his native China. His mother expects him to manage the family businesses and property while his father is making the family fortune in the "Land of the Golden Mountain," the United States. After his father and uncle return home for a brief visit, Otter wants to leave with them when they go back to the United States. He is, however, bound by his loyalty to his mother and stays in China until a misadventure necessitates that he join his father and uncle.

Increasing Reliance on the Peer Group

In *Princess Ashley* by Richard Peck, Chelsea, a newcomer in school, wants desperately to be part of the in-crowd. The most popular girl in school, Ashley, takes her into her group, but eventually Chelsea realizes she is being used and must confront a serious conflict in their values.

While the role of the peer group is often portrayed negatively, some books show the positive interactions between young people. For example, Monica Hughes's *Invitation to the Game* depicts a group of young people who must learn to work together to make lives for themselves in a futuristic urban wasteland. Their reactions to each other are human and believable. Eventually, they realize that each member of the group has unique talents that are valuable to the survival of the group as a whole.

Accepting Physiological Changes and Emerging Sexuality

In the true account of becoming a teenage mother in Janet Bode's *Beating the Odds,* Pawnee tell of becoming pregnant at fourteen and having the baby's father talk her into keeping the baby. She takes responsibility for her action and learns about babies, nutrition, and exercise. She does everything to help make the baby's life good and safe, while working and continuing her education.

In Jenny Davis's *Sex Education,* a high school biology teacher addresses high school students' lack of knowledge and awareness about their sexuality. The main characters, Livie and David, are increasingly aware of their own emerging feelings for one another, but their relationship is clouded by a class assignment that goes awry.

Learning to Relate Appropriately to Members of the Opposite Sex

Todd Strasser's *A Very Touchy Subject* is the story of Scott, who, by his own accounting, spends "an average of 47% of each day thinking about sex." Scott finds that his next-door neighbor, Paula, might be the perfect person to fulfill his fantasies. But Paula's family troubles make her vulnerable, and Scott must make difficult decisions about how he will treat her.

In *Ring-Rise, Ring-Set*, Monica Hughes presents the conflict of cultures in a world frozen by a coming ice age. Liza is a part of the life in the city, where scientists seek ways to combat the ice. Liza ends up in the wilderness and is adopted by a primitive tribe. She learns a great deal about kindness and humanity, especially through her relationships with her boyfriends from each culture.

Planning for Future Careers

One of the themes in *I'll Love You When You're More Like Me* by M. E. Kerr is making career choices. Wally Witherspoon wrestles with his own desire for independence and his parents' expectations of him—they expect him to take over the family mortuary and be an undertaker like his father. Wally, however, has no interest in the family business. He wants to go to college and have a life of his own.

Norma Fox Mazer and Harry Mazer create four serious and highly focused young people who are involved in a summer intern program for a group of small local newspapers in *Bright Days, Stupid Nights.* They strive to refine their skills and judgment while preparing for careers in writing and journalism. Chris, the only male in the group, wants to be a novelist; Elizabeth wants to be a famous columnist so she can influence how people think; Faith, who is never without her camera, wants to be a photographer who changes "people's perceptions of the world" with her pictures; and Vicki wants to be "the best newspaper reporter in the world."

In *Shizuko's Daughter* by Kyoko Mori, the main character, Yuki, uses her painting and her plan to become an artist to deal with the emptiness of her life after her mother's tragic death. Her art is a release and an escape, and it also helps Yuki to clarify her own life's direction.

Making Decisions about Education

Verna LaVaughn, called LaVaughn, is fourteen, poor, and living in a rough neighborhood, but she and her mother have a dream that she will be able to make a better life for herself by getting an education. In *Make Lemonade* by Virginia Euwer Wolff, LaVaughn takes a job babysitting to make money to save for college, but the job entails more that she expected.

In Isabelle Holland's *The Man Without a Face,* education becomes an escape and a haven from a troubled family situation. For Charles, the thought of his older sister's not returning to boarding school provides the impetus for his decision to go away to school. His decision is complicated because he has already deliberately flunked the admissions exam—he will have to spend the summer preparing to retake the exam.

In *Jumping the Nail* by Eve Bunting, Dru has a scholarship to go to Northwestern University, two thousand miles from home. Her boyfriend is staying home, going to college part time to get a business degree, and working in his father's construction business. With Mike's future planned and secure, he pressures Dru to stay and go to a local college. She, however, holds on to her dream to go to Northwestern to pursue the possibilities her gift for languages presents.

Determining Values, Ethics, Morals, and Political Views

Fergy, in James Lincoln Collier's *Outside Looking In,* is sick of his parents' nomadic life. His father has never gotten beyond being a self-styled hippie who lies, steals, and cheats. He justifies his behavior by saying that the problem is with the corrupt, materialistic system. Because of his father's lifestyle, Fergy has attended school only twice, for brief periods. Fergy wants a stable home; he also wants to go to school. Fergy makes the decision to change his life and to find a more stable environment for his little sister, Ooma. He takes her and sets out to find his maternal grandparents whom he has never met. From his mother's fond memories of her childhood, he knows that they will help Ooma and him to have a normal, stable life.

Cab's visit to spend the summer helping her grandmother is filled with surprises in Jenny Davis's *Checking on the Moon.* Her grandmother's restaurant is in a neighborhood that has declined and become dangerous since the steel mills closed. When there are problems in the community, Cab decides to take action.

Renegotiating Relationship with Parents

In Margaret I. Rostkowski's *After the Dancing Days,* Annie is frightened and shocked as she sees the maimed young men who are returning from the First World War. Her father, a doctor, announces that he is going to practice at the local military hospital. Annie visits the hospital and befriends an angry young man whose face was hideously burned by gas. Her mother, objecting to Annie's exposure to the horror of the patients' injuries, forbids Annie to visit the hospital, but Annie disobeys her mother. When her mother finds out, they have to renegotiate with one another. Annie must understand her mother's position, and her mother must realize that Annie is capable of making some of her own decisions.

In Virginia Euwer Wolff's *Probably Still Nick Swansen,* Nick, a sixteen-year-old with a learning disability, struggles to be independent and to fit in at school. His parents are protective, but Nick wants to be his own person. As he asserts himself, his parents have to let him try and even fail. They have to accept that they cannot shield him from the realities of his life.

In Anne Fine's *The Book of the Banshee,* we experience the worst-case scenario of adolescence. Will, a self-proclaimed war correspondent, describes the war zone that is his home as his sister Estelle hits adolescence and turns against the whole family.

> ### Bridging
> #### *Bridging a Poem with a Novel*
> Use the relationship between the narrator and the father in Theodore Roethke's poem "My Papa's Waltz" as a bridge to looking at the relationship between Chris and his father in <u>Bright Days, Stupid Nights</u> by Norma Fox Mazer and Harry Mazer.

Characteristics Illustrated in *Stotan!*

Each of the characteristics we have just discussed appears in Crutcher's sensitive story of camaraderie and challenges, *Stotan!* High school senior Walker Dupree, the main character, is one of four members of the school's swimming team who are lifelong friends. As they go through their last year of high school, Walker, Lion, Jeff, and Nortie are making the best of their time, yet they are looking forward (dealing with issues of identity and seeking a sense of independence). They are challenged by their swimming coach, Max, to give up their first week of Christmas vacation to participate in Stotan Week (*Stotan* being a combination of *Stoic* and *Spartan*). Although they are unsure of what they are getting themselves into, they all volunteer. The intensity of the week—the most exhausting physical endurance and mental training they have ever

Talking with Chris Crutcher

If you want to see how something works, look at it broken.

Selected Titles

Athletic Shorts
Chinese Handcuffs
The Crazy Horse Electric Game
Ironman
Running Loose
Staying Fat for Sarah Byrnes
Stotan!

Chris Crutcher grew up in a small lumber and logging town in the mountains of Idaho. He spent almost ten years as a teacher and then director of an alternative school in Oakland, California, for inner-city kids who couldn't make it in the public school system. Tired of spending almost a third of his life standing in line, he left the city to live in Spokane, Washington, and to work as a child and family therapist specializing in abuse cases. Chris Crutcher's books are consistently designated ALA Best Books for Young Adults. In 1993 he received the ALAN Award for Outstanding Contributions to Young Adult Literature. Several of his books are currently under contract as screen projects.

I am a better therapist because I am a writer and a better writer because I am a therapist. I am a better therapist because I process human pain through my imagination and a better writer because I'm forced to listen. I don't take a story right out of therapy and put it in a book, but the inspirations for discovering true heroes come from there. One of my favorite lines is from "A Brief Moment in the Life of Angus Bethune" in *Athletic Shorts* when Angus's stepdad tells him that Superman is not a hero. "It's guys like you and me that are brave, Angus. Guys who are different and can be crushed—and know it—but go out there anyway."

I write to tell people what kind of stories are out there, often in response to the astonishing things I hear in my work. Sitting in every classroom is at least one kid who seems nasty and repulsive, but that is because we don't know his story. If we did, we would treat him much differently, and we would learn about ourselves from him. The worst thing I've ever heard a kid say is, "I don't think they see me."

I want kids to know that there are adults out there who will go to the wall for them and there are ways to find those adults; there are also adults to stay away from.

That's true in real life and it should therefore be true in literature. I often use interpretive adult characters in my stories to put things together: Dakota in *Running Loose,* for example, and Max in *Stotan!* I believe adult perspectives are as important as kid perspectives in young adult literature. In fact, I never think about whether I am writing for kids or adults; that's a publisher's decision about marketing. I don't think there should be much difference between young adult literature and adult literature. The only real difference is the age and perspective of the main characters.

I was pretty much a mainstream kid growing up. I was fairly popular, but athletics was king in my small town, and I always wanted to be a better athlete. I think I saw myself as weak. I now believe some of that "weakness" was sensitivity, but sensitivity wasn't even a word where I grew up. I also found that I could talk my way out of almost anything, and did.

My mom and dad were voracious readers, and books were a big deal in our house. As a little kid I read a lot, though that came to a virtual standstill during high school and college. I was rebellious for rebellion's sake, and adults' desire for me to read was plenty of reason not to. I found all kinds of creative ways to keep from doing any schoolwork, which was in itself, of course, a full-time job. I wrote "creative" book reports by inventing titles and stories to go with them, choosing my authors from the telephone directory. I did read Harper Lee's *To Kill A Mockingbird* in high school. I loved it, though I wouldn't have admitted it at the time. That story still influences my writing.

Writing a novel is like never having your homework done. But it is also extremely personal and intimate, and it seems to me to be a perfect way for an American male to show emotion. You can let your characters take the heat. Being able to express that way is a wonderful feeling to me.

Louie Banks in *Running Loose* is probably the character closest to me. He thinks like I thought. I was never as heroic as Louie, but his voice—that voice of the person who stands up for him- or herself—is the voice I look to as a writer.

encountered—brings the four close friends even closer together. Along with the fifth member, Elaine, they talk about their group being a substitute for their families (increasing reliance on the peer group). Together the group confronts racism, abusive behavior, a potentially fatal disease, and the inevitability of growing up and apart (determining values, ethics, morals, and political views). The group rescues Nortie when his father beats him once too often. They provide Nortie with an escape from his abusive home (renegotiating relationship with parents). The bond among the Stotans sustains them through their personal crises and their public victories in swimming.

Walker goes through a period of confusion as his longtime friendship with Elaine changes. He realizes that he wants to break up with his girlfriend, Devnee, so he can start dating Elaine; however, he also realizes that this type of involvement with Elaine might alter their friendship. He also suspects that Elaine would reject any sexual overture from him (learning to relate appropriately to members of the opposite sex). He feels guilty about his relationship with Devnee because she likes him better than he likes her, and he realizes that much of the bond he feels is lust (accepting physiological changes and emerging sexuality).

As high school seniors, Walker and his friends are looking toward the future. They all plan to go to college the next year (making decisions about education), and Walker speculates about the careers that each will pursue (planning for future careers). Walker says, "Me, I'd like to be a writer of some kind; maybe a journalist, maybe a storyteller" (p. 16).

Conditions Facing Students

As we stated earlier in the chapter, a number of challenging conditions confront students today. Janet Bode's *Beating the Odds* provides graphic and inspiring true stories of young people as they face and overcome difficult obstacles. The following are some of their plights: living in a welfare hotel, drugs, teenage pregnancy, abusive homes, conflicts between American lifestyle and familial cultural heritage, and immigration troubles. The young people in the book manage to overcome their problems with perseverance, optimism, and hope for a better future. Bode's book is appropriately subtitled *Stories of Unexpected Achievers.*

Mary Dowling Hahn has her two young protagonists, Matt and Parker, find a murdered body and uncover a drug ring in their quiet small town in *Dead Man in Indian Creek.* The reality they face is complicated when they discover that Parker's mother is involved with the drug dealers.

Differing Opportunities and Roles for Women

In Caroline Cooney's *Operation: Homefront,* a high school brother and sister and their preschool-aged brother have their lives changed dramatically when their mother's unit is called up for active duty in preparation for Operation Desert Storm. The family is turned upside down as each member struggles with having the core of the family gone.

Although her career of librarian is one that has long been open to women, Judith Wayland, mother of the main character in *The Drowning of Stephan Jones* by Bette Greene, plays a unique and courageous role in a conservative southern town. She, often without any support, speaks up on issues of tolerance, equality, and honor. She is the conscience of her community.

> ## Bridging
>
> *Bridging a YA Novel with a Classic*
>
> Chris Crutcher's novel <u>Stotan!</u> presents the friendship among a group of high school boys. This novel and the relationships in it can serve an an appropriate bridge to John Knowles's novel <u>A Separate Peace</u>.

Changing Family Structures

A family is totally disrupted when the parents are killed in a plane crash in Harry Mazer's *When the Phone Rang.* A phone call informing them of the crash changes the lives of Billy, his younger sister, and his older brother, who leaves college to keep the family together. Refusing to leave each other to live with relatives, they struggle to redefine their family, to learn new skills and roles, and to handle adult responsibilities.

In *Whatever Happened to Janie?,* the companion book to *The Face on the Milk Carton,* Caroline Cooney presents the confusion and pain that a young woman goes through when she returns to the family from which she was kidnapped twelve years earlier. Janie/Jennie's whole life changes. She is no longer the only child of wealthy parents, but one of five in a middle-class family. She must make adjustments and so must her birth family, which has lived with the pain of her disappearance.

Increasing Awareness and Sensitivity to Ethnic and Cultural Diversity

Laurence Yep brings to life the trials and the contributions of Chinese Americans in his books based on family stories. In *Dragon's Gate,* he captures the inequities and cruelties that Chinese workers experienced while building the

---

Bridging

Connecting Fiction with Nonfiction

Growing up is never an easy process. One element of quality fiction is that it often leaves the reader wanting more and speculating what would have happened to the characters beyond the covers of the book. Mildred Taylor in her Logan family saga satisfies the reader's desire to know more. From <u>Roll of Thunder, Hear My Cry</u> to <u>Let the Circle be Unbroken</u> to <u>The Road to Memphis</u>, readers learn about Cassie's life as she grows toward adulthood. Her experiences can be used as a bridge to experiences in the growing up of another young African American contained in the three-part autobiography of Maya Angelou, <u>I Know Why the Caged Bird Sings</u>, <u>Gather Together in My Name</u>, and <u>Singin' and Swingin' and Gettin' Merry Like Christmas</u>.

---

transcontinental railroad. *The Star Fisher* describes the experiences of the first Chinese American family to live in a small town in West Virginia during the 1920s.

In *Racing the Sun* by Paul Pitts, Brandon's family has left its Native American heritage and tradition behind. His father even changed his name from Kee Redhouse to Keith Rogers. By his own admission, Brandon knows little about his Navajo culture until his grandfather comes to stay with them. His grandfather gives Brandon lessons in their culture and a sense of his heritage.

Addressing Use of Drugs and Alcohol

Shep Greene addresses a problem that many teenagers face today in *The Boy Who Drank Too Much*. Buff's life is ruled by drinking and fear of his father, who expects Buff to fulfill his failed dreams to be a great hockey player.

In his novel *No Kidding,* Bruce Brooks treats the problem of alcoholism in a futuristic society. Kids in this world are forced to assume adult roles because many adults are alcohol dependent. Although some readers have found the novel to be a heavy-handed treatment of the issue, it does address the problem of drinking.

Facing the Dangers of AIDS and Other Sexually Transmitted Diseases

For thirteen-year-old Debra, life takes an awful twist when her "perfect" older sister, Ellen, tests positive for HIV in Fran Arrick's *What You Don't Know Can Kill You.* As her parents and sister struggle with the terrible implications of the disease, Debra finally puts things in perspective and makes decisions about getting on with her own life.

In *When Heroes Die,* Penny Raife Durant examines the pain that twelve-year-old Gary experiences as he realizes his Uncle Rob is dying of AIDS. His uncle has always been the strong male role model in his life. He has to face his grief and the stereotypes that accompany the disease.

Adolescence is truly a period of upheaval. It is a time when youths undergo so many changes that many can neither gain a stable perspective on their own lives nor accept overt adult help in establishing perspective. The characteristics of adolescence are unique; young adult literature speaks to that uniqueness. Repeatedly, we have heard students say of a book with which they have connected, "I never knew anyone else felt that (or did that or thought that)."

The connection with books that accurately reflect youths' turmoil and triumphs helps them to establish a perspective of who they are and what they are doing. In the next chapter we will explore further the connection of youths with their reading.

Sharing the Connection

What You Don't Know Can Kill You

Fran Arrick

After reading this book, I would recommend that students in seventh grade and up should be exposed to it and have discussions about it. This book has really haunted me since I read it. Maybe because I have a young daughter that I constantly worry about even though she is a great kid or because I know that young people are so sure that things like AIDS aren't going to happen to them. Young people think they are super human and maybe this book might help dispel this myth.

Evelyn Tenbusch, pre-service teacher

Summary

An understanding of the characteristics and developmental tasks of adolescence helps teachers as they seek to promote the growth of adolescents as readers. Current societal influences and ethnic and cultural changes also affect adolescents as readers. Young adult literature speaks to the uniqueness of adolescence and enables youths to see themselves in books written for them.

Suggested Activities

1. In your journal, discuss how you think reading young adult literature can help adolescents to understand themselves and their interactions with others.

2. Describe a teenager you are familiar with in terms of the characteristics and developmental tasks of adolescence presented in this chapter.

Literature Involvement Strategy

Character Awards

We know that one of the significant values of literature is that it helps young people to understand themselves and others. The exploration of characters plays a crucial role in developing these understandings. Frequently, students rely on simple physical descriptions or explicitly stated views of a character when they are asked what that character is like. In this strategy, we ask students to look at fictional people in new ways by nominating them for awards that reveal something about their characters. This strategy effectively involves students in looking at characters in nontraditional ways.

The teacher should provide a model for the activity, such as the following:

The award for the person I would most like to have on a camping trip: Brian (<u>Hatchet</u> by Gary Paulsen)

The award for the person to whom I would tell my most guarded secrets: Park's mother (<u>Park's Quest</u> by Katherine Paterson)

The award for the person I would most like to have guarding my house: Pluto (<u>The House of Dies Drear</u> by Virginia Hamilton)

The award for the person I would most like to have as an older brother: Jim (<u>Father Figure</u> by Richard Peck)

Although there are many possible variations on this strategy, two in particular are useful. In the first variation, the teacher provides the award categories for students to make their nominations. Students then have to explain their choices for the awards. In the second variation, students, usually working in groups, create the award categories and then make their nominations. They also have to explain their categories and choices.

---

3. In what way are these characteristics and current societal influences apparent in the young adult literature you are reading?

4. Using the Character Award activity described in this chapter's Literature Involvement Strategy, plan a class discussion focusing on memorable characters in some of the young adult literature you have read.

CHAPTER 4

Connecting Young Adult Literature with Students

Books, novels, stories, are one way we can reach out to one another without losing face, one way of saying: "We are not alone, not in our fears, not in our hopes, not in our nightmares, and not in our dreams."

Sandy Asher

Journal Writing: Responding

Reflect on the young adult literature you are reading along with this textbook. What insights into yourself or others have you gained from these readings?

Books that make a lasting impression on readers are those that connect with their lives and personal experiences in significant ways. Avid readers often talk about "watershed" books that literally change their lives. What they remember "was the emotional impact of the book, the insights it provided whether for self or others, and the growth that it stimulated in the reader. . . . [They] described books as kindling the imagination, creating visions of life's possibilities, giving expression to the reader's own inarticulate feelings, as well as affecting their emotions, intellectual pursuits, and attitudes" (Carlsen and Sherrill, 1988, p. 86). Although it is impossible to predict with total accuracy what books will connect with adolescent readers and stay with them forever, we do know the conditions that foster this type of connection. Many teachers have identified Gary Paulsen's *Hatchet* as a book that has changed more students than any book they have ever used. They report that students who have never read a book to the end have not only finished *Hatchet,* but have reread it and then moved on to other works by Paulsen.

In this chapter we explore the role that young adult literature can play in helping students make connections with all literature. We provide a rationale for using young adult literature that addresses student needs and interests as well as the educational aims of schools. Additionally, we describe the adolescent as a reader and the role that the reading and writing processes play in helping students to construct meaning, all within the context of using young adult literature in the classroom.

Reading and Literature

Reading has an ongoing, pervasive impact on our lives. The printed word surrounds us—from street names on a map to the menus in a restaurant. In our complex, technologically advanced society, young people must be able to read to follow directions, to gain new information, and to succeed in school. Although these routine uses of reading are important, reading also has a power to transform individuals. The reasoning that individuals do when they use the written word is what separates human beings from other animals and allows for the advancement of civilization. It provides the reader with infinite possibilities for knowledge, enrichment, and wisdom. Finally, written language has the power to evoke memories and emotions, to create pictures in our minds, to soothe or arouse passions, to persuade or dissuade, and to provide insights and flashes of brilliance.

Louise Rosenblatt (1991) identifies two ways of reading: *aesthetic* reading—the reading of literary texts—and *efferent* (from the Latin for "carry away") reading—nonliterary reading (p. 444). She states that

> instead of thinking of the *text* as either literary or informational, efferent or aesthetic, we should think of it as written for a particular *predominant* attitude or stance, efferent or aesthetic, on the part of the reader. We have ignored the fact that our reading is not all-of-one-piece. We read for information, but we are also conscious of emotions about it and feel pleasure when the words we call up arouse vivid images and are rhythmic to the inner ear. Or we experience a poem but are conscious of acquiring some information about, say, Greek warfare. To confuse matters even further, we can switch stances while reading. And we can read aesthetically something written mainly to inform or read efferently something written mainly to communicate experience. Our present purpose and past experiences, as well as the text, are factors in our choice of stance. (p. 445)

Probably no literary theorist has influenced the teaching of literature as much as Rosenblatt who, from the first publication of *Literature as Exploration* in 1938 through its fourth edition in 1983, has focused attention on the transaction that takes place between the reader and the text. These transactions are unique, according to Rosenblatt. All readers bring to reading prior knowledge and experiences that influence their perceptions of the text. Meaning evolves for individual readers as they interact and respond to the text. This recognition that meaning is an individual awareness frees both teachers and students to view literature as a vehicle for affirming personal meaning, for exploring values, and for gaining new awareness and insights about the world.

Reflecting a social constructivist perspective, Langer (1994), in her role as the co-director of the National Research Center on Literature Teaching and Learning, examines current directions in teaching literature. She believes that "a literary orientation involves 'living through the experience.' It can be characterized as *exploring a horizon of possibilities.* It explores emotions, relationships, motives, and reactions, calling on all we know about what it is to be human" (p. 204).

Young Adult Literature to Meet Student Needs

Young adult literature has the potential to meet the needs of young people as it promotes self-knowledge, the knowledge of others, and knowledge of a world view. Literature has many benefits for readers. The reader witnesses the lives, the trials, the victories, and the defeats that characters experience. This framework allows readers to compare their beliefs and reactions with those of the characters. For example, students who have read Avi's *Nothing But the Truth* react strongly to Philip's dilemma, while they also are torn by the conflicting perspectives of justice in the book. Readers clarify their beliefs as they measure their values and responses against those of the characters. Chambers (1985) states:

> I believe literature belongs to all the people all the time, that it ought to be cheaply and easily available, that it ought to be fun to read as well as challenging, subversive, refreshing, comforting, and all the other qualities we claim for it. Finally, I hold that in literature we find the best expression of the human imagination, and the most useful means by which we come to grips with our ideas about ourselves and what we are. (p. 16)

Additionally, students read about cultures and customs that they might never experience directly. As students read of worlds beyond their own experiences, they begin to recognize that the characters who live in these unfamiliar settings are like them in many ways. Such heightened awareness can promote understanding and tolerance. For readers of literature, books activate their imagination, allowing them to imagine what it is like to be someone else or to visit somewhere new. The reader travels to Japan with Lincoln and Tony in Gary Soto's *Pacific Crossing* and experiences the merging of three cultures, that of boys from the United States who value and share their Mexican American heritage, and that of their Japanese hosts.

Literature is not simply a reading activity; it is an aesthetic experience and creative experience. Approaching literature both cognitively and affectively promotes an involvement that has the potential to move and to change students through that involvement. Readers are provided opportunities to examine and articulate their values. The role of young adult literature in students' lives can provide them with opportunities to explore major issues confronting youths. For example, Harry White in James Lincoln Collier's *When the Stars Begin to Fall,* knows what it is like to be a outcast in his town, and his troubles increase when he decides to expose a local manufacturer who is polluting the river. Harry must then face several difficult realities.

Rosenblatt (1985) describes what she calls the literary evocation, or "the process in which the reader selects out ideas, sensations, feelings, and images drawn from his past linguistic, literary, and life experience, and synthesizes them into a new experience" (p. 40). This is the essence of the aesthetic response to literature, a response which, unfortunately, is minimized or ignored in many classrooms. Traditional approaches to literature tend to ignore the importance of providing students with the opportunity to experience literature, rather than just analyze it. Literary analysis is largely a cognitive process that does not capitalize on the whole range of affective responses that students may have when reading literature. Involving students with literature affectively as well as cognitively can help to avoid a purely academic exercise in which students are taught simply to analyze a work.

Monseau and Salvner (1992) present a rationale for using young adult literature:

> To adolescents, the advantage of young adult novels is that these books harmonize well with the experiences they have had in their young lives. As a result, instead of merely learning *about* the literature they read in school, as so often happens when they analyze literary classics, students become involved *in* the literature as a result of the connections they make between their experience and the text. (p. xii)

Young Adult Literature Promotes Self-Knowledge One of the most widely accepted arguments for young adult literature in the classroom is that as readers reflect on their interactions with texts, they relate to characters, their life situations, their challenges, and their successes. As Sandy Asher (1992) said, "[Books] give you the words to explain yourself to yourself, words you can use to create your own life, to recognize your options and to make your choices, to separate as an individual and to reconnect as a member of the human race" (p. 82). In this process of relating to and empathizing with characters, readers of any age may gain a critical understanding of themselves. For example, most students would be able to identify with Margaret and Elizabeth as they are harassed by Gordy, the class bully, and his buddies in Mary Dowling Hahn's *Stepping on the Cracks*. As Margaret and Elizabeth learn about Gordy's life and the reasons for his behavior, they must make decisions about how to react to him and his problems. As readers identify with Margaret and Elizabeth, they will be able to examine how they would react to similar situations.

"Do you know what happens to deserters?" Gordy asked her. For once he didn't yell. Instead he leaned toward Elizabeth, almost like he was begging. "Stuart could be shot or put in jail or sent straight to the front. Some Nazi would kill him the first day. Do you want that to happen to him?"

"Huh," Elizabeth said. "It would serve him right." She flicked her eyes at Stuart. "I don't feel sorry for him, not one bit. I'd rather see him die than Joe." She turned to me. "How about you, Margaret? Wouldn't you be mad if Jimmy died and old sissy baby Stuart was right here, safe in the woods?"

Without wanting to, I looked at Stuart. His long, dark hair hid most of his face, but I could see how thin he was. Like me, he was all elbows and knees and wrist bones. How could I wish him dead? I didn't want anybody to die. Not Jimmy, not Joe, not Stuart. I just wanted the war to be over.

When I didn't say anything, Stuart said, "There's been too much killing already. Even if they catch me and send me overseas, I won't shoot anybody. War's wrong."

"Tell Hitler about it," Elizabeth said scornfully. "He started it, not us. Him and the Japs. If we don't kill them, they'll kill us. Is that what you want?"

"Of course not," Stuart said. His voice faltered and he coughed. Running his hands through his hair, he looked at all of us. His face was very pale. "It's so complicated, I can't explain it. Killing's wrong. Wrong of them, wrong of us. I know it is." Stuart stared at Elizabeth and me as if he hoped we'd understand what he meant, but we didn't say anything. (p. 80)

The youthful patriotism that Margaret and Elizabeth had felt is challenged by their reactions to Stuart and his desertion from the army. They wrestle with their beliefs and emotions as they weigh their choices and make life-altering decisions about the actions they will take. They must make a significant decision that will shape their understanding of the war. The type of moral dilemma that Margaret and Elizabeth confront is reminiscent of the dilemma Huckleberry Finn faced when he found Jim on Jackson Island. Our literary heritage is filled with examples of characters choosing between the easy way and their moral dictates. By presenting serious ethical problems, young adult literature provides an appropriate preparation for students to gain an understanding of the moral issues confronting characters in the classics.

Developmentally, many adolescents are still operating at a level of concrete reasoning—they see their world in terms of absolutes. Using a book like *Stepping on the Cracks* provides readers with opportunities to explore significant issues that demonstrate the relativity of values and beliefs. In reading about the choices that Margaret and Elizabeth make, youths will be able to realize that situations are complex and require complex solutions. Thus, young adult literature helps students to move beyond concrete thought by promoting self-knowledge that encourages higher-level thinking. For example, in Paul Pullman's *The White Mercedes,* the protagonist, Chris, is governed by emotions and naiveté. As he misjudges people and situations, the reader questions Chris's judgment and analyzes the circumstances.

Young Adult Literature Promotes Knowledge of Others Young adult literature promotes an empathetic understanding of the life circumstances of the characters. It helps young people to broaden their perspectives and to move out of an egocentric way of thinking to consider other perspectives and values. It has the power to enhance reader sensitivity toward and understanding of others, including those of varied backgrounds. As Stover (1991) indicates, "There is today an extensive array of young adult novels available to teachers and students which present diverse perspectives. Novels for adolescents exist by adults who grew to adulthood within minority cultures in the U.S. and who write about those experiences—Black, Hispanic, Eskimo, American Indian, Amish, Appalachian" (pp. 13–14). Such literature helps youngsters from minority groups to affirm their own cultural identity as well as helps all young people to grow in their knowledge and understanding of others. This awareness is illustrated in Virginia Hamilton's *Zeely.* While visiting her uncle for the summer, Elizabeth, who is calling herself Geeder, encounters the majestic Zeely. Zeely is well over six feet tall and slender, with high cheekbones that set off her deeply set eyes. Geeder sees how much Zeely looks like a picture of a Watutsi princess. Seeing Zeely's pride and dignity, Geeder is sure that she is, in fact, a princess herself. From Zeely, she gains a sense of her heritage and a new identity.

An inherent value of literature is that it lets readers know they are not alone. Youthful readers find situations and characters with whom they can identify. This process of identification is a vital connection that makes the relationship between the reader and the text personal. In *Stepping on the Cracks,* Gordy, Doug, and Toad are ongoing threats to Margaret and Elizabeth until they begin to see the circumstances that make Gordy mean.

> "Is Gordy here?" Elizabeth asked.
>
> "He's not home from school yet," Mrs. Smith said. Her voice was flat and unfriendly. She neither frowned nor smiled. Even the baby looked sullen and suspicious. Elizabeth and I glanced at each other. Without knowing it, Mrs. Smith had just told us where Gordy probably was.
>
> "You have a nice cat," I said, hoping to make her smile.
>
> "That scrawny old thing?" Mrs. Smith frowned at the cat, but the little girl opened the screen door.
>
> "Mittens, come here," she called as it ran inside, dodging the fingers reaching out to grab it.
>
> "Shut the door, stupid," a man's voice rumbled from inside. "You trying to freeze me to death?"
>
> As Mrs. Smith glanced behind her, Elizabeth stared through the screen door. I knew she was dying to go inside and see everything in Gordy's house, including the owner of the deep, nasty voice.
>
> Just as Mrs. Smith started to close the door, a man strode down the hall toward us. He was tall and skinny, as pale as Gordy and Stuart, and his eyes were small and mean. In one hand, he held the squirming cat by the nape of its neck. The little girl ran behind him, crying.
>
> Mrs. Smith stepped aside as he opened the screen door and hurled the cat past Elizabeth and me. Horrified, I watched it fly through the air, land on all four feet, and run off through a hole in the hedge. (p. 92)

This glimpse into Gordy's home life provides Margaret and Elizabeth with a new awareness of him and Stuart. Through this awareness, a new type of relationship begins to evolve.

Young Adult Literature Promotes Knowledge of a World View   Young adult literature presents readers with the opportunity to examine significant themes of the human experience. It allows readers to have vicarious experiences that heighten their understanding of the human condition. Books can transport readers to share the danger and fear that Annemarie and Ellen experience in Lois Lowry's *Number the Stars* when the Nazis occupy Denmark or the danger and fear that Tara and her family experience in an internment camp after they flee the Iraqis in *Kiss the Dust* by Elizabeth Laird. Rosenblatt (1983) talks about the shared experience of the reader with the text:

As the student vicariously shares through literature the emotions and aspirations of other human beings, he can gain heightened sensitivity to the needs and problems of others remote from him in temperament, in space, or in social environment; he can develop a greater imaginative capacity to grasp the meaning of abstract laws or political or social theories for actual human lives. Such sensitivity and imagination are part of the indispensable equipment of the citizen of a democracy. (p. 274)

Young adult literature also enables readers to build a storehouse of basic information, references, and allusions that provide a foundation for understanding material in a wide range of subject areas. Young adult literature also provides opportunities for improving the readers' thinking. Critical reflection helps adolescents to reflect on issues greater than the individual self. For example, *Stepping on the Cracks* promotes the readers' sense and understanding of the Second World War. The following quotation illustrates how much the war was a daily part of Margaret's and her parents' lives.

Quietly, I slipped into the house, hoping Mother wouldn't take one look at me and know exactly what I was planning to do. My face always gave everything away.

I needn't have worried. As usual, Mother was too busy to pay much attention to me. If I was quieter than normal at dinner, neither she nor Daddy noticed. They had more important things on their minds.

The Germans had started a big campaign against us in France and Belgium, and things looked worse every day. Mrs. Wagner told us about it in school. Pointing to a place on the map called the Ardennes, she said that was where we were fighting the Battle of the Bulge. According to Daddy, Jimmy was probably right in the middle of it, and he and Mother talked of nothing else. (p. 108)

Readers can readily perceive how Margaret's view of the world expands to include the European theater of operations. She is taught current events and geography in school, while she lives their ramifications at home.

Young Adult Literature to Meet the Educational Aims of the Schools

The ultimate aim of education is to prepare students for meaningful membership in society. Educators seek to help young people develop into literate, knowledgeable, and productive members of society. Because of the three-faceted perspective of the knowledge that students can gain from young adult

Talking with Joyce Hansen

Writers have a responsibility to give young people something, to show them possibilities, to show them not only what is, but what can be.

Selected Titles

Between Two Fires (nonfiction)
The Captive
The Gift-Giver
Home Boy
Out from This Place
Which Way Freedom?
Yellow Bird and Me

Joyce Hansen grew up in the Bronx. A language arts teacher in the New York City schools, she has worked with students with reading problems. Currently, she is a staff developer helping other teachers. She also teaches literature and writing at Empire State College. She has received several awards, including the Coretta Scott King Honor Book for Which Way Freedom? and the Parents' Choice Award for Yellow Bird and Me.

I try to reach that audience that does not often see itself reflected in books. When I started out I had in mind primarily the African American youngster and the Hispanic youngster—the kind of students that I ran across in the schools where I worked. I've always taught in New York City, but I'm finding that there are a lot of other students who are responding to these books. They are responding for other reasons than the race of the characters. They are responding to the fact that I deal with families who have economic problems and while that's not what the books are about, that's the reality of the lives I write about. And they respond to the struggles of the characters. I try to create books that give the readers something of substance. I don't want to be didactic and I think teachers, especially those teachers who write, might have the tendency to be didactic. But I do want to offer young people a story that leaves them with a sense of hope and leaves them with some understanding of the world they have to deal with. Young people need to see how they are connected to other people; they need to understand that there are more similarities than differences among people in this world.

I was an avid reader as a child. I grew up in a predominantly black, working-class, poor neighborhood in the Bronx. Reading opened up so many worlds to me; it was something I could do without anybody bothering me or interfering with me or what I thought in my imagination. I had dreams of being a writer, and in high school I fancied myself possibly becoming a writer. Reading and writing were the only two subjects that came easily for me—I struggled with everything else, but I loved to read and loved to write.

I wrote my first book as an assignment for my master's degree. I didn't want to do a

research project; I wanted to do something creative. I had been trying to write short stories and poetry for adults, unsuccessfully. After I wrote it [*The Gift-Giver*], the professor said he thought it was publishable. With my first book, I realized this is what I am supposed to be doing. This is what I know, this is where I belong, this is where my writer's voice is. I was with kids all the time; I had my audience and I had my characters.

My ideas start with a very small seed that grows. I get a lot of my ideas from my students and I also love history. I would have written *Which Way Freedom?* even if no one wanted to publish it. I wanted to write a story that was really exciting—showing, telling, teaching something about the slavery experience. I had never written historical fiction before so I was afraid when the book was published. I was afraid that I might have created some horrible stereotype or made some terrible mistake; I was very concerned about the reaction to it. I was thrilled when I received the Coretta Scott King Honor Book for *Which Way Freedom?* It was one of the proudest moments of my life.

Which Way Freedom? and *The Gift-Giver* really came straight from the heart and that's the best way to write. I really have a problem writing on demand. I can't just churn books out—I have to get involved in

my stories and with my characters. It takes me a long time to write. Summer is when I start a book because the first draft is the most difficult for me. I take a notebook and a pen and I just start to write, letting all kinds of ideas come out. It is very rough and it's not organized at all, but I do have the central idea of the book even though the narrative strands are not yet connected. Then I type all that rough stuff up, triple space, and now I have these notes. Then I begin to really try to focus and to find the story. During the school year when I am teaching, I write on weekends and sometimes early in the morning, but it is hard to find the time.

I think literature can help young people make some sense out of the world. I think it can help establish a connection between the imagination of the reader and what the writer is trying to show the reader. Kids need a lot of experiences in literature. They need to be exposed to different kinds of literature. I write from a reality base, but I'm not putting down fantasy. They need that, too. You learn to read by reading, you learn to write by writing. If we give our students good reading materials and help them understand that reading can be pleasurable, then the reading scores will go up. We have to truly speak to our youngsters in these books we write.

literature (knowledge of self, knowledge of others, and knowledge of a world view), students have the potential to develop and mature through their interactions as readers. Through these kinds of explorations, students are challenged to think and to see their world in broader, more abstract terms. The following passage by Clifford is cited by Don Aker (1992), a secondary English teacher, as an explanation of why this should be a priority:

> (It) is only in the hearts and minds of wholly literate people that a different society can be envisioned. The spirit of a critical literacy hopes for change, for social justice in a more humane democracy. . . . [Flawed] institutions change only when the people who inhabit them are transformed, when they can see differently. A critical literacy hopes that students and teachers will become agents of change, enactors of attitudes and beliefs rooted in democratic values, in a celebration of informed and problematized differences. (1990, p. 2)

Curricular Concerns   Literature serves many purposes in the school curriculum. Rosenblatt (1987) identifies the importance of literature in the curriculum: "Literature has a special role to play on two considerations: first, literary texts inevitably offer potential insights into values. Second, in evoking a literary work from a text the reader carries on a kind of activity that differs from the process required for reading natural or social science texts" (p. 66). These two insights about the nature of literature (one concerning the content of literature and the other, the potential for literature to provide an aesthetic experience not available in other kinds of reading material) provide assistance to teachers in making curricular decisions. In reflecting on Rosenblatt's first point, it is important to distinguish between the potential for helping students to understand values better and the ability to change values. The purpose of literature is not to teach values; it is to *explore* values. This exploration is vital as it provides readers with a context in which they can develop their own values.

The literary tradition in the schools has been one of using classics or the works of major authors with well-established reputations. Exclusive use of traditional selections raises legitimate questions of their relevance to young adults. Carlsen and Sherrill (1988) in *Voices of Readers: How We Come to Love Books,* a study of thousands of avid readers, note

> It seems fairly clear that most of these people's taste had to reach a certain level of maturity before the classics were appreciated. Some mention their

senior high school English classes as being responsible for their interest in the classics, but more often, it was not until their college English courses that they began to understand the reasons for labeling a literary work as "classic." Even then, some respondents had been so traumatized by their earlier exposure to a particular title that they could never overcome their distaste for it. (p. 135)

They also remind us that it was during the 1890s that the Committee on Uniform College Entrance Requirements selected a limited number of books to test high school students on for college entrance; these books remain today a fundamental part of the literature curriculum for secondary schools (p. 129). At a time when there are concerns about the reading ability and habits of today's youths, teachers need to encourage students to read. Logically, the likelihood of students reading increases when they have opportunities to read books that reflect their interests and the world in which they live.

Adolescent interests have a tremendous impact on what students are willing to read and how much of themselves they are willing to invest in their reading. Research studies (Bintz, 1993) confirm teachers' experiences that after elementary school, many students' reading abilities no longer continue to grow. Additionally, their interest in reading seems to decline, although some experts argue that the decline is in *school* reading, not reading per se. Young people say that their diminishing interest in reading stems mainly from having more interesting and important things to do such as participating in sports and clubs, working at after-school jobs, watching television, playing video games, and "hanging out" with their friends.

In his study of resistant readers in secondary schools, Bintz describes students who read a variety of materials outside of school and find that reading to be meaningful and useful, but who express a dislike for school reading and find it boring and of little value. He states: "For many students, reading per se is not the problem. What is the problem is the fact that they are forced to read materials that they have no voice in selecting. They regard such school reading as an imposition, inconvenience, and interference with current reading interests" (p. 612). Some of their comments are

I like to read. I'm a good reader when I really want to read something. I'm not so good when teachers require me to read something, and it is just boring. Most of school has been that way. I've always felt like I had to squeeze in my own reading. (p. 612)

In school, I'm not happy about being limited to five or six books that we are required to read. I'd rather be trusted to pick my own books. School doesn't make much time for me to read my own books. (p. 612)

I don't even read some assigned chapters in my textbooks. I just listen to the teacher and take notes. On my last test I barely skimmed the chapter and was still only a few points from a perfect score. Or like in English, it's all essays, and so I just have to basically know what is going on so you can BS. (p. 612)

Bintz concludes with this sobering observation:

It is important to note, however, that this form of resistance to reading can be counterproductive. It didn't appear that students fully understood the long-range implications of their resistant behaviors and attitudes. They understood the benefits of using shortcut and survival strategies in the short term, but it did not appear that they understood the implications of using these strategies in the long term. Specifically, they were not aware that these strategies might hinder them from becoming highly proficient readers. Thus, I have come to believe that by resorting to shortcut and survival strategies, students were participating in their own deskilling. (p. 613)

Gallo (1982) found similar results in his study of the reading interests of 3400 students in fourth through twelfth grades. In junior high school, thirty-five percent of the girls and forty percent of the boys said they "seldom" or "never" liked the novels and books they were assigned to read. In senior high school, twenty-three percent of the girls and forty-one percent of the boys gave the same response. Of all students, only one in five indicated that they "usually" or "always" liked the assigned books.

In recent years debate has raged about the nature of the school literature curriculum. For traditionalists, the classics have value demonstrated throughout years of use and remain at the core of the school curriculum. In contrast, others maintain that defining our literary heritage in such narrow terms excludes much of the field of young adult literature, as well as much of the work of women writers and most of the work by authors of color. Some decry the attempt to continue to mandate the classics exclusively (all those books by "dead, white, male writers") as sexist and racist. Although those charges will probably be debated for years, a more germane issue revolves around the need for the school curriculum to be responsive to the characteristics, needs, and interests of students. It is interesting to note that Harmon (1993) found that more high school anthology pages are devoted to Edgar Allan Poe than any other writer; yet, in our experience, many students find Poe's work "boring," "hard to understand," and "just plain weird." Even if one enjoys Poe's work, it is difficult to justify this depth of treatment. If increasing student involvement with literature is truly a goal of our schools, then teachers must have the opportunity to use literature that students will read and that they will respond to by making connections with it.

Students from diverse ethnic and cultural backgrounds frequently experience even more disaffection with traditional assigned reading. An author of young adult literature, Nicholasa Mohr (1990) speaks of her own experience:

> Growing up, I had never seen or read *any book* that included Puerto Ricans (or Hispanics, for that matter) as citizens who worked hard and contributed to this nation. In American letters, we were *invisible*. Writing has given me the opportunity to establish my own sense of history and existence as a Puerto Rican woman in the literature of these United States. . . . With this magic, I can recreate those deepest of personal memories as well as validate and celebrate my heritage and my future. (p. 146)

Another author of young adult literature, Harry Mazer (1992) gives us his perspective:

> Literature is greater, broader, wider, more encompassing than the classics. Literature is an ocean. The classics are like an inland sea. We don't need "great" books to bring our kids to literature. We need readable hooks that enchant and inform and move kids to want more.
>
> Why teach the classics? Why struggle to make meaningful what belongs in a history program or in an advanced literature class? At a time when our kids are not reading, when we need all our inventiveness, imagination, and flexibility to keep the desire to read alive, the classics keep us doing things in old, tired ways.
>
> Much has been heard from the few, little from the many of humankind. Literature needs these other voices. Blacks, women, Native Americans, Hispanics, and the voices of children and teenagers. It's only in contemporary literature, in books that are being written now and will be written in the future, that we have a chance of hearing these voices—these voices who are us. (p. 8)

Au (1993) speaks to the need to develop students' critical literacy through multicultural literature:

> For all students, literacy achievement is a matter of heart and motivation as well as of mind and cognition. Critical literacy . . . is also a matter of conscience and responsibility, since it involves a perception of the world

and transformation of the world through practical action. Having students read and discuss culturally conscious works of literature is one way of developing students' critical literacy, because they have the opportunity to learn about a variety of life experiences and to become aware of issues of social justice. In discussions of multiethnic literature, teachers guide students not only to interpret the text but also to reflect upon the ways that they might carry democratic values forward in their own lives. Teachers with a commitment to the values of democracy and diversity accept the challenge of using new patterns of literacy instruction to help the students who are in their classrooms today. Through their positive actions and those of their students, they also work toward a future when the United States will be a more just and fully democratic society, offering all children a wealth of educational opportunities. (p. 189)

J. A. Appleyard (1990), author of *Becoming a Reader: The Experience of Fiction from Childhood to Adulthood,* provides an insightful perspective on adolescent readers that can be helpful to teachers seeking to understand young people and provide them with meaningful reading experiences. He describes five stages of reading development: Early Childhood: The Reader as Player; Later Childhood: The Reader as Hero and Heroine; Adolescence: The Reader as Thinker; College and Beyond: The Reader as Interpreter; and, Adulthood: The Pragmatic Reader. As with any stage theory of development, it is important to recognize that the stages describe only general patterns of progression. Stage theories are not tied to specific ages of readers; progression through the stages is an individual matter.

Appleyard found that when questioned about their responses to particular stories, adolescents tend to give three kinds of responses:

1. They explicitly mention the experience of *involvement* with the book and *identification* with the character ("it was just like I was there," "you can sort of lose yourself in it," "It could have been written about me," "I couldn't get into it").
2. They talk about the *realism* of the story ("it was true to life . . . believable," "the characters have flaws like a normal person," "I know kids just like that").
3. And they say that a good story *makes them think* ("I like things that force me to think," "a story that keeps you reading and constantly thinking about what's going on"). (p. 106)

Involvement, identification, realism, and *a good story that makes them think* are terms that characterize young adult literature that helps adolescents understand themselves, their relationship with others, and the world.

Purves (1992) describes three views of the goals of literature in the curriculum. Some educators think these are competing and conflicting views, but Purves believes they are complementary and should be part of a balanced program. These three views are "that literature is an adjunct of the language arts, that it comprises a distinct body of knowledge, and that it is an aspect of aesthetic perception. Thus literature is seen alternatively as a stimulus for reading and writing, as an aspect of the humanities, and as one of the arts" (p. 23).

These studies and commentaries and others like them provide a powerful argument for the use of meaningful literature that speaks to the needs and interests of adolescents. This means we must create a balanced curriculum that addresses both the aims of the schools and the needs and interests of students. Implicitly, these studies also address the need for a model of instruction and strategies that facilitate the use of literature in a manner that makes a connection with youths.

> **Bridging**
>
> *Bridging a YA Novel with a Classic*
>
> Robert Cormier's <u>After the First Death</u> serves as an appropriate bridge to William Golding's <u>Lord of the Flies</u>, a classic novel of a group of boys stranded on an island.

Instructional Concerns Teachers encounter a multitude of instructional concerns in planning and implementing a literature program. As we have discussed, one result of students' gaining self-knowledge is their improved thinking. The challenge of actively responding to their reading provides students with opportunities for critical thinking. Through varied teaching strategies such as the ones presented in this text, students can be encouraged to be active readers who interact with the characters and their experiences and who learn to think critically.

The Reading Process

How we define reading has significant implications for how we teach literature. For many years, reading was thought of as the *product* of recognizing words, comprehending their individual meanings, and then accurately extracting from the text its meaning as determined by an authority figure. In the literature classroom based on this theory of reading, students do such things as identify the main idea and define key vocabulary terms (frequently using commercially prepared worksheets) or write character sketches and essays about the author's use of symbolism. Factually based tests, often true/false and

Literature Involvement Strategy

Discussion Continuum

Teachers are often frustrated when only a few students contribute while the rest sit back apathetically during a whole-class or small-group discussion. The discussion continuum is a strategy for involving <u>all</u> students in a lively discussion. The teacher draws a continuum on the board with opposing statements at either end. As the students enter the classroom, they write their initials somewhere along the continuum on the spot that best specifies their own position on the issue. During the discussion, the students explain their positions, often using references from their reading to back up their points. The only rules are that everyone must have a chance to speak before someone can speak for a second time and that all positions must be listened to respectfully. Initially, the teacher may structure the discussion so that students representing views at opposite ends of the continuum alternate speaking. It is our experience, however, that once students get involved they take over the discussion themselves and are soon responding to each other rather than using the teacher as the person who must keep the discussion going. It is also our experience that some students decide to change their position and thus their place on the continuum as a result of the discussion.

The discussion continuum works well as a springboard for writing or for further research on an issue or creative project. As students become familiar with the discussion continuum, they can create their own opposing statements in their Student Sharing and Study Groups or with their Learning Partners. Having students create their own statements helps them to develop critical thinking skills and to internalize what they are reading at a deeper level. The following are examples of a discussion continuum with young adult literature:

<u>Fell</u> by M .E. Kerr

| It is all right to change one's identity for money. | It is dishonest to assume another's identity. |

•————————————————•

<u>Nothing But the Truth</u> by Avi

| Philip was taking an ethical stand. | Philip was playing a power game. |

•————————————————•

<u>Waiting for the Rain</u> by Shelia Gordon

| The author provides a balanced view of conditions in South Africa. | The author provides a biased view of racial conditions in South Africa. |

•————————————————•

multiple choice, are used to determine if students have read and "really" understood the material.

Based on extensive research on learning and cognition, more recent theories have resulted in redefining reading as an interactive *process* in which readers actively construct the meaning of a text by connecting it with their prior knowledge. Reading is viewed as a participatory process, with social and cultural contexts playing significant roles. In the literature classroom based on this social constructivist theory, students read selections by a variety of authors and share their responses, both affective and cognitive, through such activities as journal writing and discussion groups. Literature portfolios and creative projects are more likely to be used to assess student growth than tests.

A process model of reading incorporates three phases: pre-reading, during reading, and post-reading. This model describes how readers think about and respond to a selection before they read it, while they are reading it, and when they have finished reading it. For most "good" readers, this process operates primarily at an automatic, subconscious level. For many students, however, this process remains mysterious and is one with which they have limited success, especially with school reading. As teachers, we frequently assume that all of our students have a greater sophistication with the reading process than they actually do. This was brought home to us when working with a group of middle school students who were struggling to understand their assigned literature selection. We enthusiastically reacted to a particularly descriptive passage by exclaiming, "Oh, can't you just see it!" The students were dumbfounded by our comment and responded with, "But there aren't any pictures." The concept of visualizing what they were reading was unfamiliar to them and certainly helped to explain, in part, why they thought reading was a boring and laborious task.

Teachers using the process model of reading recognize that learning occurs when students are actively involved in connecting new information and ideas with what they already know. In many classrooms, the instructional emphasis is placed on post-reading activities; teachers make the mistaken assumption that all students are successfully and independently performing the pre-reading and during reading functions. For students who need this kind of assistance, teachers model the reading process and provide a scaffolding to help them learn to internalize the process themselves.

Writing is used extensively at every phase of the reading process to aid students in connecting their experiences with, exploring their responses to, and interacting with others about what they are reading. Reading and writing are complementary processes that help students not only to construct meaning but also to develop critical thinking skills and greater conceptual understanding. Teachers who understand the process approach to writing find the process approach to reading compatible with it.

Young adult literature provides the teacher with an excellent opportunity to meet the needs and interests of adolescents and to implement the process model of reading with its emphasis on constructing meaning through the connection of the reader's prior knowledge with the text. As Rosenblatt (1968) emphasizes, the making of meaning is the most important reason for having adolescents read literature:

> There is an even broader need that literature fulfills, particularly for the adolescent reader. Much that in life itself might seem disorganized and meaningless takes on order and significance when it comes under the organizing and vitalizing influence of the artist. The youth senses in himself new and unsuspected emotional impulses. He sees the adults about him acting in inexplicable ways. In literature he meets emotions, situations, people, presented in significant patterns. He is shown a causal relationship between actions, he finds approval given to certain kinds of personalities and behavior rather than to others, he finds molds into which to pour his own nebulous emotions. In short, he often finds meaning attached to what otherwise would be for him merely brute facts. (p. 42)

The Pre-Reading Phase

In the literature classroom, the pre-reading phase involves engaging students in the selection as well as helping them to activate and apply their prior knowledge and to establish purposes and strategies for reading. Traditionally, teachers have focused classroom instruction on post-reading activities. Pre-reading instruction has typically consisted of a brief introduction to the selection and an assignment to be completed after reading it. A more extensive and thoughtful approach to the pre-reading phase, however, helps to ensure that readers' curiosity is aroused and their prior knowledge activated so that they connect more authentically and deeply with the selection, thus enhancing the success of post-reading activities. Lee Patton (1993), an experienced high school English teacher, resource teacher, mentor, and author, changed his teaching approach to provide what he calls an "emotional activation of prior knowledge" during pre-reading instruction. He found that fostering a personal, emotional connection before reading resulted in a more critical reading of a selection. He describes how he might do this before reading *The Adventures of Huckleberry Finn*:

> Before my students take off downriver with Huck Finn and well before Huck himself lights off for the territories, we will be reflecting on abusive parents, puritanical relatives, the possibility of friendship across age, caste, and race, and any crises of conscience we've wrestled with. Passing out the

book will not be the way we start with a novel, it will be one of the ways we continue to proceed. (p. 136)

The following questions and directions are some general ways to assist students with the pre-reading phase:

- Based on the title and the book cover, what do you think this book will be about? What does it make you think of?

- What do you already know about this topic and genre?

- Are you familiar with anything else the author has written?

- Why did you select this book? What expectations do you have of it?

- Read the introduction, if there is one, and the first page or two.

- Plan how you will go about reading this book.

- What kind of reading strategies will you need to use?

Using the Book Cover for Pre-reading   The front, back, and spine of a book may provide readers with helpful clues to prepare them for reading. For example, the cover of Peter Dickinson's highly regarded book, *Eva* (Laurel-Leaf Fiction edition) provides the reader with a number of clues. The back cover includes quotes from reviews, including one calling it a "daring, often horrifying adventure story" (from the *Horn Book* starred review), whereas another calls it a "dramatic science fiction story" (from *Bulletin of the Center for Children's Books*). The back cover text reveals that thirteen-year-old Eva has been in a coma for a long time since an accident and that some unknown techniques were used to keep her alive. Eva senses that something has happened that she does not understand and that there is "some other price she must pay to be alive at all." The back cover text provides an ominous, but intriguing hook for the reader. The picture on the front shows a strip of a face including pale blue eyes. Above the eyes, a sun sets behind a large tree. Students might be asked to speculate why we are shown only the eyes; why a wilderness scene takes the place of the top of her head. They might also speculate about the possible consequences of her accident. They may look for other clues on the book jacket. Once the cover picture and other information have been examined, students can apply their knowledge to make more informed determinations about the book. Students might also look at the structure of the book and make some assumptions about the book based upon the three parts—"Waking," "Living," and "Dying"—and the chapter titles, all of which refer to time. Using book covers and a brief survey of the contents in this way will often help to raise questions in the readers' minds and encourage them to read and to interact with the text.

These types of speculations help to prepare students to approach the book. In other words, pre-reading activities are those in which the reader focuses on and mentally prepares for the experience of reading.

The During Reading Phase

The during reading phase includes assisting students in making connections and associations while reading as well as using strategies for self-monitoring their understanding. In the during reading phase, students might be directed in the following ways:

- As you read, stop periodically to let your mind absorb what you are reading.
- It is all right to reread passages so you understand them better.
- Think about what that this book reminds you of, such as people, places, or experiences you have had.
- Visualize in your mind the setting, characters, action, and events.
- What feelings are you having while reading this book?
- Ask yourself questions about what you are reading.
- Use sticky notes to mark passages that you especially like or sections or words you don't understand. Take brief notes with page numbers so you can refer back to them.
- Talk to someone else about what you are reading.

The during reading involvement with *Eva* necessitates that readers make some imaginative leaps and visualize what they have never actually seen. Some readers may be confused about the technical aspects of the experiments; they can be encouraged to use sticky notes to jot down questions. Students may also be expected to raise crucial ethical issues as they read.

Strategies for engaging in the during reading phase will vary depending on the type of material being read and the purpose of reading it. Skillful readers approach nonfiction differently than they do fiction. Reading for study purposes must be approached differently than leisure reading.

Bridging

Characterization

M. E. Kerr's <u>Gentlehands</u> and Jay Bennett's <u>Skinhead</u> deal with people who believe in the principles of Nazism. The character of Gentlehands earned his reputation during the Second World War; Mitch and Carl in <u>Skinhead</u> are contemporary neo-Nazis. Readers can reflect on questions such as Is the only bridge between these characters their political philosophy? How are these men alike and how are they different?

The Post-Reading Phase

The post-reading phase involves opportunities for students to clarify, elaborate on, and extend their understandings. Throughout this text, we will provide you with a variety of learning experiences for this purpose.

In the next chapter, we elaborate on the three-phase model of reading and show how writing is an integral part of it. We describe in detail a Model of Young Adult Reader Involvement for the teaching of young adult literature. More reading and writing ideas are presented in Chapters 10 and 11.

Summary

Young adult literature meets student needs by promoting self-knowledge, knowledge of others, and knowledge of a world view. Studies of adolescent attitudes toward reading provide a powerful argument for using literature that addresses their needs and interests. A balanced literature program that includes young adult literature helps to meet the fundamental educational aims of the schools and addresses curricular and instructional concerns. Current theories define reading as an interactive process in which readers actively construct meaning.

Sharing the Connection

The Drowning of Stephan Jones
Bette Greene

Stephan Jones was a powerful and moving story. I think that the format of the story made it very easy to read and because of the sensitive subject matter, I felt this was important. A clear picture of Stephan and Frank and Andy and Carla was presented so the reader didn't have to decipher actions and motives. Also, there were no inappropriate references that might offend the reader. I have never read a book that evoked such emotion. There were times I felt my heart racing because I was so involved; I wanted to jump in and save Stephan. I was humiliated for him, enraged, and so many other things I get worked up just thinking about them.

Kim Essex, secondary English teacher

Suggested Activities

1. In your journal, describe how reading young adult literature can promote self-knowledge, knowledge of others, and knowledge of a world view. Use examples from books you are currently reading to illustrate your points.

2. Relate the studies on reading interests either to your own adolescent reading experiences or to those of the students you teach.

3. Using a young adult literature selection you have recently read, develop a Discussion Continuum as described in this chapter's Literature Involvement Strategy. If you are teaching, use it with your students.

4. Observe one or more middle school or secondary literature class. Describe whether the instruction seems to be based on theories of reading as a product or reading as a process.

Establishing the Connections with Young Adult Literature

Part 2 is composed of four chapters. The first two chapters focus on involving students with their reading of young adult literature. The last two chapters in this part shift the focus to the role and direction of the teacher in using young adult literature.

In Chapter 5, The Literature Curriculum: Involving the Young Adult Reader, we discuss the literature curriculum and the importance of encouraging authentic student responses to literature. We describe the Young Adult Reader Involvement Model and present six approaches for structuring the literature curriculum. Chapter 5 also includes our interview with Marion Dane Bauer, author of realistic fiction and fantasies.

Chapter 6, Implementing the Young Adult Reader Involvement Model, presents scenarios of students and teachers using the model. In this chapter, we talk with Laurence Yep, prolific author for children and young adults.

Chapter 7, Teacher Roles for Teaching Young Adult Literature, serves a dual role. First, we discuss the teacher roles as reader, expert guide/reading coach, and researcher in connection with the Reader Involvement Model. Then the roles are related to teacher responsibilities to read widely, to communicate effectively, and to know the history of young adult literature. Virginia Euwer Wolff, author of three highly regarded young adult novels, shares her experiences in this chapter.

The last chapter of this part, Chapter 8, Selecting Young Adult Literature, examines teachers' roles and responsibilities in selecting what students will read, communicating the nature and purpose of their curriculum, and addressing possible questions and potential challenges from censors. Additionally, in this chapter we provide a brief overview of the history of young adult literature so that teachers may be knowledgeable about the field. Graham Salisbury, a new and highly regarded author, talks with us.

CHAPTER 5

The Literature Curriculum: Involving the Young Adult Reader

Reading makes immigrants of us all—it takes us away from home, but, most important, it finds homes for us everywhere.

Hazel Rochman

Journal Writing: Responding

What benefits do you receive when you have opportunities to share what you are reading with others? What ways of sharing do you enjoy the most and why?

Reading literature in the classroom should not be a random exercise. The literature curriculum should have the breadth to include young adult selections as well as classics, paperback books as well as anthologies, and student recommendations as well as teacher selections. It should include a range of literary types—from novels to nonfiction to short stories to poetry. But more importantly, the literature curriculum must engage the young adult reader.

In this chapter, we discuss the status of the literature curriculum and the importance of providing authentic connections for students. We present a Model of Young Adult Reader Involvement, followed by a description of six ways to structure the literature curriculum.

The Literature Curriculum

Langer (1992), Applebee (1992), Purves (1992), and others have found that literature study in the schools has largely remained static in recent years in spite of concern about writing instruction and efforts to implement process approaches to writing. Secondary literature classes continue to be organized primarily around genres—eleventh graders study the traditional canon of American classics and twelfth graders study the British classics. Middle school programs vary widely. Although some middle school teachers pattern their classes after Nancie Atwell's reading workshop approach, many middle school teachers have no paperback books in their classrooms. In some cases, they do not even have literature anthologies. They are expected primarily to teach grammar, spelling, and writing. When literature is taught, it is frequently used as a vehicle for teaching comprehension skills rather than as a means for students to learn about themselves and their world.

Literature study at all levels is predominantly whole-class instruction. All students read the same selection, discuss it, write papers about it, and take tests on it. When individual differences are taken into account, poorer readers are usually tracked or grouped and given less to read, when what they need is more. Also, teachers may assume that if more able readers have the ability, they also have the maturity and interest to become immersed in the classics, thus, they are given even greater doses of them. The state of literature instruction, then, is not significantly different from what it was almost a hundred years ago. It sorely needs a transfusion to meet the needs and interests of today's students.

We believe that the study of literature should be based on a curriculum that is accessible to students. Often English teachers assume that because they have read the classics and even had authentic connections with many of them, their students should have similar experiences and be able to make the same kinds of connections.

Jack Thomson, author of *Understanding Teenagers' Reading: Reading Processes and the Teaching of Literature* (1987), describes his own university experiences studying to become an English teacher:

> The more I listened to the lectures, the more I realised that it would be unwise to try to do any thinking for myself or to record my own honest responses in essays or examinations. Like many others, I read the set books dutifully and then found out what was important to know about them by reading and making extensive notes from books of literary criticism. It was digests of these notes that I swotted for examinations, which I duly passed. (pp. 11–12)

Jack Thomson's experience is more typical than we would like to believe, and unfortunately it often results in teachers who attempt to teach literature in the same manner they were taught. Students learn to play the school game through producing the expected responses while deadening their own authentic connections with the text and author. As adults, we can choose not to read most things that we don't have an authentic experience with, but that is a luxury that we seldom allow our students. Too often we treat literature assignments as if they were medicine—"Read this; it's good for you."

The issue of relevance remains significant if students are to establish meaningful connections with their reading. Monseau (1992) explores the role of literature in the classroom:

> Robert Probst suggests that in designing a literature course teachers ask themselves this question: "What do we want the literature students to experience and learn in our classes?" If we don't do this, he says, "we assume that the goals of the professional literature student are also the goals of the secondary school literature student, though instinct, common sense, and brief experience in the classroom all tell us that this is not a safe assumption." Most high school students will not become literary scholars, yet literature courses are commonly designed around objective analysis of classic texts. As Rosenblatt says, "In our zeal to give our students the proper literary training, we constantly set them tasks a step beyond their powers, or plunge them into reading that requires the learning of a new language" (1988, 215). She goes on to say that intensive analysis of the classics often forces students to work so hard understanding the language that the work loses its power to affect them. This kind of classroom encourages students to indulge in what Bloome calls "mock participation," where students employ deceitful behavior (72–73). In the literature class this may mean copying the answers to the study questions from a classmate, extracting an "interpretation" from *Cliff's Notes* and presenting it as one's own, or simply parroting information from lecture notes. None of these activities requires a true understanding of a literary work or even a reading of it. (p. 88)

Sharing the Connection

On My Honor
Marion Dane Bauer

On My Honor has a powerful message about trust and responsibility. I read it to my students and they related to it easily. They were completely involved in the story of two boys getting carried away acting on dares with tragic results. Many of them shared personal experiences that were similar to the characters in the novel. I recommend it highly to other teachers and students as well as parents.

Alejandro Velasquez,
middle school teacher

Authentic Connections

Providing students with opportunities for making connections with literature in the classroom should be the goal of all teachers who use any type of literature in their courses. These desired connections or experiences are what we call *authentic connections* with literature as opposed to *expected connections*. We often hear students express surprise about a book they have read because they anticipated that they would react differently. Students have described authentic connections in the following ways: not being able to put a book down; feeling that they know the characters like friends; picturing scenes in their minds; being intrigued by an idea; and having other "being there" experiences as they interact with their reading. For example, Kevin, a tenth-grade student, "lived" Michael's reunion with his father in Marion Dane Bauer's *Face to Face,* as he imagined what it would be like to see his father again. Leslie, a virtual nonreader, made an authentic connection with Cab in *Checking on the Moon* by Jenny Davis because they both are crusaders. As Monseau (1992) states:

> Engagement is an element that is natural and necessary to the understanding of literature. That such an important factor is often overlooked in the literature classroom may be a major cause of student boredom and lack of interest. Perhaps it is a cause of teacher boredom as well. (p. 90)

In contrast to authentic connections, expected connections are those that someone else expects the readers to make. Some external authority, such as the author, teacher, or reading expert, predetermines how the reader should react and respond to a selection. Teachers, often unknowingly, may set up situations in which expected connections are valued more than authentic connections. For example, students may experience authentic connections while reading and discussing a selection, but then they are expected to supply certain "correct" responses on worksheets and tests, which become the official evaluation of their experience. Or students may be expected to "prove" that they understood a book by writing plot summaries or following a prescribed book report format. Teachers may also design activities in which they "guide" students to respond in a certain manner. This may be based on teachers' sincere desire to have students concur with their responses, which they believe to be the "true" interpretation of the work.

Students may also be influenced to respond to a particular work of literature in a certain way because their friends expect them to respond as they have. For example, the formula horror stories of V. C. Andrews are frequently popular among middle school students; however, some students admit that they read her books only because it is the thing to do and not because they enjoy the books. To the contrary, when teachers provide students with experiences in which they address their thoughts and feelings about a work without trying to guess the expected response, students have the opportunity to interact authentically.

Further to illustrate the difference between authentic connections and expected connections, let us describe a personal experience that one of us had as an adolescent reader. You may have had a similar experience yourself or taught students who did.

As a high school student, I had a wonderful American literature teacher who had us read many challenging and fascinating works. I liked and devoured *Walden,* but I found Emerson tedious. My papers on *Walden* were fun to write, but I struggled with the one on Emerson. My favorite novels were *Moby Dick, The Scarlet Letter,* and *Arrowsmith*—books that were as varied in quality as in content and difficulty. With each of these works, I made some type of connection. My responses both during class discussions and in written assignments illustrated that I not only comprehended these works but I also understood them and had powerful insights about the characters, their situations, and their actions. Then we read Crane's *The Red Badge of Courage,* and I was unable to make any type of connection with it. I waded through the book, but I was unresponsive in class and did poorly on the paper we had to write about it. My teacher was puzzled and accused me of not having read the book. What I understand now, and what I was then only beginning to have a superficial awareness of, was that I was not able to connect with that particular book. I had a similar experience when, later that semester, the teacher attempted to teach and involve us with Edgar Allan Poe. My earlier experiences with works with which I had made authentic connections made it difficult for me to "fake" a connection with works that meant nothing to me. The teacher then tried to elicit "expected connections" from me, but that seemed too contrived to me as an adolescent. My experiences were, I believe, typical of many students.

We believe that young adult literature can help adolescents to have authentic connections with literature. The Model of Young Adult Reader Involvement is designed to assist teachers as they seek ways to foster these connections by using young adult literature in their classrooms.

Gallo (1992) describes the importance of students' involvement:

What most students want—whether they are in advanced classes or not—is involvement with the literary text. "I want to read something with a pulse!" one exasperated high school boy told me. "I like young adult novels because they catch your attention very quick," asserts a middle school boy. In a recent study in Texas, a University of Houston researcher has noted that reading for avid readers—as opposed to students who read little—is an emotional activity; they want to interact with the text (Beers). "I like to read books about people my age . . . 'cause you can relate to it," declares Cindy, a suburban Connecticut eighth grader. (p. 20)

Some teachers mistakenly believe that they can involve students with literature simply by giving them choices—that is, by having them read one book or even several books they like. Involvement with literature, however, can be accomplished only when students are helped to establish a *process* for making connections with their reading. See Figure 5.1. This process has three phases and one ongoing dimension. In the first phase of our model, *Initiating,* readers "get into" a work. Initiating begins for students as they select what they will read or examine an assigned reading. Selection is influenced by many factors, including the sharing or recommendation of someone else. In like manner, attitudes toward an assigned reading can be influenced positively by sharing. Next, students decide how they will explore their reading. These decisions include establishing purposes for their reading as well as selecting appropriate reading strategies to fulfill those purposes. Norma Fox Mazer (1992) speaks about the importance of involving students:

> Let them choose their own books. Have a library of paperbacks in the classroom, on the windowsill or on your desk, or on a shelf along the wall. The books are there and they're available. And read them yourself. Recommending comes from the heart. Enthusiasm is contagious. Strong feelings, either for or against, are interesting. Ask for your students' help in reading the books. Take their opinions seriously. Involve them in the process of selecting books, of weighing and assessing, of thinking about who is likely to enjoy which book and why. (p. 30)

In the second phase, *Connecting,* readers are engaged with the selection; they make associations and relate what they read to themselves, to others, and to their world. In the third phase, *Internalizing,* readers incorporate ideas and perceptions into their own knowledge base and belief systems. *Sharing* is the

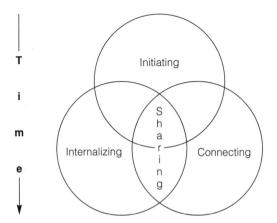

Figure 5.1   Model of Young Adult Reader Involvement

ongoing dimension of the process, when readers engage in written or oral interactions with others about aspects of the work that have attracted their attention or raised questions in their minds.

As Figure 5.1 illustrates, the remaining significant factor is that of *Time*. Students will need many opportunities across time to practice and to experience literature. Talking about it once will not help students; teachers must structure ongoing opportunities and time for students to initiate, connect, and internalize their reading. They also should encourage students to share their reading through such activities as dialogue journals, class presentations, and discussions with learning partners. Figure 5.2 describes this process in the Reader Involvement Model.

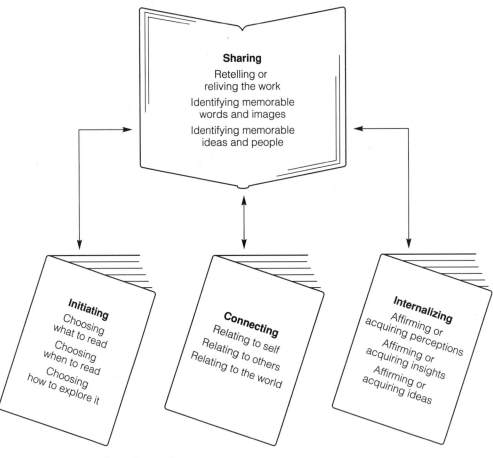

Figure 5.2   Aspects of Reader Involvement

We believe that the Young Adult Reader Involvement Model encourages positive experiences with literature for all students and that it can be used regardless of level and interest. In fact, it provides teachers with a framework to involve even poor or reluctant readers. Additionally, the model serves as a social interaction model by recognizing the importance of having students and teachers share as they read. As we have stated, the sharing component is the ongoing thread that intertwines all aspects of the readers' involvement. Experience with literature should never be presented to students as an isolated and isolating activity. Our goal is to have this sharing of involvement with books an enriching and rewarding experience for students. From making decisions about what to read to acquiring new ideas, the interaction of the reader with peers, parents, siblings, teachers, and librarians has an important influence on the reader. The process of sharing is the focus of the teaching strategy for this chapter, "Sharing the Connection," based on the Young Adult Reader Involvement Model.

Reflecting on the Young Adult Reader Involvement Model

The Young Adult Reader Involvement Model is a useful way of examining how readers relate to their reading. It is important to remember that the three phases of the model are not linear, nor are they necessarily sequential. The phases are recursive in that readers may repeat the phases at any time during reading. (Internalizing, however, occurs over a period of time as the result of reflection.) The ongoing process of sharing is crucial to achieving reader involvement.

Literature Involvement Strategy

Sharing the Connection

Students are asked to identify a book to which they had strong, positive reactions. They are asked to write about why they liked it, responding to such questions as "What did it make you think of?" "How did it make you feel?" "What was your favorite part?" and "What made you feel a connection with the book?" Sharing the Connection sheets are then posted around the classroom, in the hallway, or printed in the school newspaper. They are also used as the springboard for class discussion or group work.

Although the obvious arena for sharing is classroom interactions, the value of writing is not be ignored. The process of writing to explore one's reactions and feelings is a powerful way for students to realize how they feel and what they think. Students should have numerous opportunities to write using such activities as dialogue journals, book reviews, and Sharing the Connection responses. Through writing, students are able to clarify their thoughts by going through the process of sorting and selecting their impressions and exploring their thoughts and feelings.

Emotional Involvement   One aspect of true reader involvement with literature always includes an emotional response. As Thomson states, "Emotional

Bridging

Examining the Role of the Family

The young women students in Is that You, Miss Blue? by M. E. Kerr form a family-like unit in their boarding school. Use this book as a bridge to Louisa May Alcott's Little Women and Jane Austen's Pride and Prejudice.

response precedes intellectual understanding and seems to be a prerequisite for such understanding to have a significant impact" (p. 72).

We have often heard educators say that they want students to "experience" literature, as if there were a miraculous formula to elicit a certain type of reaction and response between a reader and the text. We, in fact, believe that readers can have many literature "experiences." Furthermore, these experiences can be varied and change according to any number of factors, including their own purposes for reading the particular selection.

The level of readers' involvement will vary as they read different genres and different works. For example, some students will relate to poetry whereas others may not; some might respond more to nonfiction than fiction. Even within a genre that students relate well to, they will not necessarily respond to all works in the same way or to the same degree. Most readers will not respond in the same way to different works by the same authors. To assume that readers, even good ones, will respond insightfully to each work of literature denies an understanding of the literary experience. Reading literature is not purely a comprehension exercise. It involves both a cognitive understanding of the selection as well as an emotional or affective interaction between the reader and the text. Reader involvement is dependent on four factors: the reader's prior knowledge, the reader's level of interest, the reader's need to know, and the reader's emotional response to the text. The significance of each of these factors varies according to the type of and purpose for reading.

Sharing   The process of sharing includes interaction between readers and others and has three components: articulating, clarifying, and verifying. Through articulating, readers express their reactions, thoughts, and beliefs. After articulating and clarifying, readers then reassess and verify their thoughts within the context of their own value systems. See Figure 5.3. Just as the phases readers go through in the Reader Involvement Model are recursive, so are these three processes. Whenever a reading experience is shared, readers go through the processes of articulating, clarifying, and verifying as ongoing parts of the experience.

When students are reading as a part of class, teachers have a responsibility to provide a nurturing environment in which students have varied opportuni-

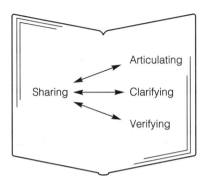

Figure 5.3   The Process of Sharing

ties for sharing. Teachers may be involved by writing responses in dialogue journals or by reacting to the books their students are reading by talking with students on a one-to-one basis. One teacher we know stays current by having his students make specific recommendations of books they like. The teacher follows up on the recommendations by reading and responding to as many as possible. One of the benefits of this process is that students gain an understanding of their teacher's interests and reading preferences while sharing their own.

Connecting   During the phase of connecting, students establish bridges between their own experiences and their reading. In Chapter 4 we advocated using young adult literature to meet student needs of developing self-knowledge, knowledge of others, and knowledge of a world view. The teacher's role at this stage is to facilitate students' making the connection through a variety of authentic learning experiences, including posing relevant questions or providing challenging writing experiences that help students to look beyond the reading.

Structuring the Literature Curriculum:
The Reader Involvement Model in the Classroom

A literature curriculum may be designed to provide students with opportunities to grow and to experience literature on a personal level and also to learn to appreciate and understand it aesthetically. Literature also needs to reflect the academic goals of the middle school or secondary curriculum. These goals may be met in the English class or through interdisciplinary uses of literature that enhance content knowledge of other disciplines. For example, science fiction provides a powerful tool for exploring the implications of scientific principles

Talking with Marion Dane Bauer

The real story isn't the surface events. The real story is what goes on inside of the characters. And all of that comes from my imagination and from my experiences.

Selected Titles

Am I Blue? Coming Out from the Silence (editor)

A Dream of Queens and Castles

Face to Face

Foster Child

Like Mother, Like Daughter

On My Honor

A Question of Trust

Rain of Fire

Shelter from the Wind

Tangled Butterfly

A Taste of Smoke

What's Your Story? A Young Person's Guide to Writing Fiction (nonfiction)

Marion Dane Bauer grew up in a small town in the Illinois River valley. She describes her childhood as solitary, even lonely. Early in her adult life, she taught college composition and high school English for a few years. When her children were young, she decided to take her writing seriously. She now lives in Minnesota where she writes full time and also teaches writing to aspiring adult writers. Among the awards her books have received are a Newbery Honor Book for <u>On My Honor</u>, the Jane Addams Peace Award for <u>Rain of Fire</u>, and an ALA Notable Book for her first novel, <u>Shelter from the Wind</u>.

My overriding purpose for writing, and I suspect this is true of most of us, is to keep working out my own issues. I keep going back to that place as a child where, for whatever reason, my needs were not sufficiently met. However wonderful our parents were, we all have a place like that. I just go back and pick it up again and work on it and make it come out this time. I grew up in a family, like many in my generation did, where feelings were not allowed; any expression of emotion was not nice. Writing allows me to authenticate feelings that I hadn't even been able to acknowledge that I had, and it gives me a place to play out those feelings. The more I write the more I am interested in the kinds of families that most of us grew up in and that most of us create. These are families with good, caring people who are still capable of missing one another in really important ways, where the child is left with profound needs that weren't met however much people cared.

When I was thirty-three and living in Hannibal, Missouri, I decided to write for

young people. The local library had a shelf of Newbery Award winners. At that time, I didn't even know what the Newbery Award was. Two of the books had a life-changing impact on me: *Slave Dancer* by Paula Fox and *Sounder* by William Armstrong. Those two books said to me that I could write something that could touch a child's life and I could write it fully and authentically and without protective barriers. At that point, I knew what I wanted to do—I wanted to tap into young people's lives with that kind of power.

I never consciously set out to teach something with my books. When I'm writing, I'm doing something for myself in that ultimately I am the reader of my own books. The only time I ever think of the reader is if I am dealing with something that I think my young reader will not understand, then I try to process it in a way that will make it clear without making it obvious. Other than that, I only think of my character, and if I have empathy and a deep connection with my character, then presumably, hopefully, that empathy and that connection will happen for the reader. When I'm writing, everything has to serve the story movement, including and particularly the language. I leave out anything

that isn't contributing to the movement of my story. Compression of time also contributes to intensity; *On My Honor* takes place during only twenty-four hours.

I was quite isolated as a child and lived very deeply in fantasy. I could distinguish between fantasy and reality, but fantasy could be a whole lot more interesting to me than anything that was going on in my real life. I did a lot of nonfiction writing such as long letters to my cousins and I kept a journal, but I was making up stories in my head all the time. They were so complex, though, that I had no idea how to get them down on paper. Some of the more fanciful ones I can still remember today. There is a very strong reality/illusion theme in my books and I am continually dealing with that line. I do a lot of research for my books, but what really fires the story is the struggle between what I can create in my mind and what happens in my life. My own years in seventh and eighth grades were absolutely horrendous. I've never been able to write about who I was then, but I can take the humiliation, the powerlessness, and the rage and bring it out in my characters. Intensity is what makes me want to write.

Bridging

Looking at Setting

The rural south has provided a rich background for many books throughout our history. Explore the role of the setting in Sue Ellen Bridgers's <u>All Together Now</u> and in Olive Burns's <u>Cold Sassy Tree</u>.

and practices with ethical issues in a science class; novels exploring AIDS may provide a human face to the disease for students in a health class; sports biographies, other non-fiction accounts, and novels about athletes can complement the activities in a physical education class.

Students' experiences with literature can serve as a springboard for further individual exploration. For instance, a high school sophomore whose class read *Dicey's Song* by Cynthia Voigt then decided to read *Izzy, Willy-Nilly* on her own. She liked that book as well and so she continued to read every book that Cynthia Voigt has written. Certainly, we hope that required reading will provide an impetus for individual leisure reading experiences. A long-range goal of studying literature is to encourage students to be lifelong readers of literature and to experience the beauty, the power, and the wisdom of literature.

By recognizing the interdisciplinary opportunities that literature can offer, teachers help students to read more widely and to read with a broader perspective. These heightened experiences and awarenesses about books will help students realize that reading literature goes beyond the English classroom and has relevance in other aspects of their lives.

There are a number of different ways to structure a literature program. In this section, we present six approaches of varying complexity. The six structures are elements of literature, genre, author, topic, issue, and theme. Figure 5.4 shows these structuring approaches on a continuum that illustrates their complexity.

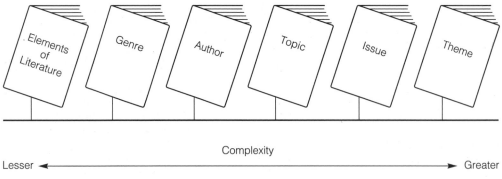

Complexity

Lesser ◄──────────────────────────────► Greater

Figure 5.4   Structures for Literature Program

Making Connections Between Works: Bridging

As we examine the six structures for literature programs, we will present ways to implement the structures. Throughout this text we have used examples of bridging as a way to identify a commonality between two or more works. Bridging is a springboard activity or experience to help both teachers and students to begin thinking about how certain works, particular characters, unifying themes, topics, or issues may be related to one another.

As we explore the six organizational structures mentioned above, we will use bridging experiences as initiating activities. Bridges can be established in a number of ways—such as between one genre and another, between young adult literature and the classics or more traditional selections, between fiction and nonfiction, or between any other combination with some type of connection that enhances and broadens the reader's knowledge and understanding.

Elements of Literature The elements of literature approach provides opportunities for students to examine specific literary elements such as characterization, conflict, setting, or any other major element. (Literary elements are discussed in Chapter 8.) This benefits students by providing them with an in-depth focus on one or more significant elements of a work. Because youthful readers can so readily identify with the characters and plots of young adult literature, it is an excellent vehicle for helping them to understand the elements of literature before they read more complex, traditional selections. Using an elements of literature approach is a particularly effective way to acquaint readers with the language of literature. Being able to use and apply literary terms helps students to be conversant about the various aspects of literature. For example, students might focus on ways that characters are developed in several books. Certainly, the study of literary elements will be an appropriate preparation for examining literature when students are expected to be able to analyze the structure of literature.

Genre The term *genre* refers to the categories into which works of literature are grouped. For example, novels are a broad category; young adult novels form a specific category within this genre, as do historical fiction and science fiction. Holman (1975) describes the categories of genres as "useful descriptions but rather arbitrary ones." In spite of this

> ### Bridging
>
> #### A Look to the Future
>
> In Lois Lowry's futuristic novel <u>The Giver</u>, Jonas, the protagonist, struggles as he remembers what life used to be like. His actions and reactions to his community can serve as a bridge to the science fiction classic <u>Fahrenheit 451</u>, by Ray Bradbury.

Bridging

The Novels of Cynthia Voigt

The best known of Cynthia Voigt's books are probably those of the Tillerman family saga, <u>Homecoming</u>, <u>Dicey's Song</u>, and <u>A Solitary Blue</u>, among others. These books can serve as a bridge for students to examine her other works such as <u>The Callender Papers</u>, <u>Building Blocks</u>, and <u>Jackaroo</u>. This experience will provide students with insights into the work of this prolific and popular author.

---

arbitrariness, a genre study provides students with extensive experiences with the traits and aspects of particular types of books. This approach lets students gain insights into those characteristics shared by the genre. The bridging example on page 105 with *The Giver* and *Fahrenheit 451* could serve as a springboard for creating interest in a unit on the genre of science fiction.

Author In the research on reading preferences of secondary students in Michigan (Brown, 1990), fifty percent of the female respondents, grades 9–12, and thirty-four percent of the male respondents, grades 9–12, indicated that the author of a work has an influence on their selection of reading material. This interest among students can be capitalized on by using several works by the same author to organize units of study. For example, one middle school teacher we know used Gary Paulsen's *Hatchet* and *The Foxman* as an introduction and then had her students read *Dogsong* and *Canyons*. The class looked at patterns in character development, plot, and style. The in-depth study of Paulsen's work provided the impetus for several of the students to read more of his books independently.

Another teacher organized his class around the works of four authors—Robert Cormier, Cynthia Voigt, Virginia Hamilton, and Robert Peck. The authors' works represent a range in style, complexity, and content; students were allowed to select one of the four to examine in depth. The students reading each author then became extended collaborative learning groups; within each, smaller groups evolved to examine different aspects and perceptions of the author's work. The advantage to this approach is that it provides students with a focus for their study. A disadvantage is that only authors who are known for both the quantity and the quality of their work would be appropriate for this kind of intense examination.

Topic Using topics as the organizing structure for instruction can be one of the broadest approaches. Topics might include sports, families, neighborhoods, friends, school, peer groups and gangs. A topical organization has the advantage of presenting a familiar idea to the students. Since they all bring some prior knowledge and experience to the topic, all students will have something to contribute. The bridging experience with secret societies, right, provides readers with an opportunity to gain a heightened perspective on a particular type of group interaction. This bridging experience might serve effectively as a springboard for broader topics such as gangs or peer groups.

Issue Whereas a topical approach is very broad, an issue orientation is more narrowly defined. For example if we were to continue with the topic of gangs mentioned above, an issue orientation to the idea could be used. The organization of the unit would focus on one aspect of gangs. An issue might be that gangs make it difficult for individuals to make their own decisions and to act according to their own beliefs. Among the books that might be used to examine this issue are S. E. Hinton's *The Outsiders,* Theresa Nelson's *The Beggar's Ride,* and Walter Dean Myers's *Won't Know Till I Get There.* In exploring an issue, at least two clearly differing positions must be evident, so that students can examine the positions and then decide what they believe. Essentially, in organizing around an issue, teachers begin with the breadth of a topic and then begin to narrow it by articulating a position that will elicit responses from students as they take stands on the issue.

> **Bridging**
>
> *Books with Secret Societies*
>
> The mystery of secret societies is intriguing. Use the secret groups in Lois Duncan's Daughters of Eve, Robert Cormier's The Chocolate War, and M. E. Kerr's Fell series to bridge with the issue of secrets and deception in Gloria Whelan's The Secret Keeper.

Theme Lukens (1986) defines a theme in literature as a

> significant truth expressed in appropriate elements and memorable language. The significant truth is an element that is essential to turn a simple narrative into literature. This truth goes beyond the story and comments on human beings. This discovery holds the story together so that long after details of plot are forgotten, the theme remains. (p. 111)

Themes are the underlying ideas of a work—the unstated but implied ideas that provide an organization to a work. Themes are broad and powerful ideas that have universal applications. Because of the breadth and universality of literary themes, they serve as an appropriate unifying element for teaching units. In selecting themes, we recommend that teachers use as guidelines the benefits of literature for adolescents described in Chapter 1: knowledge and understanding of self, of others, and of a world view. The Bridging example on page 109 connects two novels with the same theme.

Bridging

Religion

In her Newbery Honor Book, <u>A Fine White Dust</u>, Cynthia Rylant demonstrates how religious faith can be abused. Use this book as a bridge to <u>Elmer Gantry</u>, by the Nobel Prize winner Sinclair Lewis, by exploring the issue that self-styled preachers are often charlatans.

A thematic approach to teaching literature provides many benefits for students and teachers. It creates an environment in which a community of learners can discover genuine connections among selections and link powerful ideas together in significant ways that relate to their own lives. It allows for a depth and breadth of learning while providing coherence to what often seems, to students, to be fragmented and unrelated lessons and activities. The construction of meaning through the activating and developing of a foundation of prior knowledge is facilitated by the common strands and interrelationships in the selections. Through the opportunities for choice, students develop more ownership in and positive attitudes toward what is being studied. For teachers, a thematic approach is an effective way to meet those aspects of teaching that frequently seem to be terribly at odds—specific curricular requirements and the needs of diverse learners within the time constraints of the regular classroom. Additionally, it provides teachers with the flexibility to incorporate goals related to critical thinking skills, greater conceptual understanding, and aesthetic appreciation. Also, thematic approaches are essential for teachers seeking to integrate content learning across subject areas or working to establish multidisciplinary connections.

A serious limitation of using thematic units is that they may be too prescriptive. Students may read only from the perspective of looking for the development and ramifications of the theme. Teachers can minimize this problem by encouraging students to realize that many themes are present in any work and to see a broader perspective of the work.

Putting It All Together

As we introduced the Reader Involvement Model in this chapter, we presented a process for helping students to be actively involved in their reading. The connection between students and their reading is dependent on a number of conditions. On a fundamental level, students must be willing to read. Their willingness is often consistent with their perceptions of the relevance of a work. Additionally, their reading experiences must be within a learning context that encourages and supports sharing and experiencing reading. The six instructional structures we discussed have the potential to take students through all three stages of the Reader Involvement Model—from initiating to connecting to internalizing. Examining three recent books by Cynthia Voigt, *David and Jonathan, Izzy, Willy-Nilly,* and *Orfe,* provides an overview of both the use of the model and of the instructional structures.

Elements of Literature Focusing on character development in Voigt's novels *David and Jonathan, Izzy, Willy-Nilly,* and *Orfe* will give students an opportunity to examine their reactions to the main characters. They can see how the characters are alike or different from the people they know and whether they can relate to the characters.

Genre Each of these novels is an example of realistic contemporary fiction. Students will assess the "realness" of the books as they interact with the texts. An obvious criterion for realistic fiction is that it must be believable; young adult readers do not readily suspend their critical reactions about how and why characters act and react. As students make connections with believable characters, they feel that they are meeting new friends. A believable, realistic young adult book presents readers with a different group of peers to respond to.

Author Using the works of an author as accomplished as Voigt provides the students with opportunities to view and discuss the author's style and development. These books could be read in conjunction with some of her earlier books, including *Homecoming* or *Dicey's Song,* for a comparative look at style, theme, character development, and other facets of the work. This type of in-depth study of an author's work will heighten students' understanding and feeling for the author's work.

Topic These books have a significant similarity in that they depict a friendship between two characters. Therefore, the topic of friendship would be an appropriate one to use as a unifying one in discussing these books. Obviously, the topic is a central interest and concern to adolescents and will elicit their active involvement. Beyond connections with the characters, students will be able to internalize their reactions because of the importance of friendships in their lives.

Bridging

Coming-of-Age Novels

An ongoing theme throughout literature illustrates the maturation, or coming of age, of the book's protagonist. In Theodore Taylor's <u>Sniper</u>, Ben must face and overcome numerous physical challenges. In Chris Crutcher's <u>Running Loose</u>, Louie Banks also faces challenges (both physical and psychological). Both these characters mature through their experiences. Use <u>Sniper</u> as a bridge to explore the theme of coming of age in <u>Running Loose</u>.

Sharing the Connection

Juliet Fisher and the Foolproof Plan

Natalie Honeycutt

I really liked this book because I could relate to it. It is funny, yet also true. The book made me think of a snotty girl in school who told on everyone and didn't think anyone was better than she, but deep down inside she wanted to be like the popular people. My favorite parts were when Lydia always came in late to class and "bothered" Juliet Fisher at her desk. I could just picture the scene.

Krista Denkins, student

Issue   The friendships presented in these books are not without pain and difficulties. The topic raises a number of issues, in general; however, specifically referring to these books, students might respond to the issue that a close friendship can hinder the autonomy of the individual. This issue evokes strong reactions from their own experiences.

Theme   In these novels the theme of searching for identity is an important one for the main characters; indeed, it is an important theme throughout literature. It is also particularly appropriate for adolescents because searching for identity is a significant task of the teenage years.

In the previous chapter we emphasized the importance of making a connection between the reader and literature. This chapter has built on that connection by providing a model of involving students with their reading. In Chapter 6 we present four scenarios in which the model is implemented.

Summary

The literature curriculum in many schools needs serious revision. Young adult literature in the classroom offers readers opportunities to make authentic connections with literature. The Model of Young Adult Reader Involvement provides teachers with a framework for involving students with literature. It consists of three phases—initiating, connecting, and internalizing—and one ongoing dimension—sharing. The literature program can be structured using a number of approaches including elements of literature, genre, author, topic, issue, and theme.

Suggested Activities

1. In your journal, describe an experience in which you made an authentic connection with what you were reading. What factors contributed to your

ability to make an authentic connection? What factors inhibited you from making authentic connections?

2. Reflecting on the Young Adult Reader Involvement Model, describe how you might use it to foster student involvement with literature.

3. What do you see as the strengths and limitations of each of the six approaches to structuring the literature curriculum described in this chapter? Prepare a unit using one approach or a combination of these approaches.

4. Using the bridging format presented in this chapter as a model, develop a bridging activity between two or more selections you have read.

Bridging

Friendships

Use <u>David and Jonathan</u> and the complexity of the relationships as a bridge to the relationship between Finney and Gene in <u>A Separate Peace</u> by John Knowles. This bridging serves as a springboard to exploring the nature of relationships.

Implementing the Young Adult Reader Involvement Model

"No more," I said, dropping to my knees.

He turned sideways. "Try."

But I was beyond hope. "I just can't live up to my father. I can't live up to you. I'm no hero."

He came back to me and leaned down. Snow had transformed his eyelashes into white wires. "There's no magic. It's what's inside you."

Lawrence Yep, *Dragon's Gate*

Journal Writing: Responding

Recognizing the range and diversity of readers in a classroom, how do you think young adult literature can help a teacher to meet their needs?

_____

In Chapter 5 we introduced the Reader Involvement Model. In this chapter, we present four scenarios that demonstrate the Reader Involvement Model in action. The first scenario is with a capable reader; the second, an at-risk reader; the third, a bilingual reader; and the fourth is a dialogue between two teachers. The first three scenarios show students' interactions with reading and writing in classrooms where teachers are dedicated to providing a range of learning experiences with literature. In all of these cases the teachers seek to help their students interact meaningfully with their reading.

A Capable Reader

In this first scenario, we explore the experience that Jeremy, a high school sophomore, has with reader involvement. He is a capable reader, but he does not often read nor does he enjoy reading. The following is his account of several days of reading involvement in English class.

Day 1. I used to like to read when I was in grade school, but then it got to be a real bore because all the teachers ever cared about was if you got the questions at the end right. So I would figure out the important words in the questions and find them in the story or the chapter and copy the answer. It was dumb, but the teacher was happy. This year we've got a pretty rad English teacher, Ms. Amon, but she says we are going to "read,

read, read" and "immerse ourselves in literature." That immersing business sounds like taking a cold shower to me. Anyway she has all these paperback books in the room and she took us to the library and Mr. Graham had put together a display of other books that they thought we might like. I guess there's no escape. I looked at the books, trying to find something really short. I found a copy of *The Red Pony* by Steinbeck and it was short. I thought I had that wired, but Ms. Amon said, "I've always loved Steinbeck, Jeremy, but frankly, I thought you would select something more contemporary, especially one of the books about sports. Why don't we take a look at some of them?" Then I knew there really would be no escape. She was going to keep tabs on us and make recommendations. This was getting serious. There were books in a bookcase in the back of the room and also in two racks like you see at the store. She started pulling books and handing them to me. "Let's see, you're a pitcher, aren't you? These books should interest you."

As I looked over the stack of books she had pulled off the shelf, two caught my eye. I looked at the first because of the title. It was called *Baseball in April*. But the cover wasn't too interesting, just a bunch of kids riding in an old red pickup truck. The cover also said "and Other Stories." I guess I would rather read one story than a bunch of shorter ones.

So I looked at the second book. It looked more interesting. The picture on the front is of a catcher lifting a pitcher in victory. The book is called *The Crazy Horse Electric Game,* by some guy named Chris Crutcher. On the front it says "Willie's the hero of his home town. He thinks nothing can stop him now." So I figured it's one of those overcoming adversity kind of books, but if it's got baseball in it I guess I'll give it a try. I showed Ms. Amon the book and she said: "Excellent choice, Jeremy. I'm sure you'll enjoy it. After you've read that I'll share my favorite Chris Crutcher book with you. It's called *Running Loose.*" That made me nervous, because if English teachers say stuff like "excellent," it usually translates as big-time boring.

We were supposed to read either the first fifty pages or first five chapters, whichever got us into the book further. Then we were to write about it in our response journals and be ready to share the writing with our learning partner the next day in class. We were assigned learning partners and I got this new girl who is real quiet. I'm sure she'll really like a book about baseball. Yeah, sure!

I started reading the book while I waited for my orthodontist's appointment. I read the first chapter about these guys who have a flower shop sponsoring their ball team so they have these nerdy roses on their batting helmets.

Day 2. Today on the way to school Ted asked what I was reading for English. He's reading *Fallen Angels,* which he read for a book report in ninth grade, but he really likes the book. I said he chose it just so he wouldn't have to read anything, but he claims that he is reading it and that he likes it even better this time. I told him that my book is really good. The main character, Willie, is like a real guy and he is a fantastic athlete. I didn't tell Ted, but Willie's father reminds me of his father. The guy is really pushy, like it is him out there on the field rather than Willie or Ted. I'm glad my dad isn't like that.

When we got to class, Ms. Amon said that she had some poems for us to look at. A bunch of the kids moaned and she asked why. People talked about poetry being boring and about dumb things. Ms. Amon said she thought we might be surprised by the poems she had for us to look at. It turns out she had a poem that was kinda related to our books in some way. She must have had a different poem for everyone in the class. My poem was called "The Base Stealer" by some guy named Robert Francis. I'd never heard of him, but I guess I haven't heard of many poets. I didn't know anyone ever wrote a poem about baseball. I thought poetry was supposed to be about dying or love or stuff like that. There were some good things about my poem. First, it was only nine lines long. Like the title says it's about this guy getting ready to steal a base. The description is pretty good, I could actually see him going through the motions, trying to rattle the pitcher. I've done that, but I never would have thought to write a poem about it. After we read the poem and wrote a short paragraph about how it made us feel or what it made us think about, we used the paragraph to introduce ourselves to our learning partners.

Day 3. In class we took our journals and exchanged them with our learning partners. I had never talked to Melinda before yesterday, when she talked about how she liked the images in the poem about the base stealer. Then today I liked what she wrote in my journal. I think it's going to be OK working with her. In my journal, I wrote: "I'm reading *The Crazy Horse Electric Game* because I thought it would be about baseball, but baseball is just a small part of the book. At the end of Chapter 5, there is a water skiing accident where Willie, the main character, almost drowns. From the back cover, I guess the rest of the book is about him coming back. I liked Chapter 3 because it was where they talked about the game. But what I like best is Willie's friend, Johnny, who makes up these long involved jokes that are real groaners. He cracks me up. I guess that is what is good about the book; it's funny sometimes, but it's also serious and sometimes it's even

Bridging

Bridging a YA Novel with a Classic

Walter Dean Myers captures the horror and futility of war in <u>Fallen Angels</u>, his powerful story of one young soldier in Vietnam. This book, while brutal, captures the waste and pain that soldiers face daily. This book can serve as a bridge to a twentieth-century classic, <u>All Quiet on the Western Front</u> by Erich Marie Remarque. Although these books are set on different continents, about fifty years apart, they have significant similarities, including the disillusionment of the soldiers with war and the significance of camaraderie among soldiers.

sad. I think the book is very lifelike." Melinda wrote back to me: "My favorite books are ones that are both funny and serious ones. I used to like Paula Danzinger's books because they were funny, but they also talk about school problems and stuff that is serious too." When we talked about the book, I told her about Willie's girlfriend who is a really good athlete, and she told me that she was going out for the basketball team and the softball team. Maybe she *would* like a book about baseball.

Day 5. Today was the fifth day of talking about our books in class. We started a new class activity, called "I recommend or don't recommend _____ because _____." All students had a chance to talk briefly about their books, but no one had to talk today. Ms. Amon said we could wait until we were ready. I went ahead because I figured that I could recommend the book even without finishing it. I said: "I recommend my book, *The Crazy Horse Electric Game,* because it is a book about not giving in when things fall apart. The main character, Willie, is seriously hurt in an accident and he can't do all the things that he has always been good at like sports, but he doesn't quit. His family falls apart and so he finds a place where he can get better on his own."

I really like the way Willie takes charge of his life, and it is believable because his life doesn't get easier when he leaves home.

When we went to lunch, a couple of the guys asked about the book because they said it didn't sound boring like a lot of stuff we do in English. I told them that I really liked it and I thought they would like it too, because it is funny and serious all at the same time.

Day 6. Ms. Amon asked me and three or four others in the class to write a Be a Critic Review of our books because of the interest that we created yesterday when we talked about our books. She said we would get credit and that she collects reviews over the years and keeps them in a file next to the bookcases in the back of the room so that students in all her classes can look at them when they're trying to figure out what they'll read next. First we had to write to our learning partners in our journals and now we write reviews for other students. I've never had any teachers before who didn't just want us to write to them. Ms. Amon talks about authentic learning a lot and I guess this is part of it.

Day 7. I finished my book last night but most people are still reading their books. Today in class I told everyone that I am even more convinced that they all should read the book. Melinda, my learning partner, has already decided to read the book because I convinced her that it is more than just about baseball. Ted and several other guys want to read it. Ms. Amon says I've been such a good advocate for the book that she is going to have to get a couple of other copies so there will be enough for others to read it. When I read the part about Willie going home, I thought, oh no, don't go back. I kept thinking about going back to spend the summer at my grandparents' a couple of years after we moved away. I was really excited to see all my friends again, but everything was different. I felt like an outsider the whole summer. But my summer wasn't as disastrous as Willie's. I knew when he left home that he was in better shape than his parents, but I didn't expect his father to fall apart so totally. Makes you wonder who's the adult. I guess one of the things that the book is about is that when things are really bad, then you can really only depend on yourself.

In the last few years I have read three books that I really have liked. One was *The Old Man and the Sea,* which I decided to read because it was really short, but then it reminded me of fishing with my grandfather. I thought it was a very good book. The next one was *All Quiet on the Western Front,* which my dad recommended and he reread so we could talk about it. This was the third book that I have really liked. One thing I noticed about all of them was that I really hated to finish them. It was like saying good-bye to friends that you'll never see again.

Day 10. Ms. Amon says that we have to have a closure activity for our books, but we can choose what we will do, but it has to have involve a writing component about our book. She met with me yesterday to talk about what I will do. I'm going to write a paper about Willie as a hero.

Day 15. I think about Willie a lot. He really was courageous when he was hurt to leave home so he could get well. Maybe that is the saddest thing about the book—that he had to leave so he could get well and then when he went back, people still didn't accept him very much except maybe Johnny. The more I talk and think about the book and work on my paper the better I like the book.

Day 17. I have decided to read Ms. Amon's favorite Crutcher book, *Running Loose,* for my next book. I think I may then write a paper about the way he uses sports in his books. But that idea may change when I get into *Running Loose* more. Ms. Amon suggested that I spend some time writing about my expectations for the book before I begin to read it. That sounds hard, but she says that sometimes when people read a book that they really like they have unreal expectations about other books by the same author. This way you think about it and write about it so it is out in the open, and maybe you won't be so disappointed.

As we examine Jeremy's reader involvement experiences, several points are apparent. He is a bright and perceptive student who, though he was initially skeptical, obviously enjoyed the process of selecting what he would read. The teacher played a crucial role in the initiation process by being aware of his interest in baseball and guiding him to books with which he might easily make connections. Jeremy's observation about the book covers illustrates that many youthful readers ignore the old cliché "Don't judge a book by its cover." The impact of a book's cover may serve as an initial form of connecting between the reader and the reading experience. In this case, Jeremy, a pitcher, is drawn to the visual image of a pitcher being lifted in celebration by his catcher. Thus, the initial connection is made.

The teacher certainly recognizes the importance of the ongoing principle of sharing by creating learning partners, response journals, and book recommendation talks. Jeremy's enthusiasm about his book and his willingness to talk about it both informally and in more structured class activities indicates that he is actively sharing his experience. Inherent in Jeremy's level of enthusiasm is also a sense of connectedness, because readers cannot generate strong feelings without relating the characters and their circumstances to themselves. The sharing that he and his learning partner, Melinda, do is significant in fostering all three phases of the model. Jeremy also does an interesting job of relating his reading with others. For example, not only does he see similarities between Ted's father and Willie's, but he goes one step further in contrasting his own father with Willie's, even early in the book.

Jeremy makes an important connection when he compares this book with others that he has liked (see Figure 6.1). His recognition of the theme of self-reliance is an important insight about the book. This recognition provides an appropriate springboard to have him analyze his opinions and responses. It would be interesting to have him determine what, if any, elements are shared by his three favorite books.

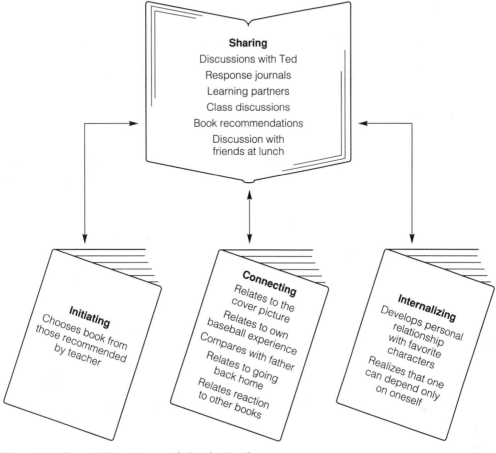

Sharing
Discussions with Ted
Response journals
Learning partners
Class discussions
Book recommendations
Discussion with
friends at lunch

Initiating
Chooses book from
those recommended
by teacher

Connecting
Relates to the
cover picture
Relates to own
baseball experience
Compares with father
Relates to going
back home
Relates reaction
to other books

Internalizing
Develops personal
relationship
with favorite
characters
Realizes that one
can depend only
on oneself

Figure 6.1 Jeremy's Experience with Reader Involvement

An At-Risk Reader

The second scenario is about Kevin, an eighth grader who is not a particularly good student and who never reads unless he absolutely has to. The teacher's role in facilitating his reading choices is complicated by Kevin's apparent lack of interest in anything. He claims not to have hobbies and says he spends his free time "hanging out." He is in a specialized intensive reading language arts class with a whole-language philosophy. His teacher, Mr. Wesley, has a wide selection of paperback books in his classroom. All of the students are to select their first book for the year. Kevin has spent one class period looking but hasn't made a book selection. Mr. Wesley is getting frustrated because the rest of the class is already reading. Finally, Kevin realizes that the stalling techniques are no longer working and selects a book.

Day 1. I guess I'll read this thing called *The Loner,* that's what everyone calls me, so maybe it'll be OK. Reading is a waste of time if you ask me, but I know ways to get around it. We had to do book reports every three weeks last year, but I just read the book jacket and a few pages and I'd write some junk and the teacher would give me my *C* and we would both be happy. The word is that Mr. Wesley is going to be a little harder to fool.

For Monday, we are to read the first three chapters and Mr. Wesley says we'll have to do an assignment in class about the first part.

Day 2. Mr. Wesley started class by having us do a quickwrite summarizing the major ideas from the first three chapters of our books. I wrote: "This is a story about a guy named Ben who goes off by himself with his dog and goes from farm to farm picking fruit." I got done but the rest of the class kept writing so I pretended to be busy. Mr. Wesley called me to the reading center and asked to see my paper. After he read it, he told me we had a problem. It might be that I couldn't read and that was why my paper was, like he said, off the mark. Or the problem might be that I just had looked at the cover and made some wrong assumptions. Then he asked me which problem I had. I tried not to answer, but he wouldn't let me off the hook. I admitted that I guessed I had paid more attention to the cover than the words. I know they have the guys who can't read do a bunch of dumb worksheets and I figured that would be worse than actually reading a book or two. He told me to spend the rest of the period reading in the back of the room. And I was to bring in the summary the next day. I tried to listen as others talked about their books, but no one else was reading *The Loner* so I was out of luck. Mr. Wesley kept coming back and checking on me. He'd ask me questions and when I answered he'd tell me that I was right on track and that I could be a good reader if I would just apply myself. I've heard that story from just about every teacher I had in elementary school, but I thought they'd dropped it since I got into middle school. He assigned Chapters 4 and 5 for class the next day.

I read Chapter 1 in class and I got Chapter 2 read in social studies. None of my teachers would ever expect me to be reading a book, so I lucked out and didn't get caught. I kinda like the book. It's about a kid with no name and no family who just hitches with folks that go around picking beans and potatoes and other stuff on farms. His only friend gets killed so he runs off again and gets lost. An old woman and her dog find him and take him in. What I like best about it is that I know how the kid feels about being a loner. I guess I screwed up on that thing I wrote in class, so I guess that it makes sense that Mr. Wesley figured it out.

Day 3. I wish that I could read faster so it wouldn't take forever to get through this fool book. I read for so long last night that my eyes hurt. That's never happened before. I still didn't get all my assignment done. I hope I don't get caught today. Mr. Wesley puts us in groups of three. We are supposed to take five minutes to list three things we like about our book and three things that we would like to change. Things I like: I like that the boy got to pick his own name. I like that he found people to be nice to him. I like that there is a lot of action and excitement. I would change that the girl got killed. I would change that he didn't like dogs. I don't know what else I would change because I kinda like the book so far. We were supposed to share our lists with the two people in our group and they could ask questions. Gail and Andy were in my group. They both said that they thought my book sounded pretty good. I think they may read it next. I didn't get caught for only having four chapters read instead of five. But we are supposed to read Chapters 6, 7, and 8 for tomorrow and write about it in our journals.

Day 4. I wrote in my journal: "I think that the boy was dumb to leave. He thought that Boss didn't want him, but she didn't say so. It was too cold and he didn't know where he was going." We had to read what our learning partners wrote in the journal. Dale is my partner. He wanted to know why the boy left so I told him about it. He was more interested in the part about the dogs. I'm still behind in reading and we are supposed to read three more chapters for tomorrow.

Day 5. I got all my reading done and there is only one more chapter and I'll have the whole book done! We had to spend twenty minutes writing about whether we would like the main character to be our friend and why. I decided that I would like to be David's friend because he turned out to be pretty nice. He kept screwing up, but he always felt bad. I screw up sometimes when I don't really mean to so I can kinda understand. I liked the way he took care of Jup, the dog, and the way that he told Boss that he was the one that got the sheep messed up not Jup. The dogs remind me of my grandpa's dog. Mr. Wesley said that we could either read our paper or tell the class about it. I told the class about David and my paper. Some people asked questions, and I could answer them, which made me feel pretty good.

Harley talked about a boy who goes after treasure in his sailboat. The book is called *Windcatcher* by someone called Avi, that's all, just Avi. I don't know if that is a first name or a last name. Anyway the book is real skinny, but it sounds like it is OK. I think I'll read that next, maybe.

Everybody is supposed to read three more chapters for tomorrow, but I only have to read one.

Day 6. David killed the bear. That was pretty good. He didn't get scared. Then Boss knew that he really was OK. I was kinda sorry that he was going to have to go to school the next year.

Mr. Wesley said we had to do something called a closure. I didn't know what he meant, but he showed me a couple of things and said I could choose. I decided to do a character map because it doesn't take as much writing.

Day 7. I didn't work on my character map last night because I watched TV. I tried to do it when we first came into class, but I couldn't figure out how to do it. Finally, Mr. Wesley talked to me about my book and we figured out that the map should be about David and what things were like when he started living with Boss. Once I got started, I kinda liked doing the map. It was OK to use the book to get words, too.

Day 8. I told my Ma last night that I wanted to train a dog like David did, but she said she's not going to fool around with any pup.

I hurried to finish my map, because Mr. Wesley said we had to show whatever we did to the rest of the class. I don't really like to do stuff like that, but I guess I can do it pretty fast with my map. My map turned out pretty good, too, I guess.

As the scenario reveals, Kevin is a reluctant reader at best. He expects to rely on the games and avoidance that he has used in previous classes to keep from reading. One hopeful point in the initiation phase is that he feels a sense of identification with the book because he feels that he, too, is a loner. This initial point of connection, however, isn't enough to inspire Kevin to read the book. He thinks he can simply read the book jacket and a few paragraphs here and there. Mr. Wesley's questions to Kevin motivate him to begin reading the book. Kevin's responses indicate that he doesn't read very often. His responses, while valid, are more superficial and less insightful than Jeremy's. His reaction clearly demonstrates the significance of prior experience as he primarily relates

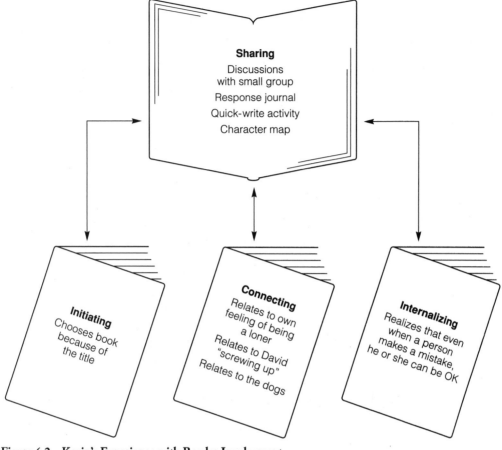

Sharing
Discussions
with small group
Response journal
Quick-write activity
Character map

Initiating
Chooses book
because of
the title

Connecting
Relates to own
feeling of being
a loner
Relates to David
"screwing up"
Relates to the dogs

Internalizing
Realizes that even
when a person
makes a mistake,
he or she can be OK

Figure 6.2   Kevin's Experience with Reader Involvement

to David's uncanny ability always to do something wrong. The task of getting the assignments done frustrates him. He experiences feelings of success when he is able to respond to his classmates' questions about "his" book and when he is able to complete a character map. His desire to have and train his own dog indicates that the story has an impact on him and that he connects with it and relates it to himself (see Figure 6.2). Kevin's experience with Wier's *The Loner* via Mr. Wesley's approach to reader involvement is the beginning of a more positive attitude toward reading literature; his reactions, however, are still tenuous and cautious—even ambivalent. It will take many more experiences of this nature to convince Kevin that reading holds something worthwhile for him.

A Bilingual Reader

As the increased cultural diversity of our society changes the demographics of our school population, teachers encounter scenarios like our third one more frequently. Kai Lee is a sixth grader who wants to relate to the books she reads. Kai Lee's family has been in this country for two years. English is her second language, and she studied it in Hong Kong in a school that bore the British influence. Her English is precise and usually formally correct, which makes her self-conscious around many of her peers. There are only three other Asian students in her entire elementary school, and none of them is from Hong Kong. Although she is a good student who does well in most of her classes, she feels isolated and sees little connection with the books that are traditionally used in the English language arts curriculum.

Day 1. Mrs. Clemens, my teacher, just finished reading *Tuck Everlasting* by Natalie Babbitt to the class and all of us had to read *The Goats* by Brock Cole. We used these books to talk about how they made us feel and what in our lives they made us think of. Then we had to do projects. Now we are supposed to find a book that we want to read in a way that would be special for us. Today the teacher took us to the school library because we had to pick a book to read. I didn't find anything that looked good, but I remembered a book I read when my family first came here. It was called *In the Year of the Boar and Jackie Robinson,* about a girl named Shirley Temple Wong who moved to America from China. I liked that book and I asked the librarian, Mrs. Sanderson, to help me find a book like it. She found me a book called *The Star Fisher* by Laurence Yep. It is the story of a Chinese American family that moves to a new town where there aren't any other Chinese families. I think I will like the book.

Day 2. When I got home from school yesterday I started reading my book and I finished it when I went to bed last night. I really liked the book. The author says that it is a story about his grandparents and their experiences. The family reminded me of mine. I've heard lots of stories about my grandfather, but I never knew him because he died before I was born. Then when we moved here my grandmother came to live with us. It is hard to move to a new place. The book made me think of people who were nice to us when we moved here. I also thought about my grandmother who lives with us. She's like the mother in the book because she speaks hardly any English.

At school today we had a free reading period to read our books, but since I had finished mine Mrs. Clemens let me go back to the library. I asked for another book by Laurence Yep and Mrs. Sanderson found one called *Dragonwings.* It looks pretty good, but it's about a boy instead of a girl so I probably won't like it as well. For homework we are supposed to write a paragraph about one character from our books.

Day 3. Today we got into groups of six and read our papers. We did a thing called PQP. The other people in the group are supposed to begin by telling us what they like about our papers or **p**raise our papers. Then they ask **q**uestions about anything they don't understand about our papers. Then we are supposed to revise or **p**olish our papers.

Day 4. We were supposed to pick our favorite scene from the book and illustrate it. Then we had to show our illustration and tell the class about it and why we choose that part of the book. I chose the scene at the church when everybody finally tried the mother's pie. I liked that part because you know then that they're going to have friends and not feel so lonely. We were supposed to tell the class why we chose that scene, but I was embarrassed to tell the real reason so I just said because apple pie is my favorite and then I sat down. Sometimes I feel so lonely and out of place here. Everybody else in my class has always lived here. Some of them have never even been to another state.

Day 5. Today Mrs. Clemens said we were to write if we would recommend our book to the rest of the class and why or why not as a closure activity before we go on to the next book. Usually I like to write a lot and the teacher says I am the best writer in the class, but I just couldn't write anything about *The Star Fisher.* Mrs. Clemens came over to check on me and was surprised when she saw I hadn't written anything. She asked me what was wrong, but I couldn't answer. She asked if I liked the book and I said yes. So she asked why and I said because it reminded me of my family and things we had done. I told her I was afraid the other kids in the class might laugh. Mrs. Clemens said everyone here came from another country and that I, like everyone else, should be proud of my heritage.

Day 6. I thought a lot about what Mrs. Clemens said and talked to my dad about it, too. He talked to me about something called a vicarious experience where people learn about things that are unfamiliar to them through reading. He agreed with Mrs. Clemens and told me stories about what my mother's parents went through to come to this country. When I came to school today, I had the book recommendation done and was the first one to volunteer to read it to the class. In my literature response journal I wrote a letter to Joan Lee, the main character in the book, and talked about the experiences I had that were like hers.

Talking with Laurence Yep

Writing is just a special way of seeing. It is a way of looking at the ordinary world with a sharper awareness than you would normally. Everything suggests a story to me.

Selected Titles

Child of the Owl

Dragon's Gate

Dragon War

Dragonwings

Liar, Liar

The Mark Twain Murders

The Rainbow People

Sea Glass

The Star Fisher

Sweetwater

Laurence Yep was raised in an African American neighborhood in San Francisco, living above the grocery store owned by his Chinese American parents. As a child, he commuted to Chinatown to school where he was one of only a few students who did not speak Chinese. After he published his first story at eighteen, he went on to earn a doctorate in American Literature from SUNY at Buffalo. He now resides in San Francisco. Laurence Yep is a prolific writer whose talents encompass several genres—science fiction, mystery, realistic fiction, historical fiction, and folktales. He also writes for the theater. He has received numerous awards including the Newbery Honor Book, Boston Globe-Horn Book Award, International Reading Association Children's Award, Jane Addams Peace Award, and the Christopher Award.

I get letters from kids who are like me when I was little—an outsider. I like being able to tell kids it's OK to be different and that at some time you will find your own peer group and you can be appreciated for what you do. It wasn't until high school that I finally met some friends with the same interests. In Chinatown the kids were all interested in sports, and while I liked playing sports up to a certain point, I was

---

Day 7. When I was in the library last week, Mrs. Sanderson told me that she had just gotten a new book in about a Korean girl called *Finding My Voice* by Marie G. Lee. She said it was the author's first book. It is about a high school senior, but her parents are really strict, even more than my parents. It is a pretty good book, but it makes me mad that when people are mean to her they call her Chink and Chinaman and things like that. It

never very good. Both of my parents and my brother were star athletes winning many trophies. I never won anything! My parents always read comic books to me. They had a rule that they would read one comic book to me and then I had to read one back to them. So all the reading skills were in place for me when I finally discovered the library, and then there was this explosion. I could never get into the stories about Homer Price and his Doughnut Machine because every kid has a bicycle and leaves his door unlocked. That just seemed unrealistic to me. So instead I got into reading fantasy and science fiction because those stories always talked about adapting and surviving. I grew up in an African American neighborhood and I went to school in Chinatown. Adapting and surviving were something I did every time I got on and off the bus; I was clearly having to adjust world views. Do you remember how libraries used to label science fiction with a blue rocket? Well,

I was the kind of kid who would go to the library and read every book there was with a blue rocket.

I started out writing science fiction for adults. I went to a Jesuit high school and I had an English teacher who said if I wanted to get an A in his class I had to get something published in a national magazine. He retracted his statement but I just kept sending things in and sold my first story when I was eighteen. It took me three months to write it, and it sold for a penny a word—earning me ninety dollars. That same English teacher taught us to write by having us imitate famous authors, which is how I learned to write so many different types of literature.

There are advantages in writing for kids. Kids are real honest critics—if they don't like what you're writing, they tell you. And

Continued

makes me mad that people do things like that anyway, but it also makes me mad that they think all Asians are the same. I know how she felt when it happens, but I think she should stand up for herself more. I also got another book called *Becoming Gershona* by Nava Semel. It is about a girl growing up in Israel back in 1958 when the country was just getting going. I liked the book because she goes through lots of the thing that I do too. In

Talking with Laurence Yep (continued)

I don't know how to put this politely, but you can't "b.s." kids. You have to write about what you see and hear and feel, not some abstraction of it. You can talk about dysfunctional families and acculturation, but when you write for kids, you have to put these in very real terms. And the most real, the most basic, terms for kids are the parent and the child.

Every book I write is special to me in a different way. *Sea Glass* is really about myself. The basketball scene is my father and me with him trying to teach me to shoot a basketball. My father was born in China and came over here when he was ten and hardly ever talked about China. My mother was born in Ohio and raised in West Virginia. I grew up with stories of life in West Virginia which found their way into *The Star Fisher.* I'm working on a sequel now about Christmas in West Virginia based on their wonderful memories. I'm also working on a sequel to *Child of the Owl,* in which Casey's daughter is in middle school in the suburbs, a product of a mixed marriage between a Chinese and an American. *Dragonwings* took a lot of blood to write. Then twenty years later, I adapted it for the stage. That was like

going to a family reunion—you recognize faces but you don't really know anyone anymore. *Dragonwings* has been seen by more than 100,000 kids across the country. It is a real joy to go to a performance, because as a writer of books, you can't really see a kid as he reads, but when it is on stage, you can actually see kids enjoying the play.

You learn from your senses. When you describe someone in writing, it is like visiting them again. In Chinese folktales you have ghosts slipping in and out of bodies so it is almost like Grand Central Station. To me that's the way a story is. I can see the structure and I can get the feeling for the style and I can almost flow into it. I usually work on several books at the same time. I go with one book for several weeks until I start running out of gas with it and then I switch to another book that has a similar theme. Psychologically I am working with the same type of characters but in different situations, so that's fun. I want to keep working on stories and plays. I've always been interested in the theater and I want to get back more to it. Basically, I am really doing what I love!

a way it helps to know that other people hear that awful stuff and it's not just me. I hope Mrs. Sanderson will keep helping me find books.

For Kai Lee, experiences with books can provide a vital link to her heritage and help her overcome her sense of isolation (see Figure 6.3). Although she is a bright, conscientious student, she appears to have trouble establishing relationships with her classmates. Her reticence in sharing her true connection with *The Star Fisher* reveals her discomfort. Mrs. Clemens seems perceptive about this problem and provides positive encouragement. Additionally, the librarian plays a significant role in helping Kai Lee find books with which she can connect.

In each of these scenarios, we explored situations in which the students were allowed to select books to read. The most typical classroom situation, however, is for the teacher to select a book for whole-class instruction. The Young Adult Reader Involvement Model can also be applied in these situations with some shifts in emphasis. For example, at the initiating stage, the emphasis shifts from student selection to the teacher. The teacher needs to introduce the book and provide prereading activities to help students make a

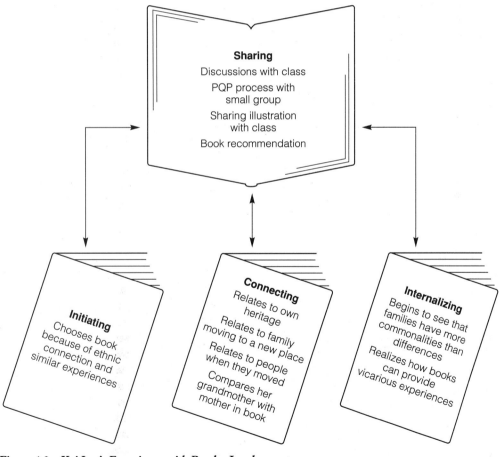

Figure 6.3   Kai Lee's Experience with Reader Involvement

Literature Involvement Strategy

Memorable Characters

This is a helpful strategy to help students focus on characterization after they have had the opportunity to read widely. Students select a character whom they have found to be unforgettable. Next, they work individually to clarify their own understanding of the character. With their Learning Partner, they assume the role of their character and introduce themselves to each other. Finally, they prepare a ten-minute interaction between the two characters to present to the class.

In one class, two learning partners choose Bobby, a Jewish boy, from Fran Arrick's Chernowitz! and Lena, an African American girl, from Ouida Sebestyen's Words by Heart to present a discussion of how discrimination affects them.

---

connection with it. When reading fiction, the type of involvement will vary significantly according to the readers' prior experiences and interests in the characters and their circumstances. Involving students in reading nonfiction demands a different type of interest and involvement. The level and degree of a reader's need to know often increases in nonfiction reading.

Teacher Discussion

In the final scenario, Mrs. Coombs, a more experienced high school teacher, is talking with Mr. Walkington, a middle school teacher. He has approached her for advice about using literature in his eighth-grade classes.

> Walkington: I remember you told me that you supplement your anthology with paperback books. I need to do something new. My kids gripe about the selections in the anthology just about every time we use it. I need new ideas. What do you do that works so well?

> Coombs: I suppose if I look for a simple answer to what has changed my class, I would say it is having students read widely, choose their own books much of the time, write about their reading, and use their writing to connect with others in the class. My philosophy is that students should read and write for authentic purposes. But let's talk about your classroom, Aaron. How do you use the literature anthology?

> Walkington: I have the students read a story like Richard Connell's "The Most Dangerous Game" and then we discuss it in class and maybe I have them do some writing about the story, like their reactions or something like that.

> Coombs: Do you always have the whole class read the same selection and do the same activities? What kind of writing are they doing?

> Walkington: Yes, Jo, we have only the one anthology. I've been experimenting with having them do some reader responses. They like doing

them, but it seems to me that they use them as an excuse to complain about the anthology.

Coombs: I've found that having whole class assigned reading is often not very productive. Many of our students don't read the assignment under those circumstances and those who do have to carry the discussion. Often over half of my students just sat passively. Now, Aaron, we both know that eighth graders seldom sit anywhere passively, but the end result is basically the same—not much learning takes place.

Walkington: That's the truth, but how do I change it?

Coombs: First, I suggest that you talk to the librarian at your school. Mrs. Mitchell at the public library is very helpful, too. Do you get fliers from the book clubs like Trumpet and Scholastic?

Walkington: Yes, lots of my kids regularly order books.

Coombs: That's a good place to begin. Do you make recommendations about the monthly book selections, or do your students pick out the books completely on their own?

Walkington: Both, but lots of those books and authors are new to me.

Coombs: Then you need to do your homework. I suggest that you start reading book reviews in the journals like *Horn Book, The ALAN Review,* and *The Journal of Reading.* The state-wide English meetings always have sessions on what is currently happening in both children's literature and young adult literature. The field is changing so fast, but there are wonderful writers that your kids will read and enjoy. Aaron, I recommend that you ask your students about what they are reading. You can get valuable information and insights from listening to your students. Have them recommend the best three books they've ever read and make a master list and start reading. That's what I did about seven years ago when I was going through the same type of frustration that you are now experiencing. You'll see that many of the students are reading formula-type books and popular series that you should probably take a look at, but I'd be surprised if you could stand to read any of them. Still, you can get insights about the students from what they are reading, and it will give you a starting place to do some bridging to better books. For

---

Bridging

Bridging a Short Story with a YA Novel

The issue of AIDS is being addressed more frequently in young adult literature. In his short story "In the Time I Get" (published as part of <u>Athletic Shorts: Six Short Stories</u>), Chris Crutcher has his popular protagonist from <u>Running Loose</u>, Louie Banks, befriend a person with AIDS. Use this story as a bridge to Marilyn Kaye's <u>Real Heroes</u>.

Sharing the Connection

The Cay
Theodore Taylor

The Cay is a book that no one should miss reading. It has a powerful message in it that is significant, especially in today's society with the problem of racism. I especially like the relationship between the main characters and how Timothy helped and protected Phillip. The lesson that Phillip learned was a valuable one.

Melanie Tetil, student

---

instance, I had a student who would read nothing but those dreadful formula romances, so I encouraged her to read some of Caroline Cooney's romance books. Once she liked her work, I got her to read some of Cooney's other books like *The Party's Over* and *The Face on the Milk Carton*. She told me that she has started to like books that "you don't always know just what is happening in them." If you guide students and are supportive of their reading, often they do start to move along on their own fairly well.

Walkington: That makes sense, Jo. I understand how it works on a one-to-one basis, but how did it change your teaching?

Coombs: As I became more knowledgeable about authors like William Sleator, Chris Crutcher, Robert Cormier, M. E. Kerr, Monica Hughes, Zibby Oneal, Virginia Hamilton, Laurence Yep, and so many others, I used them in class, letting students self-select the books that they would be reading. This is one place where the librarians can give you invaluable assistance by helping to direct your students to authors they would enjoy. This led to individual learning, small-group discussion, and writing groups.

Walkington: I've never dared do much group work with my students. They have trouble staying focused.

Coombs: When students have some say in what they are studying, they are much more willing to cooperate and become involved in all types of learning. It helped me turn my class into a center for collaborative learning.

Walkington: Thanks, Jo, you've given me lots to think about.

In the first three scenarios, we demonstrated the implementation of the Reader Involvement Model. In the final scenario, we heard the experiences of two teachers as they discussed their classes. The advice that Mrs. Coombs gives Mr. Walkington is merely an introduction to how to change his classes so that students become more actively involved in their learning. This scenario is an appropriate bridge to the next chapter in which we explore the roles of the teacher.

Summary

Four scenarios demonstrate the Reader Involvement Model in action. The first scenario is with a capable reader; the second, an at-risk reader; the third, a bilingual reader; and the fourth is a dialogue between two teachers. The first three scenarios show students' interactions with reading and writing in classrooms where teachers are dedicated to providing a range of learning experiences with literature. In all of these cases, the teachers seek to help their students interact meaningfully with their reading.

Suggested Activities

1. In your journal, relate each of the components of the Young Adult Reader Involvement Model to your own reading experiences with young adult literature.

2. If you are currently teaching, analyze how you could use the Reader Involvement Model in your classes. If you are not teaching, interview and observe a teacher to determine how students are encouraged and helped become involved in their reading.

3. Talk with one or more adolescent readers to find out what activities help them to become involved in their reading and what activities hinder that involvement.

4. Use the Literature Involvement Strategy, "Memorable Characters," presented in this chapter as a model to devise a number of similar situations. Then role play them either with adolescent readers in a school setting or in your college class.

Bridging

Bridging Poems with a YA Novel

John Crowe Ransom's "Bells for John Whiteside's Daughter" and Theodore Roethke's "Elegy for Jane" can be used to bridge to Lois Lowry's A Summer to Die.

CHAPTER 7

Teacher Roles for Teaching Young Adult Literature

The teacher-research movement has made it possible for teachers to make a difference both within the walls of our classrooms—in the lives of the children we teach—and among a world of colleagues who are ready to hear the stories of what we have learned and to reflect on these stories' meanings for the children they teach.

Nancie Atwell

Journal Writing: Responding

Describe your favorite K–12 teacher of literature, the methods used, and the learning environment established in the classroom.

The concept of reader involvement is a significant idea for teachers who believe in the power of literature to affect positive changes in the lives of their students. Simply providing students with good literature is not enough, however. It is only when students are actively involved in experiencing literature that they come to recognize fully its power and benefits. In Chapters 5 and 6, we presented the Young Adult Reader Involvement Model, which describes the processes students use when they are actively involved in their reading. In this chapter, we describe a Model of Teacher Roles and demonstrate how it relates to the Young Adult Reader Involvement Model. We present a perspective on the roles of the teacher, and we discuss teachers' responsibilities. These responsibilities include developing effective communications and having a working knowledge of the history of literature for young adults.

Roles of the Teacher in Teaching Young Adult Literature

To facilitate positive connections between students and their reading, the role of the teacher needs to reflect a new way of working and a new way of thinking in many classrooms. If teachers truly want their students to become readers of literature, they must nurture and encourage that process. The knowledge and attitudes of teachers are central in helping to change student behavior in reading. Arthur Applebee's (1989) extensive research, *A Study of Book-Length Works Taught in High School English Courses,* documents that 1) more than ninety percent of English classrooms employ anthologies, emphasizing genre in the lower grades and chronology in the upper grades; 2) familiarity is the second most important characteristic of the literature taught in junior and senior high schools—that is, traditional classics dominate the literature curriculum; and 3) most English programs make little distinction between literary works taught to college-bound students and those taught to nonacademic students. Anthologies are usually filled with traditional works that most English teachers studied in their own college literature classes. Thus, teachers often greet these works as old friends that evoke pleasant memories of intellectual challenges and stimulating times. Teachers are not likely, however, to create reader involvement for many of their students when their literature choices are primarily traditional with a dose of nostalgia tossed in.

Additionally, many teachers teach literature as they were taught. Although they love literature, they believe it their responsibility to engage students in endless dissections of a work and to arrive at its "true" meaning. The realities of teaching adolescents should rapidly make these teachers rethink both their methods and the content they teach; however, many teachers when confronted with a sea of pubescence hold tightly to their beliefs as a shield against the challenges of the classroom.

The problem is even more serious when we consider the need to incorporate the use of literature across the curriculum to help students develop a depth and breadth of understanding in all content areas. Gerlach (1992) makes a convincing case that

> teachers can facilitate reading as a way of discovering knowledge in their subject areas . . . reading literature can provide reinforcement for learning when students read about content which they can relate to and enjoy . . . no matter how the curriculum is organized, learning takes place only when learners make active connections between what they need to learn and what they already know, understand, and believe. Reading young adult novels in the content areas encourages learners to synthesize and organize their own ideas with the view presented in the novels. (p. 124)

Many teachers are unfamiliar, however, with the wealth of books beyond the basic textbooks in their subject areas that can enrich and extend their curriculum. For example, a number of excellent books are related to the history and issues of slavery. Joyce Hansen's historical novels *Which Way Freedom?* and *Out from This Place* relate the lives of African Americans during and immediately after the Civil War. *The Captive,* Hansen's newest historical novel, describes slavery in post-Colonial New England. Hansen also has written a nonfiction account of African American soldiers during the Civil War, *Between 2 Fires*. Paula Fox's powerful novel *The Slave Dancer* describes the plight of kidnapped Africans on ships bound for the Americas. Ann Rinaldi in *The Last Silk Dress* presents the compelling story of a young Southern belle who is forced to confront the racial double standard in her life. Additionally, nonfiction selections can enhance student understanding, such as *To Be a Slave* by Julius Lester, Virginia Hamilton's *Anthony Burns: The Defeat and Triumph of a Fugitive Slave*, and *All Times, All People: A World History of Slavery* by Milton Meltzer. The Collier brothers are noted for their fine historical fiction focusing on the time of the Revolutionary War. Scott O'Dell's popular and engrossing books extend the reader's knowledge of the Far West. As more teachers become involved in thematic teaching and interdisciplinary teaching, this knowledge of books and authors becomes even more crucial.

So how does a teacher make the transition? We believe that the following steps help both seasoned teachers wanting to make significant changes in their classrooms and novice teachers just entering the classroom. The steps are as follows:

1. Be observant—watch what the students choose to read.
2. Don't be judgmental about student choices.
3. Ask about the books and authors students are reading.
4. Find out how students select the books they read—that is, who and what influences their choices.
5. Ask students to recommend books to you.
6. Read the books with an open mind.

And, what about those students who don't read at all? How can teachers who want to select appropriate literature for the classroom discover the interests and needs of their nonreaders? The following questions may be helpful:

1. What do your students talk about informally?
2. What topics, issues, and events cause them to show strong emotions?
3. What do they value? React to?
4. What problems and conflicts are they struggling to resolve?
5. What entertains them? Challenges them?

All of this information, by establishing a sense of what is relevant to students, should be helpful to teachers. This is not to say that student choices should dictate the curriculum; they can, however, help teachers look beyond the traditional anthology favorites to find quality literature written for today's students.

Having the information is only the first step; finding ways to utilize it is the significant challenge. In subsequent chapters, we describe specific implementation and instructional strategies. Thomson (1987) suggests these three guidelines for teachers:

1. Encourage students to make links continually between the world of the text and the world of their own personal experiences outside it, between literature and their own lives;

2. Ensure that students do a great deal of spectator role [reflective observer] writing, sometimes from personal experience, sometimes from imagined experience, and sometimes in response to literature read; and

3. Assist students to find the books that speak to them of their immediate concerns, and try to help them to progress from the kinds of books that merely confirm prejudice and strengthen self-ignorance and self-indulgent emotionalism, to those which promote reflection, understanding and human growth. (p. 83)

Perhaps one of the most significant roles of the teacher is to encourage and foster student reading. The following list describes ways in which teachers can help students to establish lifelong reading habits:

- Rich reading environment
- Ready access to a wide range of reading materials
- Significant adults who value and share their reading
- Opportunities to discuss reading
- Opportunities to select their own reading
- Chances to order books through book clubs
- User-friendly libraries
- Positive classroom experiences
- Experiences interacting with peers about books

Another way to meet this challenge is to re-examine the roles that teachers have in creating a positive environment for student involvement with reading.

Sharing the Connection

The Hobbit

J. R. R. Tolkien

The Hobbit is an excellent book. I often found it difficult to set down, unlike many of the books I have read. I specifically enjoyed reading about Bilbo Baggins and his confrontation with the dragon, Smaug. The suspense was incredible; I was literally glued to the book. I have never had the privilege of reading another book of this quality. The Hobbit is well-written, exciting, and an overall pleasure to read.

Bethany Grzenia, student

Model of Teacher Roles

Three major roles are essential for teachers who seek to help young people become involved in reading: teacher as reader, teacher as expert guide/reading coach, and teacher as researcher. (See Figure 7.1.)

The role of the teacher is a dynamic one that changes best to facilitate students' learning. For example, the role of teacher as reader provides a significant contribution to students during the initiating stage. If teachers can draw widely from their own experiences and preferences as readers, they are more likely to be able to help their students find books that will meet their needs. The teacher as expert guide/reading coach draws upon the teacher's prior experiences as an expert reader and prior knowledge of literature and other subject areas. In this role teachers actively help students connect with their reading by drawing on their own connections with books and knowledge of instructional strategies, the reading process, and various content areas. The concept of teacher as researcher is based on what Patterson and Shannon (1993) describe as "reflection, inquiry, and action . . . In a sense, then, all good teachers participate in teacher research because they reflect about students' learning (and their own), inquire through multiple data sources (observation, analysis of artifacts, conferences, and the like), and then act on their new conclusions" (pp. 7–8).

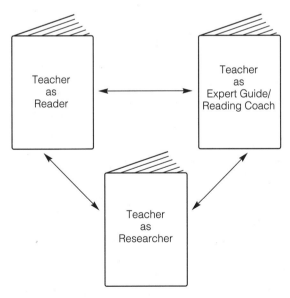

Figure 7.1   Teachers' Roles

Although the role of the teacher as researcher is an ongoing one that occurs throughout the entire reading/learning/teaching process, teachers can gain valuable insights specifically during the internalizing phase. By exploring when, how, and why students make a selection a part of themselves, teachers learn more about students, books, and ways to help facilitate connections that lead to internalization.

Although some parallel seems to exist between teachers' roles and students' stages of reader involvement, it is not a constant one-to-one correlation. For example, while students read and explore books, teachers may recommend other works by the same author, works that explore the same theme, or works that are written in the same style. So the teacher as reader may be an ongoing role, seeking to initiate new reading experiences. Furthermore, the role of the teacher as expert guide/reading coach is also an ongoing one. Whenever students and teachers share what they have read, teachers coach students to gain greater understanding and involvement—either by the questions they ask, by responding to students' insights, by sharing their perceptions, and by the instructional activities they use.

In Chapter 5, we detailed the process of sharing (see Figure 5.3). The three components of sharing (articulating, clarifying, and verifying) provide a foundation for teachers to fulfill each of their roles effectively. Sharing is the ongoing communication that makes reading come alive—whether it is students sharing with other students or teachers and students sharing together. The significance of this type of communication brings to mind the comment of a young man who stated, "I really hate to end a book. It makes me kind of sad, especially because my family members aren't readers nor are my friends. When I finish a book I like to be able to talk about it, but except for class I don't have anyone to share books with."

Each of the roles of the teacher is discussed in more detail in the next sections of this chapter.

Teacher as Reader

The role of teacher as reader plays a compelling part in facilitating the Young Adult Reader Involvement Model (see Figure 7.2). Teachers have a tremendous impact, both direct and indirect, on the reading attitudes and habits of their students. Although teachers are usually aware of their direct influence, they often are unaware of the indirect messages they send to students about the value and importance of reading. Vacca and Vacca (1989, pp. 6–7) cite the results of several studies indicating that, although secondary teachers state that

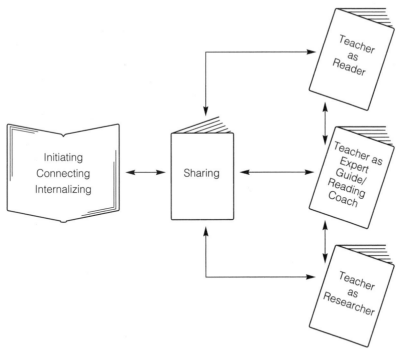

Figure 7.2 The Process of Sharing in Teachers' Roles

they believe reading is important, their classroom instruction and assignments frequently send an indirect message to students that they can succeed in school and indeed in life without much reading. Teachers may "preach" to students that they must read, but then they inadvertently reveal that they themselves are not readers. Simmons and Deluzain (1992) declare: "Students should observe that their teachers are not just *preachers* who are admonishing them to read; instead, they are genuinely enthusiastic readers, as reflected in selections on the desk and their eagerness to discuss them" (pp. 92–93).

The role of teacher as reader may also be recognized as teacher as learner. Inherent in the role of teacher as reader is an awareness that good teachers never stop learning. Some of the worst teaching occurs when teachers do the same things over and over again. Their classes are often ineffective because they have stopped learning and their lessons lack the vitality of change and relevancy. This routine is boring even to the teachers who fall into this trap. Exciting, vibrant teachers continue to learn and to communicate their enthusiasm to their students.

One of us had a colleague in a high school English department who told his high school students that they should take advantage of the opportunities he gave them to read because once they were out of school they would have more important things to do with their time. This comment caused quite a stir among the students, and they then asked their other teachers "When was the last time you read a book?" Only those teachers who routinely shared the books they were reading with their students could truly reaffirm the role and significance of reading in their lives. An interesting sidelight to the situation was that students used the responses as a gauge of approval. They would say things like, "Ms. X. reads three books at a time," or "Mr. Z. just finished reading *Winds of War,* and it has almost a thousand pages." For students who had seemed to be unaware of others' reading habits, their English teacher's implication that reading was important only as a school requirement had a startling effect. The entire experience was a powerful affirmation of the influence of the teacher as reader.

In a longitudinal research project on reading preferences of high school students (Brown, 1975, 1980, 1985, 1990), students report that teachers are among the primary influences of reading choices for both male and female readers. For teachers to facilitate student reading choices in the initiating stage of reader involvement, they must be knowledgeable about their students and the breadth of books available to them. The most effective way for teachers to recommend a book is to have read it and to share their experiences with it. Realistically, teachers may find it easier to recommend authors whose work they have enjoyed rather than identify specific books. Although it would be difficult for most teachers to stay completely up to date, given the number of young adult books published each year, teachers can keep informed about new books by reading reviews in professional journals such as *The English Journal, Language Arts, Journal of Reading, Reading Teacher, The School Library Journal, VOYA (Voice of Youth Advocates),* and *The ALAN Review* (see Appendix C for addresses for these periodicals). As readers, teachers need to be willing to share their interests and biases about books with their students; by the same reasoning, they need to be receptive to having their students share their interests and biases with them. Such communication between teachers and students is part of the ongoing sharing dimension that is crucial to implementing the model.

The Teachers as Readers Project—initiated by the Association of American Publishers and endorsed by the National Council of Teachers of English, the International Reading Association, and the American Library Association— fosters the formation of book clubs for educators designed to "help teachers to encourage students to become lifelong readers. When teachers read and enjoy quality literature with confidence, they contribute to the rich, literate environment of classrooms." The teachers involved regularly meet to read and discuss the same books. They "select at least four quality children's or adolescents' books and one professional book to read and discuss." The project is growing and more than 250 groups have registered. Group membership has expanded to include principals, librarians, and other school personnel who are interested in reading. For more information or to start a group, contact

Teachers as Readers Project
AAP Reading Initiative
Association of American Publishers
220 East 23rd Street
New York, NY 10010

Teacher as Expert Guide/Reading Coach

The role of teacher as expert guide/reading coach reflects a new philosophy of instruction. The concept of teaching as the act of bestowing knowledge on students is an outdated and untenable notion. The classroom is no longer an "us-and-them" situation; but it is now a shared experience in which the teacher guides the students as a community of learners to explore and find meaning in their reading. Norma Fox Mazer (1992) describes the type of environment in which teachers can serve as readers as well as expert guide/reading coaches.

So . . . a library in your classroom—and it's varied; it's got all kinds of sto-ries, a wide range, something for every taste. You're reading the books, and so are the students. And you're talking about the books, and you're reading out loud, too. Read to the class five minutes a day, maybe as soon as you take attendance. Read them something that has them hanging by their toes. Read them something funny or mysterious or sensational or weird or dra-matic. Read them something that makes them want to know and then what happened?

They'll listen to you . . . or they won't. Of course your hope is to read something so compelling they can't help listening. But basic to the whole process is choice. They must choose to listen. They can also choose not to listen. They must choose what they read, and they must be free to discard what they don't like. Which certainly doesn't mean you hold back your opinions. You're there to talk, persuade, recommend, and, okay, even pro-mote if it suits your style.

What you're doing is in the way of being a guide. A connection. A link. You're linking up kids and books. When the right connection is made, when children find a book that gives them that thrill of seclusion and absorption, that wraps them in the words that create a story, a world apart, then they're going to want that thrill again. And this is the way they develop GRH [good reading habits]. (pp. 30–31)

In the environment Mazer describes, both students and teachers have the opportunity to experience literature. This experience may provide a vital link in changing the entire learning experience. Atwell's (1987) reading and writing workshop approach also describes this type of shared learning experience. Inherent in the concept of teaching as a guiding or coaching experience is an awareness that students do not learn in a vacuum. Having experiences that lead to learning necessitates that students be allowed to be intellectual risk takers. Beach (1993) discusses the coaching function of teachers:

As a coach, a teacher encourages students to take risks by reading and responding in new ways to their peers, rather than simply to or for the teacher. As a coach, a teacher downplays his or her evaluative role by providing descriptive, nonjudgmental feedback to students. And, as a coach, a teacher models the process of adopting alternative roles, talking about how they read as an adult, parent, writer, critic, political being, mystery buff, and teacher. (p. 110)

The recognition of the importance of social learning may be traced to the work of Lev Vygotsky (1978) who wrote: "All the higher functions originate as actual relations between human beings" (p. 57). Vygotsky posited that learning was a social action in which students are helped to learn by teachers or by more knowledgeable peers. His theory of the zone of proximal development explores learning, initially, as an external process that is shaped and refined through the social interaction. Vygotsky describes the zone of proximal development as

the distance between the actual development as determined by independent problem solving and the level of potential development as determined through problem solving under adult guidance or in collaboration with more capable peers. (p. 86)

Through their sharing of experiences, students explore ideas externally in preparation for internalizing them later on. Developing concepts and internalizing them is a gradual process. As Vygotoky (1978) states: "The transformation of an interpersonal process into an intrapersonal one is the result of a long series of developmental events" (p. 57). The Young Adult Reader Involvement Model reflects these processes in the connecting phase as students go through a number of sharing experiences among themselves and with their teachers. These experiences are preparatory for the internalizing stage.

In *Literature as Exploration*, Rosenblatt (1983) explores the relationship between teachers and students as she says

> A much more wholesome educational situation is created when the teacher is a really live person who has examined his own attitudes and assumptions and who, when appropriate, states them frankly and honestly. He does not have to seem to possess "all the answers," which the students then need only passively absorb. . . . The teacher needs to see his own philosophy as only one of the possible approaches to life. . . . Tolerance of other points of view is extremely important for the teacher—an attitude those who are insecure and fearful of challenges to their authority find most difficult to maintain. (pp. 130–31)

Teacher as Researcher

The role of teacher as researcher has two primary facets: first, teachers should be knowledgeable consumers of research, and second, they should gather research data in their own classrooms. This first facet is two-fold. In the first phase, teachers stay current with their professional reading to learn and understand the appropriate theoretical constructs that will help their students to become more effective and involved learners. This exploration extends to a heightened awareness of teaching strategies and methodology. Beyond the professional literature, the second phase of staying current involves reading literature widely and knowing what is currently available in libraries and bookstores. Keeping up with currently published young adult books should also, as was discussed earlier, involve reading book reviews. Appendix C includes a listing of some of the major sources for book reviews and articles about books for young adults. Another resource for teachers is *Best Books for Young Adults: The Selection, the History, and the Romance* by Betty Carter and the Young Adult Library Services Association. This book offers a list of best books for young adults, 1966–93.

Once teachers have begun to develop a conceptual framework for their classroom practices, they are ready to explore classroom adaptations to enhance their students' involvement with young adult literature. In this, the second facet of the role of teacher as researcher, teachers apply theory to their

---

Bridging

Bridging a Short Story with a YA Novel

M. E. Kerr's short story "Do You Want My Opinion?" (from Don Gallo's collection of short stories, Sixteen Short Stories by Outstanding Writers for Young Adults) presents a view of a futuristic society. Use this story as a bridge to Lois Lowry's The Giver.

own classrooms through action research. They observe students' behaviors and preferences, gather data, and analyze their findings. Teachers then choose how they will act on their findings to improve learning and involvement with literature in their classrooms. Their observations serve either as the basis for proceeding or for raising questions that lead to further investigation and observation. This process is a cycle of reflection, inquiry, and action.

Teacher research in the classroom can have a profound impact on helping teachers solve perplexing problems. Jeannine S. Hirtle (1993) describes her own classroom research with disinterested eleventh-grade English students as she sought "to bring classic American literature to life for them. . . . How could I bridge the gap of time and culture? How could I help my students realize that some of the problems these writers tackle are universal and timeless?" (p. 137). She developed a plan to connect contemporary novels with the assigned classics in her school's curriculum and conducted two case studies to determine its effectiveness. Her conclusions are as follows:

> I found that when students were led into a response-based study of classic literature with novels that were developmentally appropriate and appealing to them, they became capable of transferring insights and methods of response and analysis to their reading of the more difficult literature. Through response logs, students were given a place to verbalize and develop their thoughts. The act of writing helped them reflect on their reading and, ultimately, draw on higher level skills to make personal connections and comments. When students participated in the open, supportive environment of the seminar discussions, they were able to try out their opinions, theories, concerns, and questions. This, in turn, contributed to their growth as critical thinkers and built a base of thought processes that they could transfer to formal analytic writing. (pp. 145–46)

Bridging

Bridging a Poem with a YA Novel

In "Nani," Alberto Rios pays tribute to his grandmother who helped give him a sense of his heritage. This poem may be used as a bridge to Virginia Euwer Wolff's <u>The Mozart Season</u>, in which Allegra's grandmother helps her to understand her family's background.

Responsibilities of the Teacher in Teaching Young Adult Literature

Although teachers have numerous responsibilities, we will discuss those directly related to the uses of young adult literature in the classroom. In this section, the discussion focuses on three major responsibilities directly related to the roles

Roles of the Teacher   Responsibilities of the Teacher

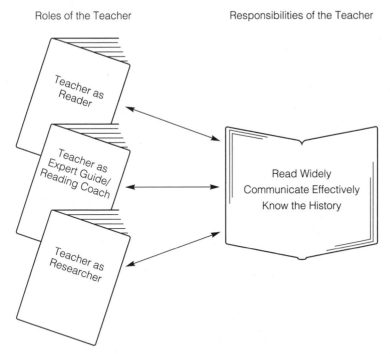

Figure 7.3   Responsibilities in the Model of Teacher Roles

that we have just described. Figure 7.3 describes the interrelationship between roles and responsibilities. The responsibilities are to be well read, to develop effective communications with others, and to have a working knowledge of the history of literature for young adults. In the next chapter, we discuss issues, responsibilities, and procedures related to selection and censorship of reading materials. Although these are, in part, separate issues, an interrelationship exists among them all. The teacher's roles as reader, expert guide/reading coach, and researcher are greatly enhanced by a knowledge and understanding of all of these issues.

Reading Widely

Inherent in the role of the teacher as reader is the responsibility of teachers to stay current. Too often we encounter teachers in the field who have not read anything since they began teaching or who rely on old reading lists to purchase books for their classrooms. Although reading reviews is helpful, there is no substitute for reading as many books as possible.

Talking with Virginia Euwer Wolff

I want to champion those who don't seem to have much of a public voice. My heart is always with the underdog.

Selected Titles
Make Lemonade
The Mozart Season
Probably Still Nick Swansen

Virginia Euwer Wolff lives in Oregon where she teaches literature and writing at Mt. Hood Academy for competitive skiers. She has played the violin since she was a child. Her first novel for young adults, Probably Still Nick Swansen, the story of a learning disabled high school student, received several awards, including ALA Best Book for Young Adults and IRA Children's Book Award for Young Adults. Her second book, The Mozart Season, a novel about Allegra Shapiro, a gifted twelve-year-old violinist, was an ALA Best Book for Young Adults. Among the awards her latest book, Make Lemonade, received are the Golden Kite Award, Top of the List from Booklist, the Bank Street Award, ALA Best Book for Young Adults, ALA Notable Books, and ALA Books for Reluctant Readers.

I have written three books for three very different audiences. In each one, I wanted to champion those without a loud voice—those with a voice that I can hear clearly. First there was Nick Swansen. I wrote it for the regular kids to get inside the slightly disabled kid's consciousness and see what it feels like in his moccasins. If this book doesn't increase the compassion quotient in some reader, I might as well as have been selling shoes or styling hair or doing something else. I'll never forget Nick Swansen's voice. Nick still lives with me. He still has a room in my house—it's not on any architectural plan, it's not zoned and I don't pay taxes on it, but Nick is in there in his bedroom studying his amphibians.

The Allegra Shapiros of this world simply weren't being written about, so I decided to do something about that. I was tired of stories about artists where we never see them practicing their art; all they do is have relationships. I believe that music is one of the most profound healers of human pain and I wanted to explore that. I also wanted to put in a word for the good kids, not that all kids aren't good, but the zealous, hard-working ones who have their dreams and their goals. These are the kids who aren't out making a disturbance in society—there may be disturbances in their own souls—

but they are as interesting as anybody else. I also thought of those mothers who say to Allegra's classmates, "Why can't you be more like Allegra?" This is really a reply to those mothers or dads. I wanted to show how, day by day by hardworking day, her family provides her with certain things, with certain "fertilizers" with which she is enabled to grow. I also wanted to surround Allegra with role models that she might choose from. Someone wrote to me saying, "I cried when I read *The Mozart Season,* not the way you cry when you are sad, but the way you cry when your children do something that makes you proud." When I started writing *The Mozart Season,* I didn't know whether or not Allegra was going to win the music competition; I knew that this would keep me writing.

In the case of *Make Lemonade,* the idea is that kids are entitled to their own vision. Society seems to have deprived some of them of a right to have a vision. I can't say it is all society's fault—society is only made up of individual human beings, but look at us! We haven't made a nice world. Those

on the top of the stairs are pretty selfish to people like LaVaughn and Jolly and Jolly's kids. I couldn't care less if any National Honor Society kids read this book—they have zillions of books on their bookshelves. This book was for a very special audience; I wanted those teen moms to read it and to know that somebody spoke for them. One of the reviewers said that LaVaughn and Jolly are not of any particular ethnic group, rather of the community of poverty. A friend told me that she thinks *Make Lemonade* is a novel written in blank verse. Well, it's not actually blank verse, but I am glad that I wrote it in that strange form even though it was stepping out so far.

I read as a child, but I read very easy stuff. I was a good student because I had a sense of language. I turned into a reader the summer of my sixteenth birthday when I read *The Catcher in the Rye. The Catcher in the Rye* changed my life, and I was just one of hundreds of thousands that it did that to. There was no other book that spoke for me at that time in my life. When

Continued

Talking with Virginia Euwer Wolff (continued)

I read it, I thought my life was livable after all; somebody spoke for me. Holden Caulfield was me. In high school and college, I chose my companions by whether they liked Holden Caulfield or not!

I have done what I have done with my life along rather jagged lines; I've never been on a track. I've been teaching for a long time and I like kids. I wrote my first short story when I was 37 years old. For years, I felt like a massive underachiever, but now I don't feel that way at all. I'm doing something with language that I hope is helping people. I feel increased dignity in my life because I have far more of a sense of who I am. Every book I start I am terrified I won't be able to do it. Of course, that helps me to defy the odds and do it! If

I can hit the word processor by 8:00 or 8:30 A.M., I can catch a few perceptions before they flee in broad daylight. Much later than that I am too self-critical, and everything I write looks like dirty socks! I take my characters very seriously, but plots don't come easily to me. I have to find the right form for each novel, and it takes me a long time. Also, I don't use my time wisely and I don't write every day. I am not conventionally self-disciplined, so I don't write as much as most writers do. But I am now quite comfortable that we are all individuals and that I am quirky. I'm a late bloomer and I am enjoying it enormously. Only when I feel I am in uncharted territory and don't have any precedents that I should be following, am I at all free to do what I do.

Communicating Effectively

The effectiveness of teachers is directly tied to their ability to communicate effectively. As expert guides/reading coaches, teachers communicate their belief in the value of reading and direct students to find books with which they will be able to make a connection. Teachers and students should communicate not only about books for required reading but also about books for leisure reading.

Teacher have additional responsibilities as communicators. The daily demands on them too often present a formidable barrier to having the time to be effective communicators with their colleagues. Unfortunately, teachers may have little idea what the teacher next door is doing and often no idea what anyone in another discipline or grade level is doing. Additionally, administrators need to be informed of what is happening in classes. We know of a number of difficult situations in which administrators failed to support their teachers when a parent or community member questioned classroom practices; this failure was traced directly to the administrators' lack of knowledge of what was occurring in the classroom and why. When they were approached, they were caught off guard. Not wanting to appear uninformed, they capitulated too quickly, rather than investigating the situation and then taking a meaningful, responsible stand. Ultimately in these kinds of situations, some culpability must be accepted by the teachers who neglected to communicate with their administrators.

Additionally, teachers need to be their own press agents to inform parents and the community about what they are doing with their students. The following are examples of actions taken by teachers with whom we have worked to keep in contact with parents. These are only a few examples of actions taken by teachers to communicate with the parents and guardians of their students.

- A teacher who had a number of difficult "reluctant learners" had a policy to call every one of his students' parents with some type of positive comment every marking period. Most of the parents had never heard from the school unless their kids were in trouble.

- A teacher and her students produced a monthly newsletter for parents that included student book reviews of required and optional reading, other samples of student work, and general information about what her classes were doing.

- Each fall, a teacher sent out class overviews, including reading lists and lists of films and videos that were in the year's curriculum.

- A teacher sent computer-printed invitations to her students' parents or guardians to visit class. She followed up the general invitation with more specific ones whenever her students were doing major presentations, dramatizations, group activities, or any other activity that would benefit from having an audience.

- A teacher had her students write letters to their parents or guardians at least once a month reporting on their own progress and describing the class activities. These letters were written and revised in the peer editing groups, and students received credit when their parents signed a sheet saying that they had gotten the letter.

- A teacher wrote a regular column for the local newspaper and another for the weekly shopper paper.

Knowing the History of Young Adult Literature

The role of the teacher as researcher can be fulfilled only if the teacher has an in-depth knowledge of the subject. To that end, teachers have the responsibility to learn about the foundations of young adult literature. The following

Bridging

Romance

Mary Dowling Hahn's <u>The Wind Blows Backwards</u> portrays the relationship between two high school seniors, Lauren and Spencer. Their relationship can be a bridge to reading about the relationship between Jane and Rochester in Charlotte Brontë's <u>Jane Eyre</u>.

historical overview will provide teachers with a knowledge base from which they can make decisions about where they will do more in-depth study.

This synopsis is intended to highlight some of the major events that have contributed to the development of young adult literature, which may be divided into four periods: pre-nineteenth century, the nineteenth century, the first half of the twentieth century (1900–66), and the contemporary period (1967–present). This last period, which is viewed as the coming of age for the genre, was described in Chapter 1.

Pre-Nineteenth Century Until the beginning of the twentieth century, the period of life we call adolescence was not considered as a separate stage. One was considered a child until assuming the adult roles of work and/or marriage—often at what would be considered by today's standards to be a very early age. Literature for most people belonged primarily to the oral tradition, with virtually no distinction made between stories for adults and stories for children. Prior to the introduction of movable type in Europe in the fifteenth century, very few people could read. Books were laboriously copied by hand, which made them expensive and scarce. The few books written for children were lesson books. These were usually in Latin and intended for the instruction of children of wealthy families. These didactic books started a tradition that dominated children's literature for hundreds of years and still is influential—that is, literature for children is primarily for their edification and should instill a moral lesson. Books for children as a source of pleasure were virtually nonexistent.

The wider use of movable type occurred concurrently with increased prosperity and the eventual growth of a middle class. Books were more readily available and less expensive. More people became literate. As the middle class became concerned with educating its children, distinctions were made between literature for adults and literature for children. Children's minds were considered to be blank slates, and adults assumed responsibility to ensure children's proper education. The Puritans were especially concerned with the responsibility of the family to ensure the moral salvation of their children. Thus, books for children were primarily religious and moralistic in nature, continuing the didactic tradition.

During the seventeenth and eighteenth centuries, children also read many books intended for adults. Such books provided moral instruction and had exciting plots that captured the interest of youthful readers. *The Pilgrim's*

Progress from This World to That Which Is to Come (Part I, 1678; Part II, 1684) by John Bunyan was an enduring favorite, combining a religious message with the excitement of an adventure novel. So was Daniel Defoe's *The Life and Strange Surprising Adventures of Robinson Crusoe,* a 1719 adventure story of a man marooned on an inhabited island where he not only survives, but manages to tame both the savages and the environment. The victory of the "civilized" man in hostile surroundings and the excitement of his adventures undoubtedly contributed to the book's lasting popularity. Another adult book popular with young readers was *Travels into Several Remote Nations of the World, by Lemuel Gulliver* (1726) by Jonathan Swift. Swift's satirical allegory masquerading as a witty adventure tale is still read today.

A significant event in the history of literature for young people occurred in the mid-1700s. Some date the advent of literature for children to 1744, when John Newbery, a publisher, made a decision that changed publishing. Newbery's business sense helped him to determine the potential for a new market in books for children, and he was among the first to publish books written expressly for them. More importantly, Newbery deliberately published books that were intended for enjoyment. The first of his pocket books, entitled *A Little Pretty Pocket-Book,* had a subtitle that read, in part, *"Intended for the Instruction and Amusement . . . A New Attempt to Teach Children . . . by way of Diversion,"* signaling a new day in literature for children. Didactic literature continued to abound, however. Probably the best-known children's book of this period was the highly moralistic *Little Goody Two-Shoes* (1765). Purportedly written by Oliver Goldsmith, it is considered to be the first short juvenile novel. With the publication of these books, Newbery and his contemporaries recognized the need to provide books written specifically for young people.

The Nineteenth Century   The nineteenth century was marked by a number of significant advances in literature for children. Books became less didactic, and different types of literature developed. Underlying these advances was a fundamental change in how children were viewed: they were no longer considered to be miniature adults. Childhood was celebrated for its charm, innocence, childish wisdom, and lack of adult hypocrisy. A major landmark at the beginning of the century was Charles and Mary Lamb's *Tales from Shakespeare* (1806), in which they rewrote Shakespeare's plays for young readers. Traditional oral folktales and fairy tales were collected and published, including those by the Grimm brothers and Hans Christian Andersen. Stories of the Greek myths were written for children by Nathaniel Hawthorne. Humor, nonsense, and fantasy appeared along with what is considered the first masterpiece for children, Lewis Carroll's *Alice's Adventures in Wonderland* (1865).

Among the most significant changes during this century was that schooling became more universal; it was no longer the privilege of wealthy young men. Literacy became a reality for the growing middle class and for many children of laboring class families. This broader base of literacy created a need for accessible reading materials. Thus the middle of the nineteenth century marked the development of three types of popular literature that had a significant impact on the reading public: family or domestic novels, dime novels, and book series.

Family or domestic stories, written primarily for girls and women, extolled traditional values and morality. These books, such as Susan Warner's *The Wide, Wide World* (1850) and Augusta Jane Evans Wilson's *St. Elmo* (1867), were stories of self-suffering and submissive female protagonists, who hated and avoided all kinds of sinful activities. They sought the only worthy goal for a woman—a happy marriage. The heroine in such books overcomes challenges to make a successful, prosperous marriage, even though she demonstrates distrust and ambivalent feelings toward men. Her challenges almost always include successfully reforming a wicked man and turning him into a dutiful, Christian husband. Such novels firmly established a tradition of gender differences for readers: while females read about the virtues of family life, male readers were enjoying adventure stories.

The second type of popular literature was the dime novel. These were, as the name implies, cheap, but they were action filled and melodramatic. Even though the plots were contrived and the characters superficial, these formula books captured the attention and interest of the reading public. Designed originally for adults, the books quickly became popular with boys and young men. Publishers then lowered their price to a nickel (although they continued to be called dime novels) and tailored them even more to a younger audience of boys. Dime novels set in the West and detective stories were the favorites, followed by stories of sports heroes and science fiction. The sensationalism of the dime novel made it the target of ministers, teachers, politicians, and parents. The concept of reading for entertainment for the young was new and unsettling to those who still regarded reading as a form of moral enlightenment. Regardless of the controversies that these early inexpensive books created, they opened the door to leisure reading. Soon, classics were also available in cheaper editions.

The third type of popular literature was books written in series. Series books for young adults, both male and female, sold extremely well. The most popular series for young women was Martha Farquharson Finley's Elsie Dinsmore series. By today's standards, Elsie was overly pious, docile, virtuous, sentimental, and weepy, but readers devoured twenty-eight volumes about her life from girlhood through grandmotherhood. The writers of books for male readers sought to entertain with stories of adventure and excitement. The male equivalent of the Elsie Dinsmore series was the series by Horatio Alger, Jr. Over one hundred of these formula books extolled the virtues of hard-working young men who overcome their meager backgrounds to succeed through their good works and, especially, through their high morals.

During the last half of the nineteenth century, some of the enduring classics for young people were written. Among these were Louisa May Alcott's *Little Women* (1867), Lucy Maud Montgomery's *Anne of Green Gables* (1904), and Mark Twain's *The Adventures of Tom Sawyer* (1876) and *The Adventures of Huckleberry Finn* (1884). In contrast to the formula novels of the time, these novels had richly developed characters and more realistic plots. While Alcott's and Montgomery's characters were lively but ultimately respectable, Twain's characters would not serve as moral guides and role models for young readers. He humorously presents his protagonists, Huck and Tom, as boys who lie, smoke, manipulate, and undertake a number of adventures. Huck and Tom are charming characters, but they were certainly not ones whom nineteenth-century parents would want their children to emulate. A significant difference between books for boys and books for girls developed during this time and continued well into the twentieth century.

First Half of the Twentieth Century (1900–66) As we discussed in Chapter 3, adolescence was first defined as a separate developmental stage by G. Stanley Hall in his 1905 publication of *Adolescence: Its Psychology and Its Relations to Physiology, Anthropology, Sociology, Sex, Crime, Religion and Education.* For the first time, a distinction was made between childhood and the period beginning in puberty. Literature reflected this emerging view by depicting more realistically the challenges and tasks of youths. The early books of the twentieth century include works of writers such as Booth Tarkington, whose *Penrod* (1914) and its sequels were humorous accounts of the escapades of a twelve-year-old. His book *Seventeen* (1916) is a dated account of adolescent first love; however, it is significant for the perspective it provides of the emergence of adolescence. Series continued to be popular. One of the more enduring ones was Laura Ingalls Wilder's Little House series, which presents a realistic historical account of life during the Western movement. Sports stories continued to be popular with adolescent male readers.

The term *Junior Books* developed during the 1930s when the publishing company of Longman, Green, and Company marketed *Let the Hurricane Roar* by Rose Wilder Lane. Other publishing companies soon established junior book divisions, publishing predominantly romances and series.

Literature Involvement Strategy

Teacher Read Alouds

Reading aloud has tremendous power to create interest and curiosity, to develop desire and excitement, to illustrate important ideas and concepts, and to foster an aesthetic appreciation of literature and language. Yet, reading aloud is sorely neglected in most middle school and secondary classrooms. Teachers in subject areas other than literature almost never think of it as a valuable teaching strategy. Junior high teacher Anne Webb (1990) has found that reading to students is the best way to encourage them to select books to read independently.

We recommend that teachers incorporate reading aloud into their classes at least two or three times a week. Five minutes of a well-chosen excerpt can reap tremendous benefits whether initiating a particular selection, topic, or theme or helping students to connect cognitively and affectively with what they are reading or aiding students to internalize their reading. Jim Trelease's book <u>Read All About It! Great Read-Aloud Stories, Poems & Newspaper Pieces for Preteens and Teens</u> is a valuable resource for teachers starting a read-aloud program.

During the 1940s and 1950s, most young adult novels emphasized the traditional values and themes of respectable middle-class America. Plots and characters were simple, superficial teenage problems were easily solved, and many topics were deemed taboo or too controversial. Maureen Daly's *Seventeenth Summer* (1942), with its realistic presentation of adolescents and their problems, is credited as one of the first contemporary young adult novels. Henry Gregor Felsen also wrote stories about real teenagers, with his books about cars particularly popular with adolescent males. J. D. Salinger's *The Catcher in the Rye* (1951), although written originally for adults, ushered in the era of realism in young adult literature with its frankness in language and theme. Although many adults did not approve of Daly's, Felsen's, and Salinger's books and the new trends they represented, such books were widely read by adolescents.

Fantasies and science fiction came into their own in the early twentieth century. They reflected moral and social issues regarding survival and the quality of life, such as the struggle between good and evil, the impact of technology on society, and the preservation of the environment. C. S. Lewis's *The Chronicles of Narnia,* written in the 1950s, have had an enduring impact on youthful readers.

The turmoil and challenges of the 1960s essentially mandated that books written for young people should reflect the realities of their world. Through the evolution of books for youths and the changes in society, the stage was set for contemporary works to present a realistic view of the world of young adults in the latter part of the twentieth century.

Summary

Three major roles are available to teachers who seek to help young people become involved in reading young adult literature: teacher as reader, teacher as expert guide/reading coach, and teacher as researcher. Teachers must develop effective communications with others and have a working knowledge of the history of literature for young adults.

Suggested Activities

1. In your journal, reflect on how teachers and schools are portrayed in the young adult literature you are reading.

2. Discuss the Model of Teacher Roles presented in this chapter. Assess and set goals for yourself for each of the roles.

3. Read a review of young adult literature using one of the journals recommended in this chapter or listed in Appendix C.

4. Prepare a read aloud to interest others in reading young adult literature.

Sharing the Connection

When Heroes Die
Penny Raife Durant

I liked the book because it dealt with a huge problem in today's society. A young boy must deal with his uncle's illness. His uncle, who is really like a father to him, is dying of AIDS. This is a serious problem, and the boy has an extremely difficult time handling it. It is a book that made me smile and laugh, then I couldn't quit crying. It is very touching and really makes the reader think about this problem and what they would do if it happened to them or someone they knew.

Sheri Wendling, student

CHAPTER 8

Selecting Young Adult Literature

Lincoln, tall and gangly, seemed plain in his rumpled suit, carrying his notes and speeches in an old carpetbag, sitting on the platform with his bony knees jutting into the air.

   Russell Freedman, *Lincoln: A Photobiography*

Journal Writing: Responding

Examine several young adult literature books. Identify and explain the factors that influence whether or not you will read a book.

_____

As educators become acquainted with types of young adult literature and representative authors and titles, questions related to selecting books that are appropriate for students and fulfill curriculum requirements become more important. In this chapter, we discuss a number of issues related to the selection of quality young adult literature, including censorship. We begin by examining selection within the broader context of discussions of quality of literature. Later in this chapter, we examine censorship issues within the same framework of quality, audience, and context.

Selection Model

The selection of appropriate reading materials presents a significant challenge for teachers because they must consider a number of factors as they make their decisions. For the purposes of this book, we do not address the issue of financial resources. Instead, we explore these three considerations: issues of quality, issues of student interest and need, and issues of curricular consistency. In other words, decisions about selection should address the text, the audience, and the context. Figure 8.1 presents a model for selection.

How Do We Determine Quality?

Selection is a thoughtful, reflective process in which professionals make determinations that they believe will be of benefit to their students. G. Robert

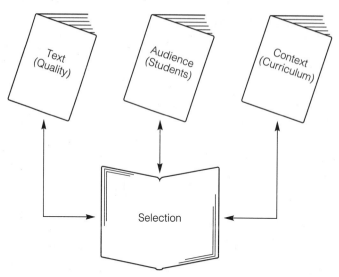

Figure 8.1   A Model for Selecting Literature

Carlsen and Norma Bagnall (1981, pp. 11–12) discuss standards for assessing a work. Carlsen identifies the following criteria:

1. *The vision presented.* What does it evoke? Does it stimulate the reader's imagination, mind, and emotions?
2. *Its stance toward the vision.* Is it one of approval, of condemnation, of neutrality? Is it intended to be serious or simply amusing? What is its voice or tone?
3. *Its style.* Does the language, imagery, plot carry the vision?
4. *The audience.* Are the book's readers at their stage of maturity ready for this vision? With teenagers we often assume readiness that is not there. (p. 11)

Carlsen speaks for a unified whole in which the work fits together—the work appeals both to the mind and emotion of the reader to combine cognitive and affective responses. Although Bagnall agrees with these points, she makes the following additions:

1. Is the work honest in the vision presented? Does the writer honestly present the theme or is trickery or purple prose used to grab attention?
2. Is the story honest to its audience? That is, does it maintain the guidelines of literature, using foreshadowing, characterization, and other literary devices honestly, or does it stretch those guidelines beyond the point of credibility?

3. Does it set up boundaries and then adhere to those limitations? In realistic fiction these limitations are already set up by the external realities we all know and recognize. But even in writing fantasy or romance, we can expect the writer to set up boundaries and then to stay within them. (p. 12)

Bagnall seeks to establish criteria that are consistent with reality. Each of her points speaks to standards of believability in fiction.

Although it is easy for most of us to think about and identify the really good books we have read over the years, it is not always as easy to explain why a specific book is good. It may be easier to identify bad books we have read or attempted to read and describe those qualities that detract from the book's quality. The reasons an individual likes a book are complex and often not entirely expressed at a conscious level. There are, however, some indicators of quality that teachers and students can consider when selecting a book:

- Believable characters. Carefully crafted characters are multifaceted people who are neither stereotypical nor prototypical.

- Coherent, but not predictable, plot

- Reasonable conflict

- Satisfying resolution of conflict

- Meaningful interaction among characters

- Significant themes

- Appropriate settings

Additionally, how a book is written influences selection decisions. These indicators of quality pertain to style:

- Authentic dialogue

- Clarity of language

- Vivid images

- Rich, but not effusive, descriptions

The third area examines questions of the integrity of a work. At the most fundamental level, readers have the right to expect to be treated as intelligent participants in the literary experience. Readers should never be exploited, and they have the right to expect the following:

- Language that is appropriate to the characters and the times

- Timeless themes that speak to timely issues

- Responsible presentation of controversial ideas

We now compare two young adult books that share one similarity—dealing with HIV and AIDS. These two books demonstrate the difference between quality literature and poor literature. One book is Fran Arrick's *What You Don't Know Can Kill You,* a sensitive and responsible accounting of a family who learns that the oldest daughter has tested positive for HIV. The second book is Charlotte St. John's *Red Hair Three,* an exploitive and superficial account of a girl who discovers that her former boyfriend is dying of AIDS. Arrick's characters are believable and likeable. The reader can sympathize with the conflict and devastation they experience, whereas St. John's characters are more caricatures, one-dimensional figures that inspire neither reader concern nor interest. The issue of AIDS and other problems in the book seem gratuitous and inappropriate. Quality fiction is the result of believable characters interacting in a well-crafted plot with appropriate incidences of conflict and resolution. For fiction to work, it must inspire caring and involvement from readers.

Primary Influences on Students' Selection of Books   Although teachers select books for classroom use based on a number of objective criteria, students are influenced by a number of subjective factors in choosing what they will read. A 1991 survey of reading preferences among high school students in Michigan (Brown, 1992) shows that friends have the greatest impact on female readers' choices. This survey was also conducted in Mississippi and Maine in 1980 and in Michigan and Montana in 1985. In each case, female students in every grade identified friends most frequently as influences on their reading choices. The primary influences on male high school students are consistently more varied. In 1991, the composite findings show that the title of a book is the most significant influence on males as they select a book to read; however, the majority of eleventh graders listed a teacher as the greatest influence, and twelfth-grade males most often listed a friend as influencing reading choices. Table 8.1 presents the data from the 1991 survey, presented by gender and grade level, indicating the number of responses for each influence and the comparative rankings of them. The last group of data includes the composites by gender with percentages and rankings.

Among the significant data in these findings are the role teachers play in influencing what students will choose to read. As students rely on their teachers to provide them with direction about their nonrequired and leisure reading, teachers are challenged to have an increased knowledge of appropriate books for their students. Appendix C provides a list of journals that regularly publish book reviews, which can help teachers become informed about current books.

Females	9th Grade	10th Grade	11th Grade	12th Grade
Friend	74 (1)	50 (1)	57 (1)	53 (1)
Parents	31 (7)	25 (7)	28 (7)	22 (7)
Sibling	14 (11)	21 (9)	15 (12)	15 (11)
Teacher	52 (4)	36 (4)	57 (1)	52 (2)
Librarian	22 (8)	10 (12)	23 (10)	11 (12)
Written Book Report	16 (9)	26 (6)	25 (9)	16 (9)
Oral Book Report	15 (10)	18 (10)	26 (8)	20 (8)
Author	57 (2)	37 (3)	48 (3)	39 (4)
Movie/TV	54 (3)	32 (5)	31 (5)	42 (3)
Bestseller List	14 (11)	16 (11)	22 (11)	16 (9)
Title	51 (5)	47 (2)	37 (4)	39 (4)
Cover	44 (6)	24 (8)	31 (5)	29 (6)
Other	6	7	0	6

Males	9th Grade	10th Grade	11th Grade	12th Grade
Friend	35 (5)	30 (4)	33 (3)	40 (1)
Parents	13 (10)	13 (10)	10 (12)	8 (12)
Sibling	11 (12)	17 (9)	11 (11)	9 (10)
Teacher	39 (2)	31 (2)	42 (1)	37 (2)
Librarian	22 (7)	5 (12)	18 (9)	9 (10)
Written Book Report	18 (8)	24 (7)	20 (7)	15 (8)
Oral Book Report	12 (11)	20 (8)	20 (7)	15 (8)
Author	29 (6)	30 (4)	27 (6)	28 (5)
Movie/TV	38 (3)	31 (2)	38 (2)	25 (6)
Bestseller List	15 (9)	13 (10)	18 (9)	17 (7)
Title	51 (1)	39 (1)	28 (4)	33 (3)
Cover	38 (3)	29 (6)	28 (4)	33 (4)
Other	1	4	2	5

Totals	Total Female		Total Male	
Friend	234 (64%)	1	138 (42%)	3
Parents	106 (29%)	7	44 (13%)	12
Sibling	65 (17%)	12	48 (14%)	11
Teacher	197 (54%)	2	149 (45%)	2
Librarian	66 (18%)	11	54 (16%)	9
Written Book Report	83 (23%)	8	77 (23%)	7
Oral Book Report	79 (21%)	9	67 (20%)	8
Author	181 (50%)	3	114 (34%)	6
Movie/TV	159 (44%)	5	132 (40%)	4
Bestseller List	68 (19%)	10	53 (16%)	9
Title	174 (48%)	4	151 (45%)	1
Cover	128 (35%)	6	128 (39%)	5
Other	19		12	

Table 8.1 Influences on Students, 1991

	Yes	No
Literary Quality		
The plot is well developed.	☐	☐
The main characters are believable.	☐	☐
The conflicts are plausible.	☐	☐
Their resolutions are probable but not predictable.	☐	☐
Minor characters play appropriate roles.	☐	☐
The book presents themes appropriate to its audience.	☐	☐
The setting contributes to the story.	☐	☐
Appropriateness of Subject Matter		
Subject matter is appropriate to my students.	☐	☐
The book contains controversial issues.	☐	☐
Controversial issues are handled with taste and sensitivity.	☐	☐
Book contains language that might be considered offensive.	☐	☐
Language is consistent with message of book.	☐	☐
Book contains sexually explicit scenes.	☐	☐
These scenes are tastefully presented.	☐	☐
Curricular Considerations		
The book meets course objectives.	☐	☐
The book meets the school's selection policy.	☐	☐
Recommendations for Use		
Book is appropriate for whole-class instruction.	☐	☐
Book might be selected by groups and learning partners.	☐	☐
Book might be used by individual students.	☐	☐
Book is not recommended for use.	☐	☐

Comments

Figure 8.2   Sample Checklist

Young Adult Literature Checklist   Teachers can develop their own checklists to aid in their selection of books, addressing many of the issues we have presented here. Figure 8.2 shows a sample checklist for realistic fiction, which can be adapted and changed to meet individual needs.

How Do We Determine Students' Needs And Interests?

The most effective way to determine students' needs and interests is to go to the source. Student surveys and inventories that teachers develop are valuable in determining issues that concern students about their reading. A key to the validity of these instruments is their clarity. The respondents need to know what is being asked, and they also need to understand what will be done with their responses. Following are five different approaches to determining student needs and interests.

Reader Autobiography Write your reader autobiography by describing your experiences with reading. Include how you learned to read, what books have had an impact on you, and what kinds of reading you most frequently do now.

Reader Characteristics Describe yourself as a reader. What are your strengths? Your weaknesses? How do you feel about reading?

Literature Type Checklist Examine the following list of different types of books. First, put a check mark by all of the types you have read. Second, identify the *five* types you most enjoy with a plus mark. Finally, *briefly* explain why you enjoy them.

_____ Fiction	_____ Science fiction	_____ Informational
_____ Realistic fiction	_____ Historical fiction	_____ Poetry
_____ Mystery	_____ Nonfiction	_____ Other
_____ Supernatural and horror	_____ Biography	(specify, please)
_____ Fantasy	_____ Autobiography	

Student Reading Questionnaire

What is the best book you have ever read? What made it so?
What is the worst book you have ever read? What made it so?
What topics do you like to read about?
What type of reading do you like most? Why?
What type of reading do you dislike most? Why?
What do you look for in a book?
Who are your favorite authors? Why?
How do you find out about new books to read?
What influences you to read something?

Survey of Reading Preferences of High School Students The survey shown in Figure 8.3 can provide a valuable tool for determining student needs and interests.

Judging a Book by Its Cover Teachers may be well advised to remember that their students often ignore the maxim "Don't judge a book by its cover." According to the data on influences on student selection of books (see Table 8.1), book covers rank sixth among female high school readers and fifth among male high

I. List five books that you have selected and read in the last two years, either on your own or in connection with school work. These may be fiction or nonfiction and may include those you have read for book reports as long as you personally selected them.

After you have listed the books, please circle the rating for each book according to the one you liked best (5), second best (4), third best (3), fourth best (2), and least (1).

1.   5   4   3   2   1
2.   5   4   3   2   1
3.   5   4   3   2   1
4.   5   4   3   2   1
5.   5   4   3   2   1

II. List five books, other than textbooks, that you have been required to read for any of your classes during the last two years. These books may be fiction or nonfiction. Please circle the rating for each book from best liked (5) to least liked (1) as you did in Part I.

1.   5   4   3   2   1
2.   5   4   3   2   1
3.   5   4   3   2   1
4.   5   4   3   2   1
5.   5   4   3   2   1

III. List five books that you are planning to read this year. Circle the *P* if the book is for pleasure reading and *R* for a required book.

1.   P   R
2.   P   R
3.   P   R
4.   P   R
5.   P   R

IV. How do you choose what to read? Check which of the following influence your choice of books. Check as many as you like.

1. _____ A friend   4. _____ A teacher
2. _____ Your parents   5. _____ A librarian
3. _____ Your brother or sister   6. _____ A written book report

Figure 8.3   Survey of High School Student Preferences

Adapted from the Survey of Reading Preferences of High School Students, which was a survey administered periodically as part of a longitudinal study from 1976 to 1991.

7. ____ An oral book report   11. ____ The book's title

8. ____ The book's author   12. ____ The book's cover

9. ____ Movies or television   13. ____ Other (specify)

10. ____ Bestseller list

V. Rate the type of books that you prefer to read. Use 1 for your favorite type, 2 for the next favorite, and so forth.

1. ____ Animal stories   11. ____ Adolescent problems

2. ____ Adventure novels   12. ____ Science fiction

3. ____ Informational (factual)   13. ____ History (factual)

4. ____ Sports   14. ____ Historical novels

5. ____ Romances   15. ____ Biographies and autobiographies

6. ____ Mysteries   16. ____ Crafts

7. ____ Horror and supernatural   17. ____ Science

8. ____ Fantasy   18. ____ How-to-do-it

9. ____ Computers   19. ____ Other (specify)

10. ____ Westerns

VI. Please respond to the following statements by circling whether you strongly agree (SA), agree (A), have no opinion (N/O), disagree (D), or strongly disagree (SD).

	SA	A	N/O	D	SD
1. I only read books that are required for class.	SA	A	N/O	D	SD
2. Reading is my favorite hobby.	SA	A	N/O	D	SD
3. I read mainly for information.	SA	A	N/O	D	SD
4. I read mainly for pleasure.	SA	A	N/O	D	SD
5. I regularly read a newspaper.	SA	A	N/O	D	SD
6. I frequently don't finish books I start to read.	SA	A	N/O	D	SD
7. I wish I had more time for leisure reading.	SA	A	N/O	D	SD
8. I would rather play video games than read.	SA	A	N/O	D	SD
9. I would rather watch TV than read.	SA	A	N/O	D	SD
10. I never read, even when books are assigned in class.	SA	A	N/O	D	SD
11. I believe that I am a good reader.	SA	A	N/O	D	SD
12. When I finish a book, I usually start a new one right away.	SA	A	N/O	D	SD

continued on next page

13. I love to read for pleasure, but hate to read for information.	SA	A	N/O	D	SD
14. I like to read when I can choose what I read.	SA	A	N/O	D	SD
15. I don't like to read what is assigned in school.	SA	A	N/O	D	SD
16. I read a lot, but not what is assigned in school.	SA	A	N/O	D	SD

Figure 8.3 (continued)

school readers. Book covers have a significant impact on the choices that students make about their reading, often leading them to make assumptions about the content and the quality of books. For example, when we taught Caroline Cooney's *The Party's Over* in an undergraduate young adult literature course recently, the students talked about their initial reluctance to read the book because the cover made it look like a romance novel. One young man in the class talked about the teasing he encountered in the dorm for reading a book that "looked like that." If teachers do not provide students with pre-reading activities when they first encounter a book, students may use a cover to determine whether or not they will read a book.

Teachers, too, often judge books by their covers. In one case, a sixth-grade teacher we know announced to his book club that he avoided reading Lois Duncan's work because she writes horror books like Christopher Pike does. His inaccurate assumption was made by looking at the illustrations on some of her book covers. The second edition (1990) of her *Daughters of Eve* has a stark black cover with an illustration of a single burning candle and a stream of blood mixed in the melted wax. In contrast, the 1980 edition shows a dated illustration of a classroom with five girls watching a teacher as she tears a picture in half. The cover of the second edition is more contemporary, and presents a much more sinister impression than the earlier edition. Another difference between the covers of the two editions is that the first is labeled on the spine as fiction, whereas the more recent edition is labeled as suspense. It is easy to see how the sixth grade

---

Sharing the Connection

Julie of the Wolves
Jean Craighead George

I liked this book! The main character is Julie but she also goes by her Eskimo name, Miyax. She gets lost in the Alaskan wilderness and meets a pack of wolves. They treat her well by giving her food and loving her. I had never read a story like this before and I learned a lot about how life was for the Eskimos. Sometimes it was hard for me to understand, but it made me think.

Katie Allen, student

teacher might have gotten his impression about Duncan's work. It is also easy to see how her work is being marketed to appeal to youthful readers who are drawn to the macabre. Typically, what appeals to youthful readers often is a deterrent to adult readers.

Publishing marketing executives know that, although adults (including teachers and parents) may find a book cover either unappealing or indicative of a type of book that they do not want to read, adolescent readers may be attracted to a book's cover and its implied promise. Both examples of mistaken assumptions described above are based on a publishing reality: book covers are designed to entice youthful readers with promises that the texts frequently fail to keep. The covers may imply greater suspense, greater romance, or greater action than the book delivers. In some cases, the cover does not reflect what happens in the book at all or emphasizes a minor event in the book. Regardless, book covers are effective in influencing students' reading selections. The Literature Involvement Strategy shown below is designed to help students become more aware of book covers and to use them in the initiating stage of involvement with literature.

Literature Involvement Strategy

Looking at Book Covers

Book covers often serve as significant aids both to encourage students to read and to help prepare them to read. This strategy is designed as a pre-reading activity to help students examine book jackets systematically. This is an activity that teachers may find useful in helping students make initial contact with their reading. The following questions provide a framework for the students' examination:

What did you notice first about the book cover?

Look at the cover illustration. What does it imply about the plot and characters of the book?

What is written on the front cover besides the title and the author's name? Is there anything about the lettering that makes an impression on you?

Does the cover make you want to read the book? Why or why not?

Does the book cover have a brief synopsis of the book? Does the synopsis make you want to read the book? Why or why not?

As a post-reading activity, have students compare their initial reactions with the insights they have gained from reading the book. How accurate is the presentation of the cover?

What is the Impact of the Curriculum on Selection Issues?

Selecting books must be considered within the context of the curriculum. Although a variety of books may be made available to promote leisure and recreational reading and to meet individual needs, specific books should be selected to meet curricular requirements. Books may be selected to meet such course goals as helping students develop cultural awareness. For example, using Rudolfo Anaya's *Bless Me, Ultima* can help students to understand the Mexican American culture of the Southwest. Additionally, books may be selected to help students meet specific course objectives, such as improved understanding of literary elements. The following discussion defines literary elements and cites examples from young adult literature to illustrate their use.

Characterization   Characterization in fiction is the depiction of people (or animals, in personified form) around whom the action revolves. Readers become involved in a selection through their interest in the characters and sensing a connection with them. The effective development of the main character may be the single most important element of the work. Well-developed main characters seem real and make the work come alive. They are believable in their actions, appearance, and thoughts and are a complex mixture of desirable and undesirable traits. Identification with the main character is an important element in young adult literature, thus, the main character is usually an adolescent or pre-adolescent.

Main characters are developed in several ways:

1. Through their own revelations. In *Shabanu, Daughter of the Wind* by Suzanne Fisher Staples, Shabanu is a young girl of the Cholistan Desert in Pakistan. She reveals much of her character by her first-person account of her love for tending the camels and how her strong-willed independence comes into conflict with the strict Islamic traditions of her culture.

2. Through their introspective reflections and thoughts. An example of a reflective character is Virginia Euwer Wolff's Allegra from *The Mozart Season.* Allegra is a thoughtful twelve-year-old who struggles to understand her musical gift, her heritage, and her world as she prepares for her first violin competition.

3. Through physical description either by the character or some other character. In Chris Crutcher's *Staying Fat for Sarah Byrnes,* Sarah Byrnes was disfigured by a childhood accident in which her face was badly burned. She uses the disfigurement to define her public persona. The scars become

a mask under which she hides who she is and how she feels from everyone except her best friend, Moby. Brock Cole's Celine, in the book by the same name, is a teenage artist who constantly analyzes her features and appearance.

4. Through the actions and reactions of others. In *Won't Know Till I Get There* by Walter Dean Myers, Steve and his friends are required by juvenile court to spend time working in a home for senior citizens. They are caught committing a youthful prank, and the senior citizens have an unexpected reaction.

5. Through their own actions. In *Invitation to the Game* by Monica Hughes, Lisse and her friends finish school only to find that they will be unemployed. All of the young people have talents that help to identify and define their roles as they make their own social group.

Supporting characters are less well developed than main characters. Although they are important to the story and may engage the interest of the reader, they are not as complex as the main characters. In M. E. Kerr's *Dinky Hocker Shoots Smack,* Dinky Hocker, Natalia Lane, and J. P. Knight are intriguing supporting characters who contribute to the book's humor and depth. Typical supporting characters in young adult literature are friends of the main character, siblings, parents and grandparents, and school staff, such as teachers, coaches, principals, and assistant principals. In *On My Honor,* by Marion Dane Bauer, the father plays an important role although he is a minor character. Laura's boyfriend, Pete, in *The Boy Who Reversed Himself* by William Sleator, is a secondary character whose immature behavior leads her to take him on a trip with her into the fourth dimension.

Plot The plot of a work is essentially the structure for the action of the work. It is a logical sequence of events and actions in which the characters are involved. For a plot to be effective, the actions should be related and provide a framework for the characters to grow and develop. Plot construction can vary. For example, M. E. Kerr's *Gentlehands* begins as a story of a boy trying to make an impression on his rich girlfriend; however, as the book progresses, it is the evolving relationship between the boy and his grandfather that becomes the most significant relationship in the book. Patricia MacLachlan's *Journey* has a linear plot in which a family learns to cope after the mother has left them.

We discuss three elements of plot: conflict, foreshadowing, and flashbacks.

Conflict is traditionally described as the opposition of two forces in a literary work. In young adult literature, the conflict is often an internal struggle in which the main characters attempt to sort out where they belong in their world and how they think and feel about themselves and their circumstances. In this respect, the primary conflict of young adult novels is often the result of the growth and evolution of the main character. Issues of maturation are integral to the conflict as the character confronts, resolves, and grows as a result of dealing with the challenges of life. This observation is not intended to diminish the significance of conflict and its impact on the characters in young adult literature. Conflict provides the support for the plot because the action in the work revolves around confrontation and its resolution. Typical kinds of conflict are as follows:

- Individuals confronting themselves. A hallmark of adolescence and therefore of the young adult novel is the turmoil that youths undergo as they struggle with themselves. This type of internal conflict can be seen in the torment that Joel goes through as he must decide how to handle Tony's accident in *On My Honor* by Marion Dane Bauer. Alice, in Marie Lee's *If It Hadn't Been for Yoon Jun,* must confront her reluctance to accept that she is adopted and that she has a rich Korean heritage to learn about.

- Individuals confronting their environment. Numerous books examine the popular survival theme. Many of Gary Paulsen's books, including *Hatchet, The River,* and *The Foxman,* pit their characters against the rigors of nature. But the conflict with one's environment may occur in a number of different ways, as is demonstrated in another Paulsen book, *The Crossing.* In this book, Manny is trying to survive the poverty and trouble of his life on the streets of Juarez, Mexico, a tough border town.

- Individuals confronting another individual or individuals. Although books such as *The Outsiders* depict the conflict between two groups, this type of conflict is most frequently exemplified by the conflict between two individuals, such as that between Bobby and Emmett, an anti-Semitic bully in *Chernowitz!* by Fran Arrick. Marion Dane Bauer presents a classic conflict between a son and his father who have a painful and strained reunion in *Face to Face.*

- Individuals confronting society or its expectations. Monica Hughes's science fiction novel *Invitation to the Game* presents a picture of society gone awry. Lisse and her group of friends, however, work together to create their own protection and support system that helps them when they are invited to play "the game." In Ann Rinaldi's *Time Enough for Drums,* John Reid defies his friends and his society by remaining loyal to the Tory cause while his friends are involved in the fight for American independence.

In Eve Bunting's *Jumping the Nail*, Dru futilely tries to help her troubled friend, Elise. Elise is pressured into jumping into the Pacific Ocean from a high cliff with her boyfriend. On the most basic level, Elise is in conflict with the forces of nature as she confronts the danger of jumping; however, she also caught in the middle of a conflict caused by her own fear of the jump and her fear of losing Scooter, her boyfriend.

Flashbacks are a device that writers use to give the reader background information that adds clarity or perspective to the plot but that does not fit into the chronological flow of the plotline. In Robert Cormier's *I Am the Cheese*, Adam tries to sort out his past through the use of flashbacks. The significant events of Nick's childhood, including the loss of his sister, are revealed by flashbacks in Virginia Euwer Wolff's *Probably Still Nick Swansen.* The use of flashbacks in *Blue Skin of the Sea* (mentioned later in this chapter) add additional layers to the story, as young Sonny has vague, recurring impressions and fragmented memories that he works to put together.

Foreshadowing is the cues or hints that an author gives readers so that they are prepared for a coming situation or event in a story. For example, author Ann Rinaldi foreshadows the love interest between John Reid and Jem through their antagonistic verbal exchanges in *Time Enough for Drums.* In Jay Bennett's *Skinhead,* the special connection between Jonathan and the dying stranger is foreshadowed when Jonathan's photograph is found in his wallet. The devotion of Parker's dog, Otis, and his ability to find his owner foreshadows Otis's rescuing of Parker and his friend Matt in Mary Dowling Hahn's *The Dead Man in Indian Creek.*

Point of View Point of view is the perspective from which an author presents a story. Authors choose to tell their stories from the following perspectives:

- *First person.* The first-person narration is a frequently used literary device in young adult literature as demonstrated in such works as Monica Hughes's *Invitation to the Game,* Lawrence Yep's *Dragon's Gate,* and Virginia Euwer Wolff's *Make Lemonade.* In addition, a popular convention is to have the main character keep a journal in which he or she tells the story. Among the books that use diaries or journals are Avi's *The True Confessions of Charlotte Doyle,* Ouida Sebestyen's *The Girl in the Box,* and Walter Dean Myers's *Won't Know Till I Get There.*

- *Multiple points of view.* Paul Zindel's *Pigman* uses two primary points of view by alternating chapters from the perspective of each of the two main characters. Avi's *Nothing But the Truth* is called a documentary novel. The story is told through the use of diary entries, memos, letters, and dialogue, providing several perspectives. Alice Childress tells the story of Benjie Johnson in *A Hero Ain't Nothing But a Sandwich* by interspersing chapters told from his point of view with chapters from the point of view of his mother, stepfather, friends, teachers, principal, and neighbors. Sue Ellen Bridgers's *Permanent Connections* allows the reader to see events through the eyes of the adults and the teenagers in the story. Theodore Taylor in *The Weirdo* presents a sophisticated perspective in which he writes from a primarily omniscient point of view but then intersperses short first-person reflections written by Chip Clewt, who is known as "the weirdo" by the local people. In using this device, Taylor is freed to make interesting time shifts because these reflections are essays written the following year for freshman English when Chip attends college.

- *Omniscient.* Although the omniscient, or all-knowing, point of view is used infrequently in young adult literature, Fran Arrick uses it to examine the impact of AIDS on the characters in *What You Don't Know Can Kill You.*

- *Third person.* Fran Arrick's *Where'd You Get the Gun, Billy?* is structured initially from an omniscient point of view, but then much of the story is based on third-person scenarios presented by Lieutenant Wisnewski as he ponders with Dave and Liz where Billy might have gotten the gun.

Setting The components of setting include location, climate and weather, time period, and time framework. The setting of a work may be the actual physical location where a work takes place; it may also refer to the ongoing routine of the characters' lives (for example the role of school in books like Paula Danziger's *The Cat Ate My Gym Suit,* Jean Davies Okimoto's *Molly by Any Other Name,* and Gary Soto's *Taking Sides*); it may even refer to the time period in which the work takes place (historical novels, such as the Collier brothers' *In the Bloody Country,* which depend on an accurate portrayal of the time period); or it may reflect the social, moral, and psychological environment in which the characters interact (*The Secret Keeper* by Gloria Whelan is set in a Lake Michigan summer resort community that has its own rules). Frequently, the time framework in young adult literature is limited to a summer vacation or a school year. *The Sniper* by Theodore Taylor occurs during one dramatic week in the life of Ben Jepson—a week that serves as a rite of passage and significantly changes how he views himself. Seldom does young adult literature take place over more than a year, with the exception of historical fiction, which usually spans several years or more. Graham Salisbury presents another exception with his realistic fiction, *Blue Skin of the Sea.* It spans a thirteen-year period through a series of eleven stories delicately interwoven to chronicle the period from when Sonny Mendoza was six until he prepares to leave for college.

The role of a work's setting may vary. It may play a significant role that has an impact on every other aspect of the book, it may be inconsequential and barely mentioned, or it may not be mentioned at all. In those books in which the setting plays a significant role, it functions like a secondary character whose role is to support the main characters and facilitate the action of the plot. In *Z for Zachariah* by Robert C. O'Brien, the valley with its unique climatic conditions provides an environment that has escaped the nuclear destruction and that still can support human life as we know it. *The Keeper of the Isis Light* by Monica Hughes take place on a remote planet whose atmospheric and climatic conditions play a significant role in the characters' actions. The setting may also establish a unique atmosphere, such as the fishing village home of Louise and Caroline on a tiny island in the Chesapeake Bay in *Jacob Have I Loved* by Katherine Paterson. Authors often select certain geographical settings for much or all of their work, such as Cynthia Rylant, who uses the setting of the hill country of Appalachia in many of her works. Jean Craighead George uses the backdrop of the overwhelming harshness and beauty of Alaska in *Julie of the Wolves* and *Water Sky*. Gloria Whelan's works are frequently set in the northern part of the lower peninsula of Michigan, and the rural environment always plays a part in her books. Cynthia Rylant (1993) talks about the impact of Appalachia on her writing:

> The next years, until I was eight, I was raised by my coal mining grandfather and my steady grandmother and whatever other relatives happened to be living in the house at the time. It was a four-room house, no running water, no indoor plumbing at all, situated in a forsaken but stunningly beautiful part of Appalachia. Days were quiet. Birds, and cowbells, the buzz of bumblebees, the baying of far-off dogs. Everything smelled good. Milk smelled good, and ripe tomatoes, bacon, and molasses. Rosebushes, honeysuckle, pine. Smoke rose from the tops of houses in winter and everyone went to church on Christmas Day. Every child got Christmas oranges and ribbon candy.
>
> I soaked it all up, every last bit of it, everything I could take at so young an age, and when I grew up I began to ease these memories out, little by little, and I led them into books. (p. 177)

Style Style is the manner in which writers express their ideas. Style may be identified in a number of ways, including word choice, imagery, sentence structure, and other traits that are uniquely and consistently used by an author. For

Talking with Graham Salisbury

If you really love something, it will come out in your writing. I love the islands and the ocean and the whole ambiance of life between the land and the sea.

Selected Titles

Blue Skin of the Sea
Under the Blood-Red Sun

Graham (Sandy) Salisbury is a new author in the field of young adult literature. Born and raised on the Hawaiian Islands, he is a descendant of the first missionary families to arrive there. He has had a number of vocations, including skipper of a glass-bottomed boat, deck hand on a deep-sea charter fishing boat, elementary school teacher, and musician. He now lives with his family in Portland, Oregon, where he manages historic office buildings and writes books. Graham Salisbury has received a number of awards. His first novel, <u>Blue Skin of the Sea</u>, received seven awards, including the ALA Best Book for Young Adults and the Parent's Choice Book Award.

I've been told that my writing has a lyrical quality to it and I think that comes from writing about something I am passionate about. Growing up on an island is a very unique experience, a very physical experience. Some people go nuts not being able to take off and drive for miles and miles. On an island you have to drive in circles. But I never felt trapped or got what they call "rock fever." For me, open country was always right there in the endless expanse of the sea. I lived right on the water, in the hissing and thumping waves of the most perfect ocean imaginable. I can still hear it, smell it, see it in my mind—sparkling in the sun, calm and easy.

I didn't read when I was young. Embarrassing as it is to admit, I was a very, very poor student, the kind who mostly got C's and D's. I wasn't a behavior problem, or anything like that, just an easy-going, non-studying kid. It's a known fact that tropical societies don't read much, and I fit right into that profile. My education slipped on by while I was out surfing and goofing off with the boys. I call it the brainless time of my life.

I nearly flunked out of my first year of college, so I quit and went back later, when I was about twenty-five. Amazing as it was to me, I got straight A's and graduated magna cum laude, simply because I *wanted* to be there, and I wanted to learn. That's the key—desire.

I started reading when my first son was born. I was thirty. I picked up Alex Haley's *Roots* and read it in the evenings while I gave my son his bottle. I just *loved* that book. I was there, I was Kunta Kinte, I was Chicken George. And I was hooked. I've been reading every single day since then, two or three books at a time and

countless magazines. A year before his death, I got to meet Alex Haley and thank him for giving me the gift of reading. His words of advice to me were, "Add to the good in the world," which I've adopted as a primary personal endeavor.

I started writing maybe five or six years ago. I had had a bad experience in a public speaking class during that first dismal year of college, an experience that just murdered my confidence. So, years later, I took a course I hoped would help me over that horrible fear of speaking in public. One of the things they had me do was write little five-minute memory pieces. I started working on them and found that I really liked writing them! But I had a hard time controlling the truth. I bent and stretched it, molded it to make my stories more exciting. Sometimes, I flat out lied, and had a great time doing it. That's when I discovered I was a fiction writer.

Basically, I taught myself how to write, starting with short stories. I submitted them to every college and university literary review I could find in Hawaii and was published by almost all of them. Then I decided to get serious about writing and enrolled in a master of fine arts in writing program in Vermont, which was the best thing I ever could have done.

I decided to write for young readers because that's where my heart has always been—with young people. I love them. I love being among them and talking with them. So I found a home in the world of the young, and made a commitment to that world. I believe that writing for young readers is more difficult than writing for adults. Unlike adults, young readers don't wait around for you to get to the point. You've got to grab them early, *boom,* right now! If you don't, you'll lose them. You've got to come right out and say something they want to hear.

I don't write to teach, preach, or criticize. I write to explore the world of feelings, and to make good use of the English language. A big issue for me is the father-son relationship. The fact that I was raised without a father accounts for that, I suppose. Actually, I had three fathers, but I didn't know any of them. I drifted around like a leaf on the sea, drifted into trouble simply by being in the wrong place at the wrong time. So I like to write about boys who feel rudderless and aimless, as I did, boys growing up without someone to help them make decent life choices. I write from the holes in my own boyhood, and hope that my fiction will help a few kids out there with holes in their lives. If the humans around them can't help. Or won't.

Bridging

The Metaphor of the Island: Comparing and Contrasting Three Books

Islands are frequently used in literature as havens for escape, as is illustrated in <u>The Adventures of Huckleberry Finn</u>, when both Huck and Jim make Jackson Island their journey's first destination. Islands have been used throughout literature in such classics as <u>Robinson Crusoe</u> and <u>Treasure Island</u>. In this bridging experience, students read two contemporary novels, Theodore Taylor's <u>The Cay</u> and Harry Mazer's <u>The Island Keeper</u>, and one historical novel, Scott O'Dell's <u>Island of the Blue Dolphins</u>.

example, Sue Ellen Bridgers's books are rich with vivid descriptive passages that transport the reader to her setting. Zibby Oneal creates word paintings in her books, which reflects her love for painting. Gary Paulsen uses an almost clipped writing style, with short sentences and sentence fragments for emphasis and to reflect characters' thoughts. Ann Rinaldi selects her titles from a phrase that is used significantly and often in her books. Chris Crutcher's style depends on a vital perspective as he presents characters who confront the harsh realities of their lives with humor. Gordon Korman's witty style and flippant humor is immensely popular with adolescents as he portrays events in their daily lives as a series of wacky adventures.

Symbol   A symbol is an object that takes on a meaning beyond its literal one. For example, the goldfish in Zibby Oneal's *The Language of Goldfish* are a symbol of the innocence of childhood. The island is often used as a symbol in young adult literature to represent the isolation of adolescence or adolescents' need for separation from the adult world in order find out who they are, to grow and change, and to prove themselves. For example, in Harry Mazer's *The Island Keeper,* Cleo Murphy, a rich, fat, unhappy girl, runs away to a deserted island after the death of her sister. In this book, as with Paulsen's *The Island,* the setting (an island) becomes a symbol. In Mary Dowling Hahn's *Stepping on the Cracks,* the railroad track becomes a symbol of the boundaries of the girls' childhood world, and when the girls go beyond the tracks, they have to see their world from an older, more responsible perspective. *Dragon's Gate* by Laurence Yep uses the dragon and the dragon's gate as powerful symbols of learning to triumph over evil and adversity in his historical fiction about the building of the transcontinental railroad by Chinese laborers in the late 1860s. Additionally, the image of the mountain as predatory tiger and of the new Chinese workers as tiger meat serve as symbols of the difficulties they encounter.

Theme   The theme of a work is the central unifying idea that underlies it. In her book *Wolf by the Ears,* Ann Rinaldi presents the theme of alienation in the author's note that prefaces the book. Norma Fox Mazer wrote two books, *A Figure of Speech* and *After the Rain,* that explore the special relationship between an elderly grandfather and his granddaughter. A theme of both of these books is the dignity of the elderly. *Scorpions* by Walter Dean Myers, Lois Duncan's *Killing Mr. Griffin,* and Caroline Cooney's *The Party's Over* share the theme of dealing with peer pressure; however, that theme is explored differently in each of these works.

Selecting Books

Teachers have a significant responsibility as they plan and select materials for their classes. This responsibility is compounded by issues of censorship.

Is It Selection or Censorship?

Every teacher has the responsibility to ensure that students have the right to explore, think, and read without oppression. The National Council of Teachers of English publishes a booklet entitled *The Students' Right to Read* that addresses this issue and teachers' role in it. Teachers have an obligation to provide students with challenging learning experiences, including a range of quality and varied reading materials. In determining what students will read, teachers need to have the confidence that their professional judgment will be supported by their administration and school board with policies and procedures to address any attempt at censorship. Schools should plan staff development experiences for teachers and administrators so that they are aware of policies and procedures and are informed about how to handle challenges.

In a 1990 survey (Brown, 1992) conducted at the fall conference of the Michigan Council of Teachers of English, ninety-one percent of the respondents indicated that they or their colleagues had experienced censorship attempts. Additionally, over one third of the respondents indicated that they did not know if their schools had policies to address censorship efforts. Only seventeen percent indicated that their schools had made any attempt to educate teachers about the policies and procedures. Certainly, these figures indicate that at the very least, schools must institute staff development experiences to inform and prepare their teachers in case of a censorship attempt.

Teachers need to have enough confidence in their professionalism to make choices about instructional materials in responsible ways that will be consistent with the curricular aims of their classes. "The first responsibility of the

> **Bridging**
>
> *Theme of Survival: The Novels of Gary Paulsen*
>
> Although the best known of Gary Paulsen's survival books is probably Hatchet, the theme of survival is well developed in a number of his other books. In this bridging experience, students explore the theme of survival as it is developed in the following books: The River, The Voyage of the Frog, The Foxman, and The Crossing.

teacher is to provide students with varied and quality learning experiences. They must be able to do this without living under a constant cloud of fear. Teachers also need to be reflective about their curricular choices in order to guard against self-censorship" (Brown and Stephens, 1994).

One facet of censorship mentioned above is closely connected to any discussion of selection: the potential problem of self-censorship. James E. Davis (1986), past president of the National Council of Teachers of English and one of the foremost authorities on all types of censorship, identifies self-censorship as a significant problem: "Self-censorship means reading and selecting literature through someone else's eyes and with someone else's values. You attribute to this imaginary censor faculties which you yourself do not possess, and to the text a significance it does not have. Thus anything and everything can look censorable." For teachers, perhaps the most basic rule is to be faithful to their best professional judgment.

In its reprint from *Language Arts* (1978) entitled "Censorship: Don't Let It Become an Issue in Your Schools," the National Council of Teachers of English identifies the following criteria* for selecting trade books for use in the classroom:

A) Literary Quality

Literary quality relates to style of writing or the arrangement of words and sentences that best expresses the dominating theme. It includes sentence structure, dialogue and vocabulary. Literary quality is not affected by format or illustration.

Characterization is an aspect of literary quality. An effectively realized character acts and speaks in a way that is believable for that character.

Plot is another aspect of literary quality. The incidents of a story must be interrelated and carry the reader along to its climax.

Still another aspect of literary quality is a story's theme, in which the philosophy of the author is expressed in the meaning of the story and often reflects developmental values in the growing-up process.

B) Appropriateness

Factors to be considered in assessing the appropriateness of books are children's interests, the age level and/or maturity of children in relation to the book being considered, and the content, format, and illustration. While the format and illustrations are not directly related to the elements

---

considered under literary quality, they should complement the text as well as be evaluated on the basis of artistic standards.

C) Usefulness

An important aspect of usefulness is the purpose for using books in relation to curriculum objectives. Basic to the selection of any book is the suitability of the text; but by no means is this to be construed to mean controversial materials will not be used.

Accuracy is important in nonfiction and in fiction in regard to theme, setting, characters and incidents.

Authenticity is important in fiction and biography, especially in those books with a historical background.

D) Uniqueness

All books are unique. Their uniqueness may be a result of their theme, plot, style of writing, characterization, format, or illustration. Such books may have a special place and use in the classroom and library. Teachers must know what it is about a book that makes it unique, and must share this information with others.

E) Breadth of Coverage

Books may present problems of stereotyping with respect to sex and to race. Religion, politics, and questions of morality or patriotism are issues about which there are considerable differences of opinion. The importance of such books may lie mainly, or only, in their historical viewpoint and should be presented as such to children who read them. Teachers and librarians should be aware of these considerations and should make every effort to provide materials which present alternate points of view. Historically there have always been those who have recognized the offensiveness of these materials. Children, like adults exposed to new ideas, can accept or reject them, based on input from all viewpoints. All opinions require protection under the First Amendment. (p. 7)

Censorship becomes an issue when decisions are made without consideration of predetermined criteria. Therefore, the selection of books and other instructional materials should be made by applying criteria that are consistent with issues of quality, students, and the curriculum. The careful and responsible selection of materials is the best preparation for dealing with potential censorship problems. Above all, teachers should remember that they are professionals whose critical judgment allows them to make appropriate choices of reading material.

Bridging

Novels and the First Amendment

The Ninth Issue (Dallin Malmgren), The Day They Came to Arrest the Book (Nat Hentoff), Nothing But the Truth (Avi), A Matter of Principle (Susan Beth Pfeffer), Goofbang Value Daze (Julian Thompson), and The Cat Ate My Gym Suit and Can You Sue Your Parents for Malpractice? (Paula Danziger), among other books for young adults, address issues of intellectual freedom. All of these books can serve as a bridge to examining issues of selection and censorship and students' right to read.

Preparing for Censorship— Questions of Quality

The reality of the issue of censorship is that there is no book, video, classroom practice, or teaching method that is assured of being protected from censorship. Book censorship challenges are easier to address when they are based on questions of quality, but far too often challenges are the result of some subjective perception of a group or individual. Anything can be a target of some group or individual who seeks to censor it. Although there is no safeguard against these attacks, the single best defense is attesting to the quality of the work in that teachers have a degree of protection when they use works recognized for their literary merit. Teachers and librarians are the experts about content, and their judgment should be recognized and appreciated.

We explore the issue of censorship in an article entitled "Being Proactive, Not Waiting for the Censor" for the NCTE book entitled *Preserving Intellectual Freedom* (Brown, 1994), a collection of articles discussing facets of censorship issues. In that article, we advocate that schools initiate Intellectual Freedom Groups composed of the librarian or media coordinator, members of the English department and other concerned faculty members, representatives from the administration, students, and parents. These groups would develop and review policies and procedures concerning intellectual freedom. They could also serve as a clearinghouse for collecting and keeping files of reviews, background materials, and other information.

We also make the following suggestions:

Teachers and administrators need to establish selection criteria and apply them consistently to all print as well as nonprint instructional materials. The first responsibility of the teacher is to provide students with varied and quality learning experiences. They must be able to do this without living under a constant cloud of fear. Teachers also need to be reflective about their curricular choices in order to guard against self-censorship. Schools should plan staff development experiences for teachers and administrators so that they are informed about how to handle challenges. (Brown and Stephens, 1994)

In addition to the need for policies about selection, teachers must be knowledgeable about actions that they can take individually. First, they should carefully review all materials before adopting them or recommending them. Obviously, they cannot read every book that is published, but they can read reviews and find informed opinions on materials that they might include on supplementary lists. (Teachers, however, should never adopt a book or any other instructional material for class use without personally reviewing it.) Second, we recommend that teachers collect copies of book reviews and keep them on file. (Appendix C includes a list of sources for book reviews.) Third, we recommend that teachers develop rationales for books that they teach for whole class instruction. In the winter 1993 issue of *The ALAN Review,* Margo Sacco indexes rationales for the most commonly censored books. If teachers do their own rationales in addition to collecting those already prepared, they will be able to address those elements that are unique to their situations and to their students' needs. Fourth, teachers should be informed about the policies and procedures that the school will follow if there is a challenge to instructional materials.

Guidelines for Developing Rationales

- Include complete bibliographic information.
- Summarize major elements of the book.
- Identify major controversial issues.
- Find major book reviews, especially ones that address the controversial issues.
- Develop and articulate a case for using the book.
- Quote appropriate reviews.

These guidelines provide an abbreviated approach; however, in Appendix F, we include a copy of the SLATE Starter Sheet on developing rationales, which presents a more detailed approach for teachers, curriculum directors, and librarians to create their own rationales. Appendix G includes a listing of rationales available from the National Council of Teachers of English.

In Case of a Censorship Attempt In exploring the varied roles and responsibilities of the teacher, it is obvious that the concept of the teacher as dispenser of wisdom is an archaic notion. Teaching is a complex process of learning, reading, sharing, guiding, coaching, observing, gathering data, and implementing change. In that complexity, teachers need the flexibility to assume any role that is appropriate. Additionally, teachers have the responsibility to use their

☐ 1. Does your school have an intellectual freedom statement and policy?

☐ 2. Does your school have an adopted written selection policy?

☐ 3. Does your school have written reconsideration policies and procedures?

☐ 4. Has your school provided professional development sessions to acquaint your staff with all policies and procedures?

☐ 5. Does your school have a cooperative working relationship with political, religious, and civic groups in your community?

☐ 6. Has your school established an Intellectual Freedom Group or other committee to address potential problems?

☐ 7. Is your school aware of local groups or branches of national groups that are actively involved in challenges?

☐ 8. Does your school have a record of local and state-wide experts and advocates who can help you if you experience a challenge?

☐ 9. Has your school identified writers and reporters from local media who will be supportive if there is a challenge?

☐ 10. Is your school aware of national, state, and local organizations that work for intellectual freedom?

Figure 8.4   Challenge Checklist

professional judgment as they select books and teaching materials, to communicate effectively, and to avoid attempts to censor materials. Figure 8.4 is a checklist for preparedness against challenges.

In "Censorship: Don't Let It Become an Issue in Your Schools" (1978), the National Council of Teachers of English provides advice* about what to do when there are challenges:

> IF and AFTER censorship problems arise (and before a formal complaint procedure is initiated), here are some approaches and considerations:
>
> Be sure to inform your principal of any complaint, and how you plan to handle it.
>
> Urge your principal to read or view the material objected to. Afterwards, share with him/her your reasons for using the material with children. Also, try to get a school board member and a local minister, rabbi or priest to read or look at the material.
>
> If a parent complains about material, insisting on an immediate discussion about it, defer such a discussion; make an appointment with him/her

---

* Copyright 1978 National Council of Teachers
of English. Reprinted with permission.

for a later time. At the same time, assure the parent that you have a concern for the child's interest. Neither you nor the parent should be in the position of discussing material without careful consideration beforehand of the factors that are to be discussed. Do not defend materials on the spur of the moment. Apart from being unfair to all concerned, and particularly to children, it is your professional duty to present your views thoughtfully and with consideration.

Reread or review the material in question, even though you may already be familiar with it. Identify its strengths. Put down in writing why you believe it is proper and useful in your teaching program.

Collect reviews of the material from such publications as *Language Arts, English Journal, Bulletin of the Center for Children's Books, Horn Book, School Library Journal* and other professional publications.

There may be three to five parents, other than the complaining parents, who may be particularly supportive of your teaching objectives. Request that they read or view the material being questioned and invite their written reactions, addressed to you and your principal. (p. 10)

Student Needs, Interests, and Censorship　Teachers have a special challenge to select materials that will speak to the concerns and the needs of the adolescent while not pandering to sensationalism. In Chapter 3, we discussed the characteristics of adolescents. We recognize that adolescence is frequently characterized as a period of change, turmoil, rebellion, and introspection. As early as 1977, Rinsky and Schweiker recognized the trend in realistic fiction for young adults to eliminate old barriers and to present such complex and possibly controversial issues as physical changes of puberty, teenage pregnancy, drug and alcohol addiction, changes in family relationships, and changes in gender roles. The realistic content of these books causes perhaps more concern than most other issues.

The best defense that teachers have against censors is a well-conceptualized curriculum. In curriculum planning, teachers—whether individually, in teams, or as departments—identify educational goals, outcomes, methods, and materials that they believe will help their students learn the content. Again, it is the professional judgment of teachers and librarians that should be recognized as the vital ingredient in curriculum planning.

The American Civil Liberties Union is probably the best recognized opponent to restrictions of freedoms guaranteed by the Constitution. (Appendix D lists names and addresses of other organizations that provide information and support to teachers regarding censorship.) According to People for the

American Way, the following are the most frequently challenged books from 1982 to 1990:

Of Mice and Men, John Steinbeck

The Catcher in the Rye, J. D. Salinger

The Adventures of Huckleberry Finn, Mark Twain

The Chocolate War, Robert Cormier

Go Ask Alice, Anonymous

A Light in the Attic, Shel Silverstein

Deenie, Judy Blume

Then Again, Maybe I Won't, Judy Blume

Forever, Judy Blume

To Kill a Mockingbird, Harper Lee

Since 1990, challenges have increased annually. Among the recent challenges reported to the National Council of Teachers of English are the following (it should be noted that this list is representative rather than comprehensive):

The Red Pony

Ordinary People

The Chocolate War

Ten Little Indians

Many of William Shakespeare's works

The Adventures of Huckleberry Finn.

Why Am I So Miserable If These Are Supposed to Be the Best Years of My Life?

Romeo and Juliet

A Day No Pigs Would Die

One Day in the Life of Ivan Denisovich

The Catcher in the Rye

Go Ask Alice

A Separate Peace

Of Mice and Men

The Color Purple

I Know Why the Caged Bird Sings

The Bridge to Terabithia

The Effect of Gamma Rays on Man-in the-Moon Marigolds

Blubber

I Am the Cheese

Long Live the Queen

Forever

The list of most frequently challenged materials (both books and curricular programs) for 1992–93, according to *Attacks on the Freedom to Learn 1992–93 Report* from People for the American Way (as reported in *English Journal,* 1994, p. 11), is as follows:

Pumsy in Pursuit of Excellence, a self-esteem program

Developing Understanding of Self and Others, a self-esteem program

Scary Stories to Tell in the Dark by Alvin Schwartz

More Scary Stories to Tell in the Dark by Alvin Schwartz

Quest, a self-esteem program

The Bridge to Terabithia by Katherine Paterson

The Catcher in the Rye by J. D. Salinger

Scary Stories 3: More Tales to Chill Your Bones by Alvin Schwartz

The Boy Who Lost His Face by Louis Sachar

Of Mice and Men by John Steinbeck

Summary

Selecting quality young adult literature is an important responsibility for teachers. Selection presents a significant challenge because a number of factors must be considered, including quality, students' interests and needs, and curricular consistency. Selection is often tied closely to discussions of censorship, including self-censorship. The best defense against censorship is being prepared before a challenge occurs.

Suggested Activities

1. In your journal, develop a rationale for a young adult book as a precaution against a censorship challenge

2. Using any of the interest inventories, examine your insights about your own reading. How has the reading you have been doing in conjunction

with this text affected you? If you are currently teaching, use it with your students.

3. Use the Literature Involvement Strategy presented in this chapter, "Looking at Book Covers," as a pre- and post-reading activity. Compare your responses with your classmates. If you are currently teaching, use this strategy with your students.

4. Compare the literary characteristics of two young adult literature works with similar topics or themes.

PART THREE

Making the Young Adult Literature Classroom Work

This final section of the text includes three chapters designed to help pre-service and in-service teachers incorporate young adult literature into their classrooms. We describe organizational patterns and instructional strategies that can be implemented in any classroom. These patterns and strategies are designed to help students become active readers of literature and can be applied to the study of any type of literature.

Chapter 9, Creating an Environment for Young Adult Literature, describes a four-pronged instructional framework. Additionally, we provide methods of classroom management and organization in this chapter. Our conversation is with Monica Hughes, science fiction writer for readers who think they do not like science fiction.

In Chapter 10, Improving Classroom Interaction: Making Discussion and Writing Real, we present strategies for facilitating student involvement with literature by examining literature from both a cognitive and affective perspective. Strategies for discussing and writing about literature are presented. We have a conversation with award-winning author of nonfiction, Russell Freedman.

In Chapter 11, More Strategies for Using Young Adult Literature, we present a range of strategies for experiencing and responding to literature. In this chapter we talk with Joan Bauer, a new novelist of humorous fiction.

Creating an Environment for Young Adult Literature

"Good books like these can open up worlds," she [the teacher] says standing up regally. . . .

"Why not wait until the movie comes out?" calls Mike Anderson from the back of the room. . . .

"Movies and TV are definitely entertaining," she says not missing a beat. "But did you ever stop to think about how one-track they are? Movies and TV give you an entire picture and tell you exactly how to feel—they have the scary music and the canned laughter to make sure you get it right. But books, on the other hand, give you only the words; you have to use your imagination for the rest. It's more than entertainment: your imagination will help you get things from books that you'll carry with you for the rest of your life."

Marie G. Lee, *Finding My Voice*

Journal Writing: Responding

How do you think that your understanding and appreciation of literature can be enhanced by working either in pairs or in small groups?

_____

A n underlying premise of this book is that classrooms can no longer follow a traditional format in which all wisdom comes from an omniscient teacher. We believe that the classroom must be a community of learners in which the teacher and the students learn and grow. In this type of environment, teachers provide opportunities to explore new materials and ideas so that they, too, are involved in learning. This philosophy can be implemented through a classroom structure that goes beyond the traditional methods of teaching literature.

An Instructional Framework

Typically, the use of young adult literature in classrooms falls into one of three categories. First is the classroom in which traditional works are the mainstay of instruction; all reading is done from a literature anthology. Young adult literature is viewed with disdain for a number of reasons, ranging from misconceptions about quality to fears about censorship. Second is the classroom that is primarily focused on studying the traditional classics but incorporates some young adult literature, especially selections that have received literary recognition. Though young adult literature may be allowed or sometimes even encouraged in the classrooms, it is generally only for free-choice reading and for reluctant and at-risk readers. Third is the classroom in which the teacher and students are engaged in reading and responding to a wide variety of literature, including young adult literature. Thematic units offer students opportunities to experience related selections that match their individual needs, interests, prior knowledge, and abilities. Specific selected works, sometimes the traditional classics and sometimes newer or more unconventional pieces, serve as focal points for whole-class instruction to meet curriculum requirements. Although this last scenario has a more balanced curriculum, it depends on whole-class instruction exclusively, rather than providing a variety of instructional approaches to meet the needs of all students. All of these classrooms have in common variations on traditional curricular and instructional methods that have been used over the years.

> **Bridging**
>
> *Bridging a Short Story with a YA Novel*
>
> Martha Brooks's short story "A Boy and his Dog" (from her story collection <u>Paradise Cafe and Other Stories</u>) describes Buddy's relationship with his dog. This story provides an effective bridge to Wilson Rawls's novel <u>Where the Red Fern Grows</u>.

In this chapter, we describe a four-pronged instructional framework that describes another way to structure and organize classroom practices and content. This approach allows students to have a range of experiences with literature, and it meets their diverse needs. In their work with literature study circles, Samway et al. (1991) found that students emphasize four things: "the importance of reading complete books, talking about books, being given some choice over which books they would read, and having plenty of time to read" (p. 202). Additionally, Au (1993, pp. 69–70) recommends the concept of a community of learners with varying grouping arrangements for multicultural classrooms. The approaches we present in this chapter reflect some of the above ideas. Our approaches have varying degrees of structure and include ways to involve students in whole-class, small-group, paired, and individual activities. The approaches are as follows: Classroom Learning Community (CLC), Student Sharing and Study Groups (S³ Groups), Learning Partners, and Individual Learning. Figure 9.1 places these approaches on a

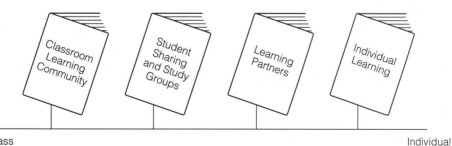

Whole Class   Individual

Figure 9.1   Instructional Framework

continuum, reflecting the type of student involvement in each. We do not advocate that teachers implement all of these approaches at one time. Instead, we recommend that they begin by selecting one or two with which they feel most confident and implement them, giving themselves time to adapt the approach to their particular teaching conditions and their own teaching style. Students (and teachers) need time to learn new ways of relating and responding in the classroom. Frequently, those teachers who find themselves unsuccessful with new instructional approaches are overwhelmed by trying to do too much in too short a time.

Classroom Learning Community (CLC)

Our concept of whole-class instruction plays a significant role in our instructional framework. Philosophically, it differs from the traditional whole-class instruction in its emphasis on the cooperative nature of learning in the classroom. The Classroom Learning Community implies that everyone, including the teacher, is a learner. Frank Smith (1986) developed the concept of the literacy club as a vehicle that enables teachers and students to share with each other what they are reading, "the way readers normally behave in the world outside school." Smith highlights the affective dimensions of the social relationships in these clubs as their most critical elements. One rule is that no coercion is allowed, because "it is the essence of clubs that their activities are entered into freely." A second rule is that no status is allowed, meaning that teachers should not be obviously in control of the club. Instead of coercion and control—which Smith says lead to intimidation, insecurity, and dependency—teachers should concentrate on providing help when help is needed by assuming the role of most experienced club member. This role is empowering to students, and the results are "growth, assurance, and independence" (p. 185). Smith also discusses the advantages of the literacy club:

> The literacy club is, of course, a club of people who use written language. Children join the literacy club the way they join the spoken language club—with the implicit act of mutual acceptance: "You're one of us," "I want to be just like you." There are no special admission requirements, no entry fees. The advantages of joining the literacy club are the same as those of joining the spoken language club or any other club. First, the activities of experienced club members are quickly revealed to new members. The newcomer is shown in the normal course of everyday activities what written language can be used for. This is no vague matter of "demonstrating the value of reading and writing" as abstract general abilities, but the

much more direct and immediate experience of making use of signs to get to intended destinations, using books for the enjoyment of a story, or making a shopping list to ensure that nothing is forgotten. These are activities which need no justification or explanation in themselves. The activities happen quite naturally, almost incidentally, to involve reading and writing. (p. 37)

Based on this concept, McMahon (1994) describes a book club in action, with students taking a leadership role in establishing a sharing community. The concept of sharing experiences provides a philosophical base for the Classroom Learning Community. The curriculum for CLC, an outgrowth of Smith's literacy club, is broadly based and provides students with a range of experiences with literature. Inherent in this type of instruction is the recognition that whole-class experiences with a particular work of literature can be valuable but are not the only way to involve students with reading. Alan Purves (1984) discusses the concept of classroom community with the study of literature:

Communities are in part held together by shared experiences, shared perceptions, and shared language. . . . Literature provides a major vehicle for creating communities, as witness the power of religious literature to hold together millions over time and space and language. (p. 18)

The ongoing process we identify in the Young Adult Reader Involvement Model is that of sharing. As students and teachers share their experiences with literature, they clarify and articulate their reactions, their ideas, and their beliefs about what they have read. According to Fish (1980), the "interpretative community" provides the social context for readers. This sense of a social community has an impact on readers' interaction with texts. Reading and experiencing literature are not solitary experiences in which the sole interactions are between the reader and the text. The reader and the text provide only two dimensions. The third dimension of the literary experience involves the social aspect when the reader shares the reading experience.

Keating (1990), in his discussion of adolescent thinking, speaks to the role of the teacher:

Students need to be engaged with meaningful material. . . . Students need experiences that lead to placing a high value on critical thinking, to acquiring it as a disposition, not just as a skill; and many of these factors occur most readily, and perhaps exclusively, when students have the opportunity for real, ongoing discourse with teachers who have reasonably expert command of the material to be taught. (p. 77)

Bridging

Bridging a Poem with a Novel

Flick Webb in John Updike's poem "The Ex-Basketball Player" and Hallie in Caroline Cooney's The Party's Over both experience difficult times after high school. Use the poem as a bridge to Cooney's book.

Student Sharing and Study Groups (S³ Groups)

The concept of sharing is prominent throughout the instructional framework. S³ Groups are designed to involve students in small-group activity to share their experiences with the members of their groups and to further their understanding of these experiences. Typically these groups involve between three to five members. Depending on the task, the teacher may decide to assign specific roles to group members, or the roles may evolve naturally during the course of group work. The composition of the groups should be dynamic rather than static. The concept of the Classroom Learning Community should be reinforced in all instructional functions. One way to accomplish this is by regularly changing the groups so that everyone has the opportunity to work with each other. This approach is particularly important with middle school students who are very much involved with their own social cliques. Study groups provide students with the opportunity to encourage and support the efforts of each other as they explore the ideas, concepts, and experiences of their reading.

Learning Partners

This approach involves two students working together. Earlier we discussed Vygotsky's zone of proximal development (1978). The notion of Learning Partners (Stephens and Brown, 1994) is a significant example of the social interaction that provides a supportive learning environment for students. Learning Partners may respond to each other in their dialogue journals, share their writings with each other or serve as peer editors, discuss what they are reading and recommend books to each other, or develop creative projects together.

Learning Partners may be student selected or teacher selected, but selection must be based on academic and social compatibility as well as similar interests and goals. Once a partnership is established and operating effectively, it is beneficial to keep it together for an extended period of time (for example, for at least a marking period). The benefit to this longevity is that the students gain trust and an increased level of cooperation. This makes the work of the partners more productive. An inherent benefit to this approach is that both partners have mutual responsibilities and mutual needs; therefore, the level of commitment and involvement is usually high.

Individual Learning

Any instructional continuum provides opportunities for students to explore on their own—pursuing interests, seeking answers to questions that intrigue them, or examining the work of a particular author in depth. Individual Learning also provides opportunities to meet individual needs and for students to take more responsibility for their own accomplishments.

Establishing a Learning Environment

The responsibilities of teachers transcend instruction: their responsibilities also include the creation of a learning environment. Included in this notion is creating a classroom climate that is supportive of and conducive to involving students with literature and learning. In establishing an appropriate learning atmosphere, teachers need to promote and encourage student involvement and positive attitudes toward reading through the instructional format and activities they use. Thomson's (1987) description of the component of the Australian National Reading Research project that examined students' reading attitudes and interests indicates that students' negative attitudes are exacerbated by certain instructional practices. These include students' being required to take turns reading aloud to the class, writing summaries and book reviews, and being required to read unsuitable material. In contrast, positive student attitudes are fostered by

> teachers who read exciting excerpts and entire texts aloud to pupils, who organise regular periods of sustained silent reading, who organise wide-reading schemes, who emphasise choice and a pupil's right to dislike a book without being penalised, who organise small-group discussion for sharing of opinions, and who arrange for more performance-oriented activities using a diversity of media. (p. 36)

Earlier in this chapter we described an instructional framework to promote student involvement and understanding that provides a necessary psychological environment for using literature. In addition to creating a positive psychological environment, teachers can increase student interest and involvement by providing a rich physical environment that focuses on books. Teachers should build class libraries that include their own books, books purchased by the school, and books donated by students and others. With students having easy access to these books, teachers can readily make recommendations. Posters about books or authors can create visual interest. Students may even create their own posters or other visuals to encourage their classmates' interest in books they have enjoyed. Some teachers have a book review corner where students use a strategy called Be a Critic to develop a rating system and critique their reading. These writings can be displayed on a wall or a bulletin board. As new reviews are displayed, the old ones can be kept in a file for reference. The strategy is described in more detail in Chapter 10.

The physical environment can also be enhanced when teachers tap an often under-utilized resource—a well-versed school or public librarian. Librarians have a wealth of information about books. They will often help with special book displays and collections or by preparing book carts for the classroom to accompany a particular unit or theme or for other purposes such as introducing an author or type of literature. A knowledgeable librarian can be invaluable to busy teachers who do not have time to research specific titles and topics. Teachers who are unfamiliar with young adult literature or just beginning to learn about it should make a friend of a librarian immediately.

Jack Thomson, in *Understanding Teenagers' Reading* (1987), describes an innovative approach to creating a physical and psychological environment for reading developed in an Australian high school:

> Many students commented favorably on various activities teachers had organised for reading and/or responding to literature. There was particular commendation of an imaginative wide reading scheme being introduced into one of the high schools. . . . In this scheme, many paper-back books were placed on shelves in the main corridors of the school and children were able to borrow on an honour system by merely writing the title and author of the book borrowed on sheets left by the bookshelves. This scheme appealed to students because it gave books a physical presence in informal surroundings allowing them to browse freely and choose at leisure. It also made borrowing less troublesome. (There seems to be great antagonism towards what they see as rigid routines, bureaucracy and the oppressive atmosphere they associate with the traditional formal library and its procedures.)
>
> [Student comments] 'Reading in school for subjects is very boring because they are rotten books. Most of the books in the library are rotten, some are okay, but it's a hassle borrowing them and you can easily get into trouble in there. The new Reading Programme at our school now is terrific.'
>
> (Obviously the programme allows the students to find what they think is 'terrific' without imposing on them what they think is 'rotten.')
>
> 'Some books are good, but lots in the library are hopeless. The thing Mr. Payne's got going now is real good, he's got good books out.'

'I like reading any book that looks interesting, such as encyclopedias, science books, science fiction, fiction. I am glad they put in the wide-reading scheme because they will get a lot of support from me.'

'In our school they have at last found lots of books that look like their [sic] worth reading.' (p. 31)

The wide-reading program that Thomson describes can be an excellent accompaniment to Sustained Silent Reading (SSR), a program that schedules a set amount of uninterrupted time for everyone (including teachers, administrators, custodians, secretaries, and aides) in the school to engage in free-choice reading. Some teachers have successfully adapted this concept to their individual classrooms when school implementation is impossible. Whatever the implementation plan, what is important is the creation of a positive physical and psychological environment that affirms the value of reading.

Classroom Organization and Management

The classroom organization and management plans teachers use have significant impact on their success in using young adult literature—or any literature, for that matter. A disorganized, chaotic approach can be as disastrous as a rigid, overly structured approach. In this section, we share ideas and strategies for developing plans for classroom organization and management that are consistent with our philosophy of using young adult literature. It is not our intention to be prescriptive or didactic, as we believe that how teachers organize and manage their classrooms is reflective of not only their individual teaching style but also a number of factors beyond their control, such as class size and scheduling. We recommend, however, that teachers consider using the instructional framework described earlier in the chapter—Classroom Learning Community, Student Sharing and Study Groups, Learning Partners, and Individual Learning.

Literature Portfolio

The purpose of a literature portfolio is to provide students with an opportunity for goal setting and self-assessment. It can also serve as a source of data for the teacher to use in evaluating both individual student progress and the program as a whole. Students establish goals and record them as the first entry in their portfolios. These goals should be for a specific time, such as a marking period, and include both individual goals and class goals promoting the concept of a community of learners. They then keep an ongoing record of what

Talking with Monica Hughes

The whole point is what you feel in your real life. If you feel passionately in your life, it is going to come across in your writing.

Selected Titles

Beyond the Dark River

Crisis on Conshelf Ten

The Crystal Drop

Devil on My Back

The Dream Catcher

The Guardian of the Isis Light

Hunter in the Dark

Invitation to the Game

The Isis Pedlar

The Keeper of the Isis Light

The Promise

Sandwriter

Monica Hughes was born in England and lived in Cairo, London, and Edinburgh as a child. During the Second World War, she served in the Women's Royal Naval Service. After the war, she lived in Zimbabwe, where she worked in a dress factory and a bank. Next she moved to Canada and worked at the National Research Council in Ottawa, later moving to Edmonton, Alberta, where she still resides. When her children were in school, she began writing full time for young people. She is the recipient of many awards, including the Canada Council Prize for Children's Literature, which she received twice. The Keeper of the Isis Light and Hunter in the Dark were both designated American Library Association Best Book for Young Adults.

Sometimes I get the sort of feeling that a book is already written; I just don't know what it is yet and I have to find it. It takes me about six months to write a book once I know what I'm writing. I'm a very quick writer, extremely quick, but I do a lot of thinking first. I don't write tentatively. I wait, thinking about the characters, the setting, the plot development, until a book is ready to explode; when my characters start talking in their own voices, then I'm ready to write. I write extremely fast in longhand. Later I use a word processor as I edit. I start thinking about every book with a question. By always starting with a question to which I don't know the answer, I continually have to go off into new fields, so none of my books is, I hope, like any of my other books. Between books I may pick a subject that sounds interesting and browse in the library.

I started dreaming about being a writer when I was ten years of age. In a sense my life has been quite pioneering. I left home to join the navy during the war, and then afterwards I went to live in Zimbabwe, again on my own. I fell into writing science fiction for young people by accident. Sheer good luck led me to watch a Jacques Cousteau movie about an underwater environment that he had built. As I watched,

I found myself asking "What would it be like to live permanently under the ocean?" and turned this into a writing question—"What would it be like to be a young person growing up under the sea?" As I continued to explore questions and write books to answer them, I began to find that the questions that interested me most were leading me away from the "nuts and bolts" Jules Verne type of story that I loved as a child, toward a "softer" kind of science fiction. I became more and more interested in the effect of human response and human values in future worlds, rather than in the excitement and challenge of the technology itself. I believe the difference between what I call "hard" and "soft" science fiction is very often the difference between books that girls hate and books that they learn to love. More than anything else I have written, *The Keeper of the Isis Light* seems to have converted reluctant readers to science fiction.

Science fiction is wonderful in that you can find future worlds to answer questions that can't be answered in any other way. Science fiction has an important place in today's world as a new mythology, making tomorrow's ogres real but within the unthreatening framework of a book. I can challenge young readers to find answers to the questions that exemplify their own powerlessness in the difficult world in

which they are growing up. But it is always hope that powers my stories. There is light at the end of the tunnel, for sure. One of the first things I read when I decided to write for young people was that you can lead a child into the darkness but you must never turn out the light. My books have positive outcomes, but they are still open-ended enough to raise questions for readers to argue about. I don't want to use my books to lay heavy burdens on the young or to preach to them, but to make use of myth within stories to help prepare them for the future, which is theirs. Armed with wisdom and knowledge, they may be able to make more informed decisions.

The difference between wisdom and knowledge is something that keeps coming up in my mind. We must never leave decision making to artificial intelligence, no matter how sophisticated or technologically advanced. That is very dangerous. The human input is vital. What makes humanity unique is our gift of loving and caring, our feelings. When you're working in the science fiction field and looking into tomorrow, you wonder what effects the decisions, or lack of decisions, of today will have on humanity. There seems to be a blind forward movement of technology. We seem to think that if it is there, we must exploit it; as opposed to thinking that if it is there, we must nurture it, which is very different.

they are reading and their activities that relate to their reading. The literature portfolio can be organized in several ways, such as by dates, by books, by authors, by themes, or by instructional format. It is important that students have periodic opportunities to review and reflect on their progress toward their goals. This self-assessment should become part of the portfolio.

Kathleen Stumpf Jongsma (1993), a middle school teacher, describes how she uses literacy portfolios with both her advanced and reading improvement (at-risk readers) classes:

> Students keep their own "literacy portfolios," manila folders stored alphabetically in large, accessible plastic crates. Most of my students pick up their portfolios as they enter the room and keep them at their desks for our 45-minute reading period; others pull their portfolios as needed. They personalize their portfolios with drawings, photographs, clippings from their favorite magazines, and messages to future portfolio readers; they fill them with materials of their own choosing as well as with writing I suggest they include. Portfolios include such things as reading response notebooks, poems, artwork, summary cinquains, story pyramids, character and topic maps, story maps, notes to one another, and tapes of our reading; materials can be work in progress or finished pieces.
>
> Students arrange their portfolios to their own liking. Many place materials in chronological order, others arrange by genre of material, and still others organize thematically. Some students organize around a specific topic—putting all the items on one book together, for example. . . . Without some organization, however, portfolios tend to become unmanageable, and conferences about contents and goals become difficult. Organizing is a crucial step for the reflection that is enunciated in conference discussions and in written pieces. . . . At a minimum, my students write down their reflections on their progress in literacy every three to six weeks. Many students, however, do this more frequently, inserting written comments into their portfolios whenever they feel the need. (pp. 123–24)

Jongsma's research indicates that all of her students, regardless of ability, were able to develop goals, monitor their own progress, and reflect on their growth.

Grading

Almost all middle and secondary school teachers have to assign students letter grades or, in some cases, numerical equivalents on a report card. Frequently, this requirement leads teachers to the practice of using worksheets or workbooks with right and wrong answers and testing students on what they have read in order to have "objective" data to justify the grade. Until letter grading is eliminated, as some experts recommend, teachers need ways to assign grades that are more reflective of current philosophies and theories of learning. One way is to establish written criteria for each letter grade and to make those criteria available to students, parents, and administrators. Such criteria describe both the accomplishments and level of quality that students must demonstrate to earn a specific grade. Students and their teacher are then engaged in a joint process of assessing their growth through the use of some form of ongoing recordkeeping system, such as the literature portfolio.

Dawn Cline (1993) explains a grading system she developed when she implemented the reading workshop approach, based on Atwell's (1987) *In the Middle.* She describes her students, who were primarily from multiethnic low and middle socioeconomic backgrounds, as reluctant readers, at best.

> For each six week period, students worked toward a page-requirement grade, a participation grade, and grades on their writing in reading logs, notes from minilessons, letters to me, and letters to classmates. For the page requirement grade, I simply assigned a letter grade equivalent for number of pages read: 250 to 300 was an A, 200 to 249 was a B, and so on, with bonuses awarded for pages read above 300. I started the page requirement at a low level to build students' confidence and raised them after the first and third six-week units. I was delighted to find that most students read more than required. In assigning participation grades I took into account involvement in discussions, engagement with books, behavior, and the like. Readings logs were simply lists of books read; grades for these and for minilesson notes were assigned based on completeness and accuracy. (pp. 118–19)

Cline indicates that this grading system has the advantage of encouraging success while letting students know what is expected of them and making them responsible for their own achievements.

Some teachers find that a contract system is effective. Thomson (1987) describes such a system developed by teachers at a high school in New South Wales.

> Each student was given a copy of the Wide Reading Contract, which included:
>
> 1. A statement of the aims of the unit (to read more widely, to read more critically, to read for greater enjoyment, to develop your written responses to literature).

2. Ten categories of literature, with an example of each, from which they were to choose their reading material. The categories were: Australian fiction, Biography/autobiography, Children's 'classic,' Famous author, Fantasy fiction, Historical fiction, Poetry (ten poems minimum), Science/speculative fiction, Teenage 'problem' fiction, Other fiction (crime, mystery, spy, etc.).

3. Details of the three levels (A, B or C) for which they could contract:
   C Level:
   - read five books from at least four categories
   - keep a Reading Log for each book
   - write an essay of about 750 words on a set topic.

   Topic: Imagine you are a member of the selection committee for Casino High School Memorial Library. Prepare a paper for the other members of the committee which ranks the five novels in the order you would recommend their purchase and which justifies your choice.

   B Level:
   - read as for C and two additional books by one author already read
   - keep a Reading Log for each book
   - write an essay of about 1000 words on a set topic.

   Topic: Discuss the three novels of the author you have read for this unit, pointing out the similarities and differences among them. Decide which of them you would recommend as the first purchase for C.H.S. Memorial Library, and justify your choice.

   A Level:
   - read as for B and two further books from another two categories
   - keep a Reading Log for each book
   - write an essay as for B and a further essay of about 500 words on a set topic.

   Topic: What have you learned about human problems and human nature from the nine novels you have read? (Do not try to cover the plots of the nine novels. Try, instead, to deduce common aspects among the novels, and to illustrate them by reference to the novels.)

4. Details of the level contracted for, the duration of the contract, the signature of the student and the counter-signature of the teacher.

Students were given an extensive Recommended Reading List to help them to make their selections. Most of the books listed were chosen specifically for their appeal to adolescents. They also received a suggested format for their Reading Logs which emphasised their personal response as readers. (pp. 248–49)

Book Charts

This is a tool to provide quantitative data about how much students read in any given period. One of the major benefits of this approach is that it gives students a sense of accomplishment. Additionally, it has been used successfully in classes that have shifted to a literature-based reading program from a reading series or an anthology. Students chart the number of books that they read. The three components of the basic chart include the title of the book, the date completed, and some type of rating scale for the book. (See Figure 9.2.)

The process of keeping book charts may be implemented in a number of ways. For example, using book charts in a class of reluctant readers is a touchier situation than in a class of involved readers. For reluctant readers the charting might be done in file folders that are not publicly displayed. In a class of students who read a lot, a followup to the individual charting approach might be significantly different. For example, students, in their S³ Groups, might demonstrate their accomplishments by combining the number of books that group members read in a bar graph that they display. Figure 9.3 shows the record of one group during a six-week period. As the figure shows, the group members collectively read more during the second week than the twelve-book

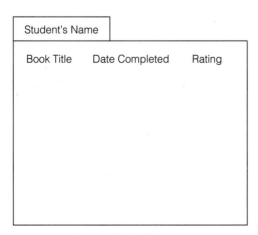

Figure 9.2   Sample Book Chart

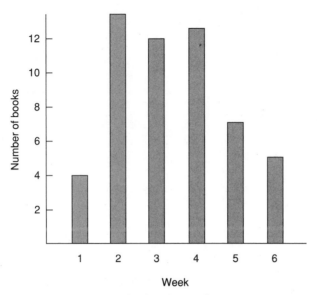

Figure 9.3   Sample Book Chart for an S³ Group

maximum on the chart. In a case like this, the teacher may decide to revise the chart appropriately for the next six-week period.

Exploration Records

We have found that if students are given total freedom to read anything that they wish they tend to read narrowly. That is, they will read one favorite author, or only nonfiction, or only a particular genre. Exploration records are designed to help the teacher serve as a guide for expanding their students' view of literature and to help them select a variety of books. This guidance may include helping students make informed judgments about quality and types of books. The chart may take a number of forms, such as the examples on the following pages.

The discovery record is designed to encourage students to read new authors and to examine both the positives and negatives about their experiences with a book. The final question asks that students realize that even books that do not appeal to them may appeal

Bridging

Poetry Springboards

Robert Hayden's poem "Those Winter Sundays" and Langston Hughes's poem "Mother to Son" speak eloquently about the relationship between a parent and child. These poems can bridge to Walter Dean Myers's novel <u>Somewhere in the Darkness</u>. The poems serve as a springboard for discussing Jimmy's relationships with Crab and Mama Jean.

Discovery Record

1. I discovered a new author named

   _____ .

2. What I like best about his/her work is

   _____ .

3. What I like least about his/her work is

   _____ .

4. I am/am not (circle the appropriate choice) going to read another
   book by him/her because

   _____

   _____

   _____ .

5. I am going to recommend this book to _____

   because _____

   _____

   _____ .

to other readers. This reinforces students' use of critical judgment about their
reading within the context of sharing in a learning community.

   To encourage students to explore genres other than those they usually
read, teachers might prepare lists of books on particular topics and match student interests with a variety of books, stories, and poems. For example, if a
student reads only nonfiction about sports, especially basketball, the teacher
might put together an introductory list of books, stories, and poems such as
the following:

Genre Record

Novels: *The Moves Make the Man* by Bruce Brooks
   Chinese Handcuffs by Chris Crutcher
Short Story: "Ain't God Good to Indiana!" by John Tunis
Poems: "The Ex-Basketball Player" by John Updike
   "Jump Shot" by Richard Peck

The teacher then prepares a checklist like the following:

Genre Checklist

Date Finished

_____   *The Moves Make the Man* by Bruce Brooks

_____   "Ain't God Good to Indiana!" by John Tunis

_____   "The Ex-Basketball Player" by John Updike

_____   "Jump Shot" by Richard Peck

_____   *Chinese Handcuffs* by Chris Crutcher

_____

_____

_____

_____

Literature Involvement Strategy

Discussion Prompts

Learning partners and members of the S^3 Groups often need a structure to initiate their discussion of books. Sometimes they have too much to say, other times they don't know what to say. This strategy is based upon the work of J. A. Appleyard (1990). He categorizes three types of responses that he found when questioning adolescents about their reading. We use their responses as prompts for discussion. The prompts take three forms: 1) those that help students frame their sense of involvement and identification with a work; 2) those that give students a sense of how "real" the story is; and 3) those that evoke thoughtful responses from them. These prompts can also be used in their literature response or dialogue journals to stimulate writing. This dual use of the prompts for discussion and writing demonstrates the interrelation of the two.

Discussion prompts are as follows:

- "It was just like I was there because . . ."

- "It could have been written about me because . . ."

- "I couldn't get into it because . . ."

- "It was believable because . . ."

- "I know people just like that who . . ."

- "It didn't seem believable because . . ."

- "This book really make me think about . . ."

- "While reading this story, I kept thinking about . . ."

The blanks at the end are for the student to record her or his reading of at least one other novel, short story, and poem about basketball or sports in general.

Implementing a new classroom structure and creating a new environment for learning, while hard work and fraught with possibilities for unforeseen challenges and complications, are often the catalysts teachers and students need for a revitalized interest in learning. In the next chapter, we explore how teachers can make discussions and writing come alive for students.

Sharing the Connection

Under the Hawthorn Tree
Marita Conlon-McKenna

This book was a surprise since I never dreamed I would enjoy historical fiction so much! I couldn't believe how it captured my heart. It showed feelings and emotions of the life and times of people during the potato famine in Ireland in the 1840's. It's a story about survival, strength, determination, and family. Great book!

Ellen Terry, student

Summary

A four-pronged instructional framework provides a way to structure and organize classrooms for students to have a range of experiences with young adult literature that meet their diverse needs. The four approaches are as follows: Classroom Learning Community (CLC), Student Sharing and Study Groups (S³ Groups), Learning Partners, and Individual Learning. Additional ideas and strategies assist teachers in developing plans for other aspects of classroom organization and management such as grading and portfolio assessment.

Suggested Activities

1. In your journal, reflect on your own experiences with various approaches to classroom organization. What have you found to be most effective, and why?

2. Use the Literature Involvement Strategy, "Discussion Prompts," with the young adult literature you are reading.

3. Develop and use some form of book chart or record using the examples provided in this chapter as models.

4. Form a learning partnership with another person in the class to share the books you are reading. If you are teaching, develop a plan for implementing part or all of the instructional framework in your classroom.

CHAPTER 10

Improving Classroom Interaction: Making Discussion and Writing Real

Yes, indeed. Two whole days to devote to the revision of my paper. . . .
I picture myself leaping from the roof with a heartbreaking wail of despair.
"Well," says the policeman, rising from an examination of my broken body,
holding the note he has found with my trembling hands. "It's as I thought.
American literature has claimed another victim."

Brock Cole, *Celine*

Journal Writing: Responding

How does discussion help you understand your feelings and clarify your thinking about a selection you are reading? How does writing help you understand your feelings and clarify your thinking about a selection you are reading?

Involving students with literature depends on using teaching methods that help students be active participants in their own learning. Research demonstrates repeatedly that classroom lectures are among the least effective ways to make students active learners. As teachers look to heightened involvement in reading and responding to literature, they seek ways to provide students with opportunities for authentic learning interactions and to involve students directly and positively in their learning. In this chapter we discuss two primary ways to accomplish these goals: through providing students opportunities for meaningful classroom discussions and for meaningful writing experiences.

Responding Through Discussions

Effective discussions can help students develop higher-level thinking skills. But frequently what is labeled discussion is actually recitation. Alvermann et al. (1987) describe three characteristics of discussion: "Discussants should put forth multiple points of view and stand ready to change their minds about the matter under discussion; students should interact with one another as well as with the teacher; and the interaction should exceed the typical two or three word phrase units common to recitation lessons" (p. 7). Class discussions are not random activities. They are the product of careful planning and structure. Students must feel that they are getting valuable insights and information from class discussions if they are to participate in a meaningful way.

There is no one set approach or model for framing a discussion about literature. Involving students will depend in part on their own initial connection with a work. However, taking them beyond that initial response by helping them see others' responses, insights, and reactions requires that whole-class or small-group discussions be structured in a way that will provide opportunities for new understandings.

Discussion Model

Planning for a class discussion incorporates the principles of the Young Adult Reader Involvement Model introduced in Chapter 5: the phases of initiating, connecting, and internalizing and the dimension of sharing. For class discussion, teachers can follow a simple three-step format: setting the stage, creating a dialogue, and extending the learning activities. (See Figure 10.1.) The first step is setting the stage. This is a crucial stage because teachers need to "hook" their students right from the beginning of any discussion. If teachers do not accomplish this, students will lack focus and not be prepared to move on to more in-depth responding and thinking. In this initial stage of discussion, the teacher directs the class so that students respond by giving general reactions to their reading. The initial springboard might be a statement specific to the work being discussed. Or, it might be accomplished by using either broad, general questions or statements such as the following:

One character I really liked was . . .

One character I really disliked was . . .

When I was reading, I thought about . . .

The part that I liked best about the book (story/poem) was . . .

The part that I liked least about the book (story/poem) was . . .

Other statements and questions can be developed according to the elements of the work that the teacher establishes for students' focus.

Literature Involvement Strategy

Be a Critic

This strategy is popular with students as a replacement for traditional book reports. Teachers distribute reviews of books that are familiar to their students as models. (Or a review of a popular movie that many of the students have seen might be used.) The models should illustrate that critics have different styles or various approaches and tones. Students then become critics and write a book review, selecting a style from the models. They are not simply to rehash the plot but to make judgments about the quality of the book and decide whether or not to recommend it to their classmates. Students focus on the strongest and weakest elements of the book and develop a rating scale for their review.

For example, statements might focus on theme, tone, conflict, or any other literary element or on other aspects of students' reactions. At this stage, the teacher helps students begin to articulate their reactions to their reading. The questions and statements should be general and open-ended enough for students to express their reactions rather than try to guess what the "right" answer is.

The second step involves a two-way communication of a dialogue or "grand conversation" about books. At this point, students are encouraged to begin an in-depth exploration of their reading. James Moffett (1986) discusses the significance of dialogues:

> One of the unique qualities of dialogue is that the interlocutors build on each other's constructions. A conversation is verbal collaboration. Each party borrows words and phrases and structures from the other, recombines them, adds to them, and elaborates them. . . . Inseparable from this verbal collaboration is the accompanying cognitive collaboration. A conversation is dialogical—a meeting and fusion of minds even if speakers disagree. (p. 73)

The fusion that Moffett mentions creates a powerful change in the classroom environment. It ensures that, through dialogues, students and teachers share and communicate in ways they have not previously used. Through this type of communication, a new mutual respect evolves. Students gain a sense of being valued and listened to as seldom happens in traditional classes in which the teacher is the ultimate authority. Participating in dialogues also provides students with opportunities for critical aesthetic responses to literature, combining both cognitive and affective responses. The teachers' role as expert guides/reading coaches is significant as they plan a variety of experiences and activities to involve their students in a thoughtful dialogue. The Brown Literature Response Model, discussed later in this chapter, is an approach for creating just such a variety of experiences for students.

The third step is extending the learning activities. These are individual, small-group, or whole-class activities to engage students through further discussion, writing activities, group exploration, or other types of activities designed to improve students' conceptual understanding and critical thinking. In a Classroom Learning Community, the follow-up activities may be devised

---

Sharing the Connection

Jurassic Park
Michael Crichton

Jurassic Park really grabbed me! I had seen the movie and my mom said the book was better than the movie. Also, I was interested by the majestic title and the picture on the cover. The idea of recreating dinosaurs and how everything went wrong was interesting and I wanted to find out what happened. Having kids as the main characters made it more interesting, too.

Nathan Decker, student

and orchestrated by students as well as teachers. For example, one student or group might enjoy a book by a particular author and choose to read more of the author's work; another might seek to explore the perspective on technology in a particular work of science fiction; another, facing a family crisis, might seek comfort and understanding by reading books that speak to that problem. Students or groups might then share with the class their reactions to the new book or books. Additionally, a number of other learning experiences may be structured to provide in-depth and personalized learning. For example, students can explore ideas and extend their study of literature by doing creative projects, such as creating videos, quilts, and collages, among others.

Responding Through Writing

Responding to literature through writing is an integral part of the Young Adult Reading Involvement Model. Vacca and Linek (1992) state: "To find meaning and purpose in learning, students must be encouraged to think about what they are learning—and therein lies the power of writing" (p. 145). Much of students' writing may be informal writing in a journal or as part of a portfolio. For example, students may jot down their initial impressions and expectations or engage in making predictions before they begin reading a selection. They may make brief notes of things they want to explore or remember while they are reading. They may write reflections after reading to record their reactions

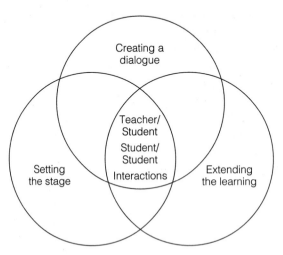

Figure 10.1   Discussion Model

to the selection or in preparation for whole-class or group discussions. They may take notes during a discussion and then write a more lengthy reflection to clarify and extend their ideas and feelings. They may respond in writing to their Learning Partner or members of their S³ Group through dialogue journals. They may make plans in writing for creative projects or for more formal kinds of writing. Teachers can encourage a "pen-in-hand" (Devine, 1987, p. 53) attitude toward informal writing that helps students come to depend on it as a natural and indispensable tool for learning.

Journal responding is a free form of informal, personal writing with no restrictions on spelling and mechanics. Hancock (1992), in her work with students using literature response journals, makes these observations: "Readers do reflect on their lives while encountering a text. The literature response journal provides the freedom and flexibility of revealing those personal reflections as they occur throughout the book" (p. 40), and "The literature response . . . is a treasure chest filled with spontaneous thoughts and ideas that otherwise would have been forgotten" (p. 41).

There are a number of different types of journal writing. Brown, Phillips, and Stephens (1993) describe a response journal approach in the following way:

> The response journal is relatively prescriptive. Students use their journal to react or respond to their reading. The journal is not used for taking reading notes; rather, it is for students to interact with their reading. In this way they are responding to the work and putting it in a context that has meaning for them. The teacher may be directive and "assign" students to focus on a particular aspect of their reading, or the teacher may leave the assignment open-ended for students to use as a process of discovery. (p. 74)

Some students are able to respond freely in a journal with little or no direct assistance from the teacher; in fact, they may find prescribed topics inhibiting and intrusive, taking the personal elements of connecting and ownership away from them. Other students, however, need teacher guidance, particularly in the beginning. They may need help to move from factual retellings and simplistic, affective responses to more in-depth responses. In providing guidance, however, teachers must guard against the journal's becoming a place to respond to teacher-developed questions or assignments. Examples of prompts that some teachers use are

The character [name] reminds me of . . .

The plot in this story seems realistic/unrealistic because . . .

I wonder why the author . . .

When I think about this book, I am reminded of . . .

To me, the most important thing that happens in this book is . . . because . . .

This story makes me feel . . .

If I could change something in this story, it would be . . . because . . .

For literature response journal writing to be successful in a classroom, students must perceive it as a useful and valuable activity. They must have specific opportunities to use it in a variety of instructional settings, such as the ones we describe in Chapter 9. One of the most powerful motivators for journal writing is to have someone else read and react to it. Teachers use a variety of different approaches to provide feedback, such as teacher-to-student on a weekly or rotating basis or student-to-student (Learning Partner) on a daily or semi-weekly basis. Brief, supportive, nonjudgmental comments combined with questions sincerely seeking additional information or clarification are the most effective approaches.

We believe that all readers can benefit from journal writing experiences. Such experiences help readers respond to literature as they record their reactions, feelings, thoughts, ideas, reflections, and opinions. A journal is a place to construct meaning, to be introspective, and to note important ideas

---

Bridging

Exploring the Holocaust

The Holocaust is one of the most painful chapters of modern history. However, from this tragic time comes a body of literature that reaffirms humanity. Traditionally, many literature anthologies have included the nonfiction work The Diary of Anne Frank. Anne's story of her life hiding in an attic from the Nazis is memorable both for her insights and because it is true. In recent years a number of other outstanding books—both fiction and nonfiction—have been written. Notable works of nonfiction that can be used are Milton Meltzer's Rescue: The Story of How Gentiles Saved Jews in the Holocaust and Renee Roth-Hano's Touch Wood: A Girl-hood in Occupied France. These books might be used with novels such as Lois Lowry's Newbery Award-Winning Number the Stars, Jane Yolen's The Devil's Arithmetic, and Ida Vos's Hide and Seek and its sequel, Anna Is Still Here. Another dimension of this tragic period is revealed in Robert Innocenti's Rose Blanche, the story of a young girl who shares her food with others imprisoned in a concentration camp outside her town. Using a combination of these books provides both a bridge between fiction and nonfiction and also a bridge between English language arts and social studies classes.

and interesting language. The data in the journal become a source for sharing, for discussions, for projects, and for formal writing experiences.

Formal writing also plays an important part in responding to literature. Formal writing is a finished product that the student publishes, or makes available to others. Traditionally, formal writing about literature focused on analytical papers designed to demonstrate that students understood the theory and interpretation they had been taught. Current trends shift the emphasis in formal writing away from a critical analysis of literature to writing that allows students to explore their responses to the literature. Fitzgerald (1992) examines recent research that indicates "having various opportunities for extended writing in response to reading stories is likely to enrich students' interpretations of what they read" (p. 90).

Sharing the Connection

The Devil's Arithmetic
Jane Yolen

This book is a real attention grabber. This book made me think about how the world is today rather than in the '40's. People still today are treated unfairly. After reading this book I felt sorry for the Jewish families who were separated, killed, and punished. I almost felt angry, too. I was mad at the people who had done this terrible thing. I think all young adults should read this book. It greatly enriched my understanding of the Jewish Holocaust.

Eric Gorney, student

Brown Literature Response Model

The Brown Literature Response Model* is designed to heighten students' involvement with literature. The model is a five-step approach to guide students to respond in a variety of cognitive and affective ways. The Brown Literature Response Model reflects the belief that students react to their reading both by thinking and by feeling. By using the various steps in the model, students have opportunities to express their thoughts and their emotions about a work. The five levels of the model are designed to describe ways in which

---

* The Brown Literature Response Model was presented initially as "A Taxonomy of Literary Understanding" in *A Two-Way Street: Integrating Reading and Writing in the Middle School* and *A Two-Way Street: Integrating Reading and Writing in the Secondary School,* eds. J. E. Brown, B. Quirk, and E. C. Stephens (Rochester, Mich.: Michigan Council of Teachers of English, 1988). Both books are available from the National Council of Teachers of English.

students may examine their responses to reading; they are not designed to pre-
scribe how students *should* react to a particular work. Inquiry, using the
Response Model, leads to greater conceptual understanding rather than
teacher interrogation. The model provides a structure of varied activities and
questions to elicit different types of understanding about literature from students through writing as well as discussion. Using a literature exploration
strategy such as this one is not a lock-step approach that teachers must follow
rigidly. It is a guide for developing a number of experiences, activities, and
questions through class discussion and writing to help students to look at
a work from a number of different perspectives, including the aesthetic.
Cianciolo and Quirk (1993) state:

> Critical aesthetic response to literature as art consists of the awareness
> and appreciation of cognitive and affective experiences evoked by the
> elements of a story (poem, drama, literary biography), the ability to criti-
> cally evaluate literary works of art according to criteria and characteristics
> defined over time and by the traditions of a specific culture, as well as the
> ability to recognize the beautiful in the selections and to prefer the beauti-
> ful in it in terms of individual taste. (p. 15)

One use of the Response Model was presented in Brown, Phillips, and
Stephens's *Toward Literacy: Theory and Applications for Teaching Writing in
the Content Areas* (1993). This use focuses on an application of the model as a
strategy for developing questions. Certainly, this is a legitimate use; however, it
is not the primary or exclusive intended use. In fact, we caution against the
over-reliance of any questioning strategy. Any strategy can be counterproductive to eliciting authentic responses from students because they may become
focused on trying to determine what the teacher wants and fail to explore their
own responses. The art of asking questions about literature is to be open-
ended enough so that the questions encourage students' reflection. This open-
endedness should appear in prompts for students' writing as well as in discussion questions. Classroom discussions based on specific questioning strategies
are frequently too prescriptive for students to explore books in ways that are
enlightening and fulfilling for them. Too often, questioning in the classroom
becomes an interrogation, with students feeling that they must try to meet a
teacher's unspoken agenda. Frager (1993) discusses the limiting effect of
purely cognitive post-reading activities:

> Many methods for helping teachers improve classroom discussions focus
> on cognitive levels of teacher questions and student responses, such as
> using *Bloom's Taxonomy of Educational Objectives: The Cognitive Domain*

(1956). While cognitive analyses of after-reading activities have significant value, much also can be gained by looking at the affective dimensions of the social relationships among teachers and students in these activities. (p. 620)

Figure 10.2 and the following discussion of the five levels of the Brown Literature Response Model previously appeared in Brown, Phillips, and Stephens's *Toward Literacy: Theory and Applications for Teaching Writing in the Content Areas* (1993).

At the Factual level, students simply relate the facts of a work. At this level, students demonstrate the most basic kind of understanding or comprehension of a work. This level provides a purely cognitive interaction with the work. A written response confined exclusively to the factual level would be similar to a newspaper article.

On the Empathetic level, students have the opportunity to relate to the characters and their situations. In this way, students are able to put themselves in the place of the characters and to realize how the characters must feel. In recent years, many basal readers and literature anthologies have included questions that ask students to "put themselves" in a character's position. Seeking this type of understanding provides students with the opportunity to relate literature to their own lives. In this way, they are able to translate the abstraction of the printed page to a concrete experience. These responses are affective and allow students to make a subjective connection with the characters and their situations.

The Analytical level requires a close reading of a work and an examination of its components. This level represents the most frequently used approach to the study of literature in the majority of English classes. Through analytic examination of a work, students are helped to understand character development, symbolism, theme, tone, and character motivation. This approach is cognitive.

The title of the Sympathetic level describes the type of response teachers seek to elicit from their students. At this level, students are expected to be able

Level 1	Factual	Cognitive
Level 2	Empathetic	Affective
Level 3	Analytical	Cognitive
Level 4	Sympathetic	Affective
Level 5	Critical	Cognitive/Affective

Figure 10.2   The Brown Literature Response Model

to react to the situations, the triumphs, and the defeats of the characters in a sympathetic way. Teachers seek to engender in students feelings of compassion regardless of whether students agree with characters' actions or share characters' value systems. This compassion can lead students to understand why characters act as they do and have sympathy for the effects and consequences of those actions. Students frequently have more difficulty in being sympathetic than in being empathetic. True compassion may be difficult for students to express because of their own limited life experiences. At this level, students are helped to go beyond the subjective, empathetic identification with the plight of the characters. They are asked to feel sympathy for and to understand problems that they have not necessarily experienced themselves. Compassion, however, is an abstract feeling that is more difficult for students to experience than empathy is. This difficulty is the result of students' inability to respond to another's plight without putting themselves in the situation, and their own limited experiences prevent them from understanding problems they have not experienced. This level encourages students to react affectively to their reading and to project concern beyond their own experiences. One student distinguished the Sympathetic level from the Empathetic level by recognizing that sympathy is a social awareness, whereas empathy is a personal response. The Sympathetic level may be recognized as a type of social contract in which an individual is able to suspend his or her subjective reactions in order to understand another's experience, action, or reaction.

The Critical level elicits a demonstrated understanding of the value or worth of the work and represents the last level of the Brown Literature Response Model. It involves students in an interpretative examination of the value or merit of a work. At this level, students are asked to identify the relationship of the author/speaker to the work and to make judgments and projections about its value and worth. This level combines both cognitive and affective understanding.

Affective Responses to Literature

Affective connections, by their very nature, necessitate an emotional interaction with a text. The levels of Empathy and Sympathy in the Literature Response Model seek to provide readers with opportunities to examine, discuss, and share their feelings about books and their personal connections with literature. The Sympathetic level allows readers to observe and understand that which they have never experienced by helping them to gain a perspective about the challenges and trials of others.

The Empathetic level provides a vehicle for readers to view their own experiences in connection with the experiences of characters that they read about. The concept of empathy was examined in a broader context by author Bruce Brooks, speaking at the 1993 ALAN Workshop of the National Council of Teachers of English in Pittsburgh. Although the Literature Response Model examines the empathy that readers have for characters, Brooks presented a different perspective as he discussed a reciprocity of empathy. He believes that an author uses imagination to create a sense of empathy, not for the characters in a work, but for the reader who encounters them. He talked about the spontaneous movement of the imagination to inhabit another life, or as he said: "a leap of imagination to share experience, to realize 'I'm curious about that person's life.'" Essentially, what Brooks explores is the ability of the author to reach out to readers and to transport them to experience the feelings that the author has created through words. Brooks believes that the connection between the author and reader is significant: "What is important is how I make you feel about the scene." The importance of the connection makes reading relevant. The significance of Brooks's reflections is his focus on the involvement and connection among the author, the reader, and the experience of reading. He also advocates that teachers help readers observe and analyze how the author has influenced the readers' response; in other words, teachers should help students explore the question, "What is it that the author does with language to create certain moods and reactions?" This type of interaction and reflection will heighten students' involvement with and understanding of the work and of themselves.

Application of the Brown Literature Response Model

The Brown Literature Response Model can be taught to students to help them become aware of a structure for exploring different types of responses to literature. By teaching students about the levels of the Response Model, teachers help them realize that there are a variety of ways to respond to their reading. Students can use and adapt the Response Model for exploring literature; it is a framework for thinking about books, characters and their actions.

Classroom Learning Community During whole-class learning, the Response Model can be used as a discussion springboard with statements generated at each level or at specific levels to elicit students' responses. These statements may be generated by either the teacher or the students. Furthermore, the statements may serve as a springboard for discussion or for writing. For example, the teacher might have students identify what they believe the conflict of the book to be (an analysis activity). As students report their responses, they might discuss how they felt as they encountered the elements of conflict and resolution. Their feelings might be characterized as empathetic or sympathetic or possibly critical, depending on the degree and type of involvement that they felt with their reading.

Student Sharing and Study Groups   In S³ Groups, students have an even greater say in shaping the direction of group exploration and discussion. For example, students might grapple with the differences between empathetic and sympathetic responses by sharing their reactions to different characters. They might also explore the critical level of responses and establish criteria for evaluating the books in a particular unit. Another type of activity is to have students articulate similarities and differences in the settings of two recently read books. This analysis activity could be facilitated by developing a comparison/contrast diagram as in Figure 10.3. Each book in this example—Theodore Taylor's *The Cay* and Elizabeth Speare's *Sign of the Beaver*—has its own circle in which individual elements are listed. Similarities between the two are listed in the overlapping areas. Comparison/contrast diagrams will be described more fully as a teaching/learning strategy in Chapter 11.

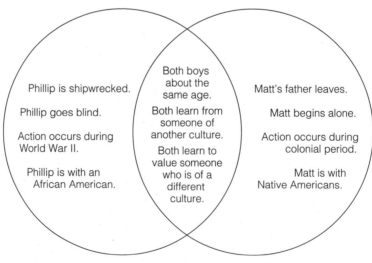

Figure 10.3   Comparison/Contrast Diagram

Learning Partners   One application of the Brown Literature Response Model is that students use it as the basis for writing about their reading in their response journals. With a framework of five types of responses, students can explore their reactions and decide how they wish to respond. For example, partners might discuss whether a book elicited primarily a cognitive or affective response from them and determine why they responded as they did.

Individual Learning   The Brown Literature Response Model provides support for students exploring literature on their own with minimal involvement and guidance from their teacher. For independent study, the Response Model provides a useful framework for helping students examine their responses and make determinations about them. One type of independent study is that which is undertaken by a student who has developed a particular interest in the work of one particular author and wishes to do an extensive study of that author's work. For example, a reader might wish to explore and examine the saga of the Tillerman family in Cynthia Voigt's books. The reader may identify the major events in Dicey's life and indicate the changes she goes through. This could be accomplished in a character chart (see Figure 10.4) in which major challenges and events are listed in a column in the left side of the paper and the actions taken by the character in the middle column. The third column is

Character Chart		
Challenges	Actions	Insights

Figure 10.4   Character Chart

reserved for exploring insights about the evolution of the character. A chart of this sort can be designed to reflect any aspect of the Response Model. In Figure 10.4, students would analyze what the character did in the column labeled "Actions." In the column labeled "Insights," students might respond critically or even empathetically.

The Response Model in Action

The purpose of the Brown Literature Response Model is to provide a framework for teachers to begin combining cognitive and affective responses to literature. The following examples apply the Response Model to books frequently used in the schools. On the middle school level, the model is applied to Zibby Oneal's *The Language of Goldfish* and on the secondary level to *Z for Zachariah* by Robert C. O'Brien. The exploration of both of these books begins with an excerpt from one of the *A Two-Way Street* books published in 1988 by the Michigan Council of Teachers of English. The excerpts include questions at each level of the Literature Response Model and some general writing activities. We have added additional experiences and activities that might also involve students with these two books.

The Language of Goldfish
Zibby Oneal

Questions for Discussion/Pre-writing*

Level 1: Factual Level
Who is Carrie's best friend?
Where does Carrie go after school every day after Christmas vacation?
Who is Mrs. Ramsey?

Level 2: Empathetic Level
How do you suppose Carrie felt when she had one of her spells?
Carrie's mother appears to deny what has happened. Carrie was surprised that she had talked to Mrs. Ramsey about it. How would you feel if you were Carrie?
Carrie felt that everything in her life was changing and that she had no control over the changes. How does it feel to lose control?

---

* Questions and writing activities are from A *Two-Way Street: Integrating Reading and Writing in the Middle School* (1988), p. 51–52

Level 3: Analytical Level
What do the goldfish represent to Carrie?
Why wasn't Carrie's mother able to talk about what happened?
Where is Carrie's island? What does it represent to her?

Level 4: Sympathetic Level
How did Carrie feel about going to the eighth-grade dances?
How does she feel about the changes in her relationship with Moira?
Why did she go to the last dance in June?

Level 5: Critical Level
What does Oneal tell us about Carrie through her art work?
What alternatives to taking the pills might Carrie have had?
How does her relationship with Mrs. Ramsey help Carrie to face change and accept it?

Writing Activities*
When you were younger, did you have a special place where you could go? If so, describe it and discuss what it was like when you spent time there.
Discuss three incidents that happened to Carrie when she returned to school after Christmas vacation that helped her accept growing up.
Carrie learned about both art and friendship from Mrs. Ramsey. Imagine that you are Carrie at the end of the book and write a letter to Mrs. Ramsey about how things have changed.

Learning Activities
(Specific directions for some of the following learning activities can be found in the next section of this chapter and in Chapter 11)

Level 1: Factual Level
Prepare a book talk illustrated by a book jacket that you have created.

Level 2: Empathetic Level
Select a scene from the book in which one character demonstrates his or her feelings or reactions. Act the scene out either with your Learning Partner or in your S³ Groups.

Level 3: Analytical Level
Complete a relationship chart showing the interactions among Carrie, her mother, her father, Moira, and Mrs. Ramsey.

Level 4: Sympathetic Level
Have Carrie write a letter to her sister, explaining how she feels about not being close to her any longer.

Level 5: Critical Level
Design a creative project (art, drama, music, crafts, among others) to represent what goldfish symbolize for you.

(Continued)

Z for Zachariah
Robert O'Brien

Questions for Discussion/Pre-writing*

Level 1: Factual Level

How was Ann able to survive without the help of her family?

How did Ann's family die?

What types of information and advice did Loomis give Ann that helped her with her chores?

Level 2: Empathetic Level

Could you have survived as well as Ann did? Why or why not?

What do you think was the greatest thing that Ann lost? Why? What do you value that you might lose in a nuclear war?

What personality traits and characteristics do you share with Ann? Are these traits and characteristics you think would aid survival? Support your answer.

Level 3: Analytical Level

Why did Ann believe others survived the contamination?

What was ironic about how Loomis became ill?

How did the diary narration build the suspense in the novel?

Level 4: Sympathetic Level

What types of things made Ann remember and grieve for her parents? Why do you think this is so?

Did Loomis feel guilty about killing Edward? What types of feelings did he have about the incident?

How did Ann feel when Faro returned? Why were her feelings so mixed?

Level 5: Critical Level

What does the author lead the reader to think about the probability of nuclear war and total destruction?

Who does the author think is likely to survive a nuclear fallout?

According to some statements in the book, of what use does the author think the military will be in the event of nuclear war?

Writing Activities*

Research your area's chances for survival in a nuclear war. Is there a plan your area or you personally could use to guard against total annihilation?

If you have seen a TV program or other types of movies that deal with life after a nuclear war, how does this book compare? Is this book more or less realistic? Which medium caused you to care more for the characters? Why?

Write what you think happened to Ann's family when they left the valley.

(Continued)

---

*From *A Two-Way Street: Integrating Reading
and Writing in the Secondary School* (1988), pp. 110–11

Learning Activities
(Specific directions for some of the following learning activities can be found in the next section of this chapter or Chapter 11)

Level 1: Factual Level
Use a comparison/contrast diagram to see similarities and differences between Ann and Loomis.

Level 2: Empathetic Level
Do a trading places exercise in which you choose to be either Ann or Loomis.

Level 3: Analytical Level
Choosing one of the two characters, do a character map.

Level 4: Sympathetic Level
Imagine that you are Robert C. O'Brien, the author of *Z for Zachariah*. Describe Ann's life during the next five days after she leaves the valley. Examine what she finds and how she feels about her experiences.

Level 5: Critical Level
With your Learning Partner, complete an opinion guide that presents your position, Ann's position, and Loomis's position.

Figure 10.5 lists the thinking processes that students use at each level.

Factual Level
Describing
Recalling
Comprehending
Relating Facts
Comparing
Stating Main Ideas

Empathetic Level
Imagining
Inventing
Projecting
Identifying with Characters
Identifying with Situations

Analytical Level
Inferring
Supporting Generalizations

Identifying Motives
Applying Literary Terms
Solving Problems
Predicting
Synthesizing

Sympathetic Level
Reacting
Relating to Characters
Responding
Perceiving

Critical Level
Evaluating
Judging
Interpreting
Speculating

Figure 10.5   Thinking Processes at Each Level

Talking with Russell Freedman

For me a good idea is a subject that excites my interest, a subject that I want to learn more about myself. Writing a book satisfies my own itch to know.

Selected Titles

Children of the Wild West

Cowboys of the Wild West

Eleanor Roosevelt: A Life of Discovery

Franklin Delano Roosevelt

Immigrant Kids

Indian Chiefs

An Indian Winter

Kids at Work: Lewis Hine and the Crusade Against Child Labor

Lincoln: A Photobiography

The Wright Brothers: How They Invented the Airplane

Russell Freedman grew up in San Francisco and served in the Korean War. Early in his career, he worked as a reporter and editor for the Associated Press and then as a publicity writer for several network television shows. He now lives in New York City, where he is a full-time writer. He is author of more than 40 books, many of them award winning, on a wide variety of subjects from animal behavior to history. Lincoln: A Photobiography is the winner of the Newbery Medal and ALA's Best of the 80's as well as numerous other awards. Among the awards that Franklin Delano Roosevelt received is the NCTE Orbis Pictus Award and ALA Best Book for Young Adults. Eleanor Roosevelt: A Life of Discovery is a Newbery Honor Book and received the Golden Kite Award.

I try to write books that lots of people will want to read willingly and with pleasure. I want students to read my books because they are interested in the subject, not because they have to write school assignments. Young people are a great audience to write for because they're so receptive and so appreciative. No author could have a better audience. The books you write for these readers will be with them for the rest of their lives. Often your book might be the first that they have ever read on that

Discussion and Writing Strategies

In this section, we describe additional strategies to use for writing and discussions. These may be used with the Brown Literature Response Model or independent of it. The goal of each of the strategies is to facilitate student involvement with and sharing of literature.

particular subject. They will come to it with an open mind and great expectations. Because you're writing for such an impressionable audience, there is no form of literature that is more powerful or influential. You have a readership that really wants to learn something. It is a very heavy responsibility, but it is also an exhilarating challenge.

I can't remember a time when I didn't want to write. I had the good luck to grow up in a house filled with books and the lively conversation of visiting authors. I knew all along that I wanted to be a writer like those strange and wonderful men and women who sat at our dinner table and exchanged incredible stories. The first book I wrote was the result of an article I read in the *New York Times* about a sixteen-year-old blind boy who had invented a Braille typewriter. That article aroused my curiosity, curiosity led to research, and research revealed that a surprising number of young

people had earned a place in history before they were twenty years old, including Louis Braille, who also was blind and sixteen when he perfected the Braille system. That gave me the idea for my first book, which was *Teenagers Who Made History*. It was a very successful book and so I woke up one morning and said, "I'm an author of a book for young people and I can do it and I'm going to do the next one."

Since I write nonfiction, my books require quite a bit of research. For my Lincoln biography, I followed the Lincoln trail from his log cabin birthplace in Kentucky to Ford's Theater in Washington, D.C., and the rooming house across the street where the President died. There is something magical about being able to lay your eyes on the real thing, something you can't get from reading alone. When I wrote about Lincoln, I could picture the scenes in my mind's eye. Much of my research is

Continued

Adding and Subtracting Meaning

Adding and subtracting meaning is a process that promotes a close reading of a short passage of a novel, poem, document, or other work of literature that might have numerous meanings. This approach is most effectively used for whole-class instruction because it includes brainstorming that is more

Talking with Russell Freedman (continued)

searching for archival photographs. It is a real thrill! There is something about seeing an old photograph that evokes a sense of history in a way that nothing else can. I feel very fortunate that I have been able to spend my working life writing books on subjects that interest me. I want to convey my enthusiasm for these subjects to the reader and I want to convey my point of view. Good nonfiction writing has to be factually accurate, but it never can be totally objective. There is no such thing as total objectivity. I believe that an author's personal vision of the material should come through in a nonfiction book. I think of myself as a storyteller, not in the sense of inventing scenes or imaginary people and events, but in the sense of using story-telling techniques to ignite the reader's imagination. It is important to dramatize factual accounts of history; it's important for readers to picture people and events and to hear people talking.

Starting a new book is a lot like trying to solve a puzzle. You have to decide what to include and what to leave out, what to emphasize, where and how to balance facts and interpretations, and how to breathe life into the subject. People spend so much time with television, which tends to per-

petuate stereotypes. A stereotype is alienating—it makes it even more difficult to understand the experiences of others. A good nonfiction book should help to dispel stereotypes and make it easier for the reader to understand the experiences of others.

I work seven or eight hours a day or maybe longer. I don't take weekends off and not many public holidays. I always work on three projects at a time. I have "mopping up exercises" on the last book, I have a "frontal assault" on the current book, and I am gathering material for the next book. I am thinking about three books at a time, but eighty to ninety percent of my time is on the current book. I am working on it in my mind twenty-four hours a day; I even dream about it. I spent one year going to bed with Eleanor Roosevelt every night and waking up with her in the morning! When I finish a book, I take three to seven weeks off, go to "Timbuktu," and then I start the next book.

I receive many letters, but my favorite is from a boy in Indiana. He wrote, "I liked your biography of Abraham Lincoln very much. Did you take the photographs yourself?"

effective with students' varied input. The process is simple. The teacher reveals the title of a selection and has students speculate about the meaning. The students are encouraged to generate as many ideas as possible. As is the case with any brainstorming activity, students are encouraged to be creative and to take risks, which depends on a supportive classroom atmosphere.

After students have generated as many possible meanings for the title as they can, the teacher then reveals the first sentence of the selection (or line of a poem, if a poem is being used). Once again students brainstorm possible meanings. This process continues until enough of the selection has been revealed that the group can take another look at all responses and start to make judgments about them. Class consensus determines whether or not a response will be eliminated. The responses that are no longer plausible are eliminated; ones for which there is not enough information remain, as do those responses that have been confirmed by the text itself. This process continues until all extraneous responses have been eliminated and the remaining responses are a viable interpretation. This process works particularly well with poetry.

Readers Theatre

Readers Theatre provides an approach that will involve students with the experience of literature: they will be involved with hearing it as well as talking and writing about it. In readers theatre, a script is presented based on the dialogue between two characters in a work. Though fiction is most frequently used, poetry and nonfiction can also be adapted. Initially, the scripts for readers theatre in the classroom are developed by the teacher. As students understand the language and interaction of characters, they can then work either individually or in small groups to develop more scripts. Latrobe and Laughlin (1989) suggest that "in order to reproduce the text through voice and bodily interpretation of emotions, the reader must experience the author's intention and comprehend fully the meaning of the entire literary work" (p. 3). The close reading that is required in doing readers theatre helps students become more intensely involved. Also, an effective readers theatre selection can encourage students to read the entire book. The process of selecting material for scripts necessitates that students read closely and critically. They also gain an understanding of the artistry of a work and an aesthetic appreciation for it as they develop scripts. Hearing a scene from a work read without props or actions helps students concentrate on a scene's meaning and what it reveals about characters. It is also an effective tool to involve students in discussions about what they have experienced.

A valuable resource for teachers is *Readers Theatre for Young Adults: Scripts and Script Development* by Kathy Howard Latrobe and Mildred Knight Laughlin. Scripts and suggestions for script development are available in other content areas, such as social studies.

Bridging

Bridging a YA Novel with Nonfiction

The period of the Civil War evokes interest even today. Two recent works of nonfiction provide readers with an effective factual background. Jim Murphy's The Boys' War and Russell Freedman's Lincoln: A Photobiography serve as an appropriate bridge to Ann Rinaldi's The Last Silk Dress.

Booktalks

Booktalks are an effective way to have students share books they have been reading independently with their classmates. They also are an important avenue for communicating the power and excitement of reading young adult literature. Joni Bodart (1980, 1985, 1988, 1992, 1993) in her five volumes of booktalks describes how teachers and librarians can use booktalks to introduce students to new books and to interest them in topics and books they may never have considered. We recommend that initially teachers model for their students how to give a booktalk so that it does not become a traditional oral book report.

"A booktalk is not a book review or a book report or a book analysis. It does not judge the book's merits; it assumes the book is good and goes on from there" (Bodart, 1980, p. 2). The purpose of a booktalk is to entice others to read it; it is to create interest, not to tell stories. A booktalk should last five to seven minutes. First, the student shows the book, gives the title, the author's name, and the illustrator's name (if applicable). Second, the student uses any of a number of approaches to tell just enough to encourage others to read the book. This might involve summarizing major events in the book leading up to the climax, or doing a character study of one or more characters, or focusing on a particular aspect of the book, or anything else that will pique the interest of others. Booktalks are especially effective in small groups, such as the S³ Groups. They benefit from flexible scheduling so students can decide when they will talk about their books.

Book Sharing

In Chapter 2 we described a teaching strategy called sentence collecting designed in part to help students gain an appreciation of an author's writing style. Book sharing is an outgrowth of this approach. Book sharing involves students reading aloud passages or sections from their independent reading, primarily in their S³ Groups or with their Learning Partners. The length of the selection is decided by the student and the teacher. The point of this process is to help students recognize the power of language by hearing how authors make characters come alive, transport readers to previously unknown locations, and evoke new feelings and reactions. Book sharing should be an optional activity because of the wide range of reading abilities in most classes. For poorer readers, the thought of having to read in front of peers can be painful, even traumatic. Students should be reminded that their goal is to encourage other students to read the book on their own The success of book sharing depends on two primary factors: a careful, thoughtful selection of the material and reading with clarity and expression. Reading aloud well requires practice and rehearsal.

Trading Places

This strategy helps students identify with and gain insight into characters. It can be used as a preparation for discussion or for a creative project. First, students write about a memorable event in their own lives, such as a challenge they have faced, an embarrassing moment, or a frightening experience. Next, they select a character that they like from their reading and identify the characteristics they admire in that character. Then they imagine that the character has their experience and describe how the character would respond.

Summary

Students can become involved in young adult literature through meaningful classroom discussions and writing experiences. Journal writing experiences help readers to respond to literature by recording reactions, feelings, thoughts, ideas, reflections, and opinions. A journal is a place to construct meaning, to be introspective, and to note important ideas and interesting language. The Brown Literature Response Model is designed to heighten students' involvement with literature. The model is a five-step approach to guide students to respond in a variety of cognitive and affective ways.

Suggested Activities

1. In your journal, reflect on a young adult book you are reading using some of the suggestions on journal writing from this chapter.

Bridging

Bridging a YA Novel with a Classic

Robin Brancato's <u>Winning</u>, Chris Crutcher's <u>Staying Fat for Sarah Byrnes</u>, and Cynthia Voigt's <u>Izzy, Willy-Nilly</u> portray youthful characters who have suffered debilitating injuries. These books serve as bridges for Edith Wharton's classic novel <u>Ethan Frome</u>.

Sharing the Connection

Won't Know Till I Get There
Walter Dean Myers

What a great book! It is a funny, upbeat story with an important message about the similar needs of both youth and the aged for independence, dignity, and respect. Written in the form of journal entries by Steve, a thirteen-year-old African American, this book appealed to all of my students. Frequently, they laughed aloud while reading it and couldn't wait to share portions with each other.

   Wayne Cole, middle school
   reading teacher

2. Use the Literature Involvement Strategy, "Be a Critic," presented in this chapter to write a review of a young adult book you have read.

3. Use the Brown Literature Response Model to develop questions and activities for a young adult novel you have read.

4. Select one of the discussion and writing strategies described in this chapter. Use it with a young adult literature selection you have read. If you are teaching, use one of the strategies with your students.

More Strategies for Using Young Adult Literature

"Winning's a fine thing, Ellie, but it's all the months and years before and after that make you who you are. . . . Grab hold of what your heart wants to tell you, honey, and you'll be one rich young woman."

Joan Bauer, *SQUASHED*

Journal Writing: Responding

Now that you have read a number of works for young adults, identify characteristics of this genre. Reflect on the similarities and differences with more traditional works.

The purpose of this chapter is to provide you with a wealth of teaching strategies to use with young adult literature. These strategies are intended to help you implement the principles of the Reader Involvement Model— that is initiating, connecting, internalizing, and sharing. They are based on the theories of reading as an interactive process and literature as a transactional, aesthetic experience. The strategies in this chapter for using fiction and nonfiction will be presented as they relate to the stages of the Reader Involvement Model, *initiating, connecting, and internalizing.* We begin with strategies that contribute to the initial involvement of readers with a work of fiction.

Strategies for Initiating—Fiction

Reaction and Reflection Statements

Teachers can use several different types of statements with students to set the stage for reading, to focus on important concepts and ideas while reading, and to aid in their internalization after reading. These organizing statements can be used when the entire class is reading the same selection or when students are reading different selections related to a common theme. We suggest using statements more often than questions because questions have been so overused and misused that many students have a negative attitude toward them.

Some teachers, however, are successful in combining reaction and reflection statements with open-ended questions.

Reaction and reflection statements are used to get students thinking about what they will read and to activate their prior knowledge. Students are asked to agree or disagree with a series of statements, usually between three and five, and to participate in a discussion about the statements. They are told that they will be reading material related to these statements and that they will have an opportunity after they read to change their minds, to respond differently to the statements, and even to rewrite the statements. They must, however, take an initial position: "I don't know " is not an acceptable response. The purpose of this is to get students engaged in the reading and to encourage a sense of ownership in the concepts, ideas, and issues being studied. As the students read, they make notes related to the statements. In the post-reading discussion, students use these notes to respond again to the statements.

This strategy works well with the Classroom Learning Community, S³ Groups, and Learning Partners. Crucial to its success are statements that challenge students to think because the statements are thought provoking or controversial. Literal statements that can be easily answered by skimming through the reading material will defeat the purpose of this approach. As students become familiar with reaction and reflection statements, they can create their own in their S³ Groups and with their Learning Partners to help them develop critical thinking skills and greater conceptual understanding. Figure 11.1 shows an example used with a historical novel about the Revolutionary War, *My Brother Sam Is Dead* by James Lincoln Collier and Christopher Collier.

Before you read
Agree/Disagree

After you read
Agree/Disagree

1. The colonists were the "good" guys and the English the "bad" guys in the Revolutionary War.

Notes:

2. Loyalty to family is more important than loyalty to a cause.

Notes:

3. "You never get rid of injustice by fighting."
(Sam and Tim's father, p. 28)

Notes:

Figure 11.1   Reaction and Reflection Statements

Talking with Joan Bauer

I've spent a lot of my life crying; I've spent a lot of my life laughing. And frankly, I'd rather laugh.

Selected Titles

SQUASHED

THWONK

Sticks (forthcoming, Fall, 1995)

Joan Bauer is a new author of literature for young adults. Born in Illinois, her early career experiences were in sales, marketing, and advertising. Now she is a freelance writer living in Connecticut. Her first novel, SQUASHED, is a humorous story about a teenage girl determined to win the giant pumpkin contest in her small Iowa town. Along the way, she learns some important lessons about herself and about life. SQUASHED is the winner of the Delacorte Press Prize for a First Young Adult Novel, a School Library Journal Best Book of the Year, an ALA Recommended Book for the Reluctant YA Reader, a selection of the Junior Library Guild, and one of New York Public Library's Books for Teenagers.

Writing, reading, and humor have always been touchstones for me. Stories and humor swirled around our house when I was growing up. My mother was an English and a film studies teacher with a great comic sense. My grandmother was a well-known storyteller. As a child, I loved to write: songs, stories, essays, letters, funny poems, and greeting cards. I was greatly influenced by the comedians of the '50s and '60s: Lucille Ball, Bob Newhart, Shelly Berman, Ernie Kovacs, Dick Van Dyke, and Bill Cosby. I was a Robert Benchley fan as a kid, but the writer who defined humorous writing at the time for me was Max Schulman (*The Many Loves of Dobie Gillis, Rally 'Round the Flag, Boys!*). I pored over his crisp, funny dialogue. I wanted to be a comedian or a comedy writer when I grew up. I wanted to make people laugh.

I took a roundabout route to becoming a novelist, with a ten-year career in sales, marketing, and advertising at the *Chicago Tribune* and, after a few stops, *Parade* magazine. At the tender age of thirty, I found the nerve to try freelance writing, starting with magazines, moving to a nonfiction book, and screenwriting. Initially, I was going to write *SQUASHED* as a screenplay. I could see the visuals of the story. Unfortunately, my screenwriting career was cut short by a crippling auto accident that made all writing for a while most difficult. When I could write again, I decided to try *SQUASHED* as a book.

The whole point of writing *SQUASHED* was to explore the life of a kid with a vision overcoming odds, and I was overcoming plenty at the time due to my injuries. I couldn't sit at my desk for more than forty-five minutes at a time; I had trouble concentrating. I had to have neurosurgery. The humor in the story kept me going, I think. Humor is a serious survival skill, not just an escape. It's a way to deal with complexity and tragedy. In my work and my life, laughter has always been a bridge between pain and redemption.

Max the pumpkin and the pumpkin festival started off as metaphors for the big things in life we try to accomplish and their ultimate success or failure. The key obstacle I had to overcome in writing the story was that I had never grown a vegetable that lived. So I went to the library and hurled myself at the librarian's feet. As I researched, I found that the metaphor was even better than I'd thought. Wimps and cowards do not grow giant pumpkins. It takes strength, vision, and determination to nurture a seed in the ground, water it, and protect it from the storms of life that will surely come. And isn't that what we're all doing when we try to turn our dreams into realities? Sometimes people don't understand, sometimes we do it in an arena in which we've never operated before. That's what happens to my girl, Ellie Morgan, in *SQUASHED*. She's competing with adults; her father doesn't understand her passion. I was able to put my heart into Ellie; I understood her dream of growing something big; I understood her disappointments. Trying to make it as a writer is hard work, too.

I've always wanted my fiction to do something—inspire, illuminate—but since I work in humor I am always engaged in a cautious dance between comedy and poignancy. I wanted Ellie to be funny and offbeat, but I also wanted her to wrestle with complex issues without losing the humor. My tendency is to go for the joke, but in finishing *SQUASHED* my editor, Mary Cash, of whom I can't say enough, forced me to look beyond the joke. That strengthened the book significantly, and it's something I'll take with me forever in my writing. It's important for young adults to look beneath the layers of a humorous passage. In literature, humor is often a way of addressing what's serious. When we can find the laughter in difficult times what we're really finding is the hope.

Reading Roulette

In this strategy, suggested by C. Anne Webb (1990), teachers select as many books as they have students in a class. The objective is to give students the opportunity to examine several books in a short period of time. Students have approximately five minutes to examine a book and then exchange books. This process can be repeated several times in a class period. During the five minutes, the students get a sense of the book by reading the book cover, information about the author, and a short selection from the book itself. Webb suggests that students keep a record by listing the author's name, book title, and either a rank ordering of books based on their interest in reading them or a brief sentence describing the subject of the book. This approach gives students exposure to a number of books and encourages independent reading.

Paired Squared

This strategy helps prepare students to read a selection by activating their prior knowledge about it. It can be used effectively with fiction or nonfiction. The teacher puts a word, phrase, sentence, or short poem related to the selection on the board and asks the students to list individually as many associations as they can. Next, students share their lists with their Learning Partners and add new associations they think of together to their lists. Then each pair shares with another pair, also generating new associations. Finally, each group of four shares its combined list with the class. The teacher uses these associations to lead the students into the selection.

The following poem might be used to initiate reading about various kinds of walls—from the walls of the concentration camps of the Holocaust to the walls of the internment camps of Japanese Americans during the

---

Sharing the Connection

My Brother Sam Is Dead

James Lincoln Collier and Christopher Collier

My Brother Sam Is Dead was a very interesting book. The author made the feeling of the colonial times very real. He brought out the younger generation's perspective and how they had to survive. I really enjoyed the plot because it was very suspenseful, and at the end brought a tear to the eye. The story really showed how it felt to lose friends and family members. It also makes the point of how it felt to see with your own eyes a stranger get killed. I felt like I was the main character at times. I highly recommend this book to students of all ages. This book is a great way to see how the younger generation had to live during the war while one of your family members was off fighting and risking his life. And when Sam is caught and killed, the author really brings out the mood of sadness. This is a book I would go out and get right away. You don't know what you are missing.

Danny Malott, student

Second World War to the Vietnam Memorial in Washington, D. C. Books that could be used include *The Cage* by Ruth Minsky Sender, *Journey to Topaz* by Yoshiko Uchida, and Eve Bunting's picture book *The Wall*, to name a few.

> Walls . . .
> Dividing, Uniting
> Connecting, Separating
> Telling Stories

Directions to students: What do you think of when you read this poem? Write as many associations as you can.

Bridging

Bridging Fiction with Nonfiction

Yoshiko Uchida wrote two novels examining the experience of a young Japanese American girl and her family during and after their incarceration in internment camps during the Second World War. These books, Journey to Topaz and Journey Home , can serve as a bridge to Jeanne Wakatsuki Houston's Farewell to Manzanar, an autobiographical account, written with her husband, James D. Houston, of her own experiences in an internment camp.

Strategies for Connecting—Fiction

ReadingMark

Students have told us that often the initial activity in their literature classes each year is to learn literary terms and then to take a quiz on their definitions. The students complain about this being boring and pointless, because "we just forget them right after the quiz." We believe that the language of literature can provide students with the vocabulary to explore literature in meaningful ways and that students should have opportunities to use literary terms and become accustomed to applying them as they read. To that end, we have developed the ReadingMark, an interactive bookmark on which students apply literary terms as they read. (See Figure 11.2.) By having the ReadingMark in hand as they read, students may respond immediately and share their reflections as they have them. This helps build on authentic student responses.

Although Figure 11.2 focuses on literary terms, the ReadingMark can also focus on helping students to gain other types of understanding in their experiences with literature. For example, if students have been reading Marie G. Lee's first novel, *Finding My Voice,* teachers could develop a variation of the ReadingMark to focus on affective understanding of the book. The story is about a first-generation Korean American high school student who struggles at home because of her parents' high expectations for her and at school with discrimination. Figure 11.3 shows a ReadingMark developed for Lee's book.

A third variation of the ReadingMark focuses on fostering an aesthetic appreciation of a work. In Figure 11.4, we have developed a ReadingMark

ReadingMark

As you read, use this marker to jot down important information about your book.

Book Title:
Author:

Main Characters (one- to two-word descriptions):

Setting:

Major events in the plot:

Conflicts:

Resolutions:

Themes:

Comments:

Figure 11.2   A Blank ReadingMark

ReadingMark

Finding My Voice
by Marie G. Lee

List every time Ellen encounters discrimination and then give your personal reaction—how did it make you feel? Why?

For example: *On the school bus the first day. It made me feel embarrassed and even angry, because she hadn t done anything to deserve it.*

Have you ever experienced any type of discrimination? How did it feel? How did you handle it?

Figure 11.3   A ReadingMark for Developing Affective Understanding

for Zibby Oneal's *In Summer's Light*. ReadingMarks can be adapted to any specific book or they can be developed, as in Figure 11.2, to apply to different books. They are valuable because they help students to interact with their reading.

ReadingMark

In Summer's Light
by Zibby Oneal

Identify ways that Oneal creates pictures for the reader.

Select images that make the book come to life.

In what ways is the book like the painting she writes about?

Select your favorite description from the book and explain why you like it.

Figure 11.4   A ReadingMark for Developing Aesthetic Appreciation

Graphic Organizers

In this section we present three types of graphic organizers that help students to make connections with literature: mapping, comparison/contrast diagrams, and relationship charts. As organization tools, graphic organizers help students to see relationships among concepts and ideas. We begin with four kinds of mapping: fiction mapping, character mapping, conflict mapping, and ideals/values mapping.

Fiction Element Mapping   A fiction element map is a structured way to have students apply literary terms to a book they are reading. The structure of the map may be adapted to different books. Figure 11.5 (p. 244) focuses primarily on the elements of action; Figure 11.6 (p. 245) focuses on the atmosphere, tone, and mood of setting. As these two configurations suggest, the fiction element map can be structured to reflect the emphases most applicable to the work being studied.

The fiction element map can be used in any type of instructional framework.

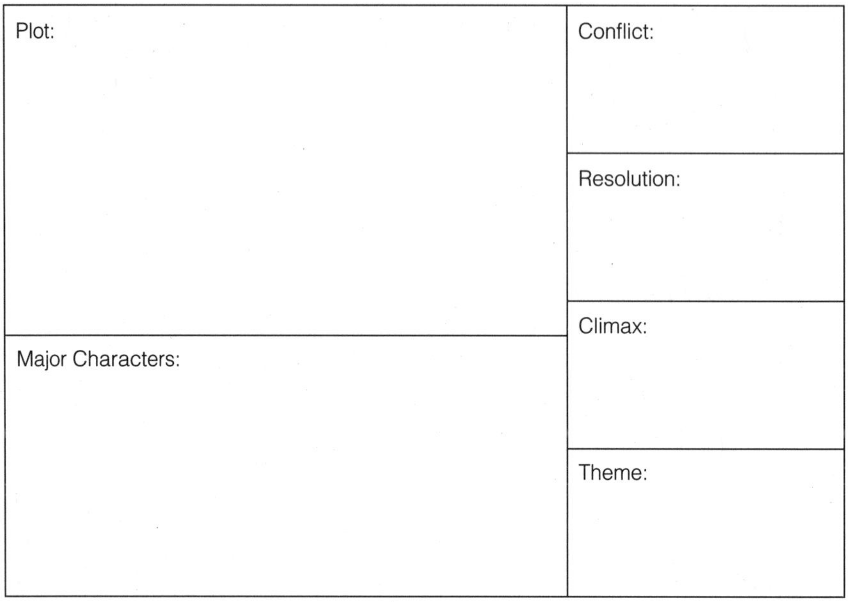

Plot:	Conflict:
	Resolution:
	Climax:
Major Characters:	
	Theme:

Figure 11.5   Fiction Element Map for Plot

Initially, it is probably advantageous for the teacher to take students through the process as a whole-class learning activity. This is especially valuable when students are unfamiliar with the literary terms or if they have simply memorized definitions previously. The value of this approach is that it gives students practical experiences with literary vocabulary.

Character Mapping   Character mapping is a useful tool to help students understand the process of characterization. In character mapping, students identify the main character in a box in the middle of their papers. They then identify characteristics and qualities of that character and list each one individually in circles around the original box. They attach these new circles to each characteristic with lines leading back to the original circle. (See Figure 11.7.)

Next, they find support or evidence for the characteristic in their reading. The evidence or support is placed in other shapes around the appropriate characteristic with lines going back to it. Students should be taught to recognize that the evidence may be found in a number of ways: the character's speech, actions, and behaviors; other characters' descriptions or comments; events; commentary from the narrator; illustrations; and implied evidence. The evidence may also demonstrate more than one characteristic; therefore, it may

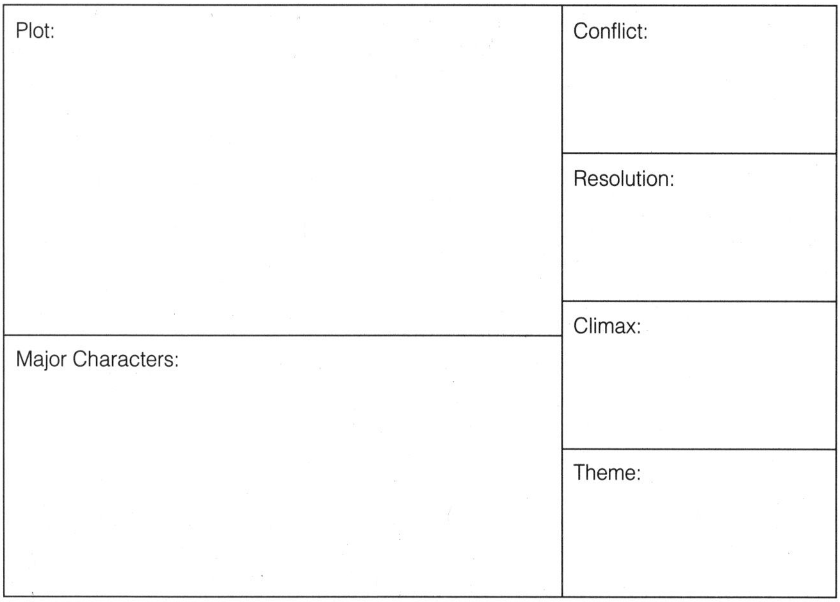

Plot:	Conflict:
	Resolution:
	Climax:
Major Characters:	
	Theme:

Figure 11.6 Fiction Element Map for Setting

have more than one line leading to more than one characteristic. Figure 11.8 is one of many possible variations. This approach focuses on the character's actions and the consequences of those actions, which provide insights about the character.

Whatever variation of the character map is used, it provides students with useful insights into characterization. Once students have completed their maps, they should write about what they have graphically represented. Among the valuable aspects of character mapping is that it can provide a foundation for students to explore characterization in their own writing.

Conflict Mapping Students today are a part of the media generation and accustomed to passively watching vivid, exciting, and even outrageous visual images that hook them and rivet their attention. Teachers frequently express their frustration with feeling that they must compete with television, videos, and movies to motivate and hold their students' attention. Students complain about anything that they perceive as unexciting. We have found that one way to get students' attention is to focus initially on the action or conflict in a work. We have developed the conflict map as an approach to capitalize on student interest in the action.

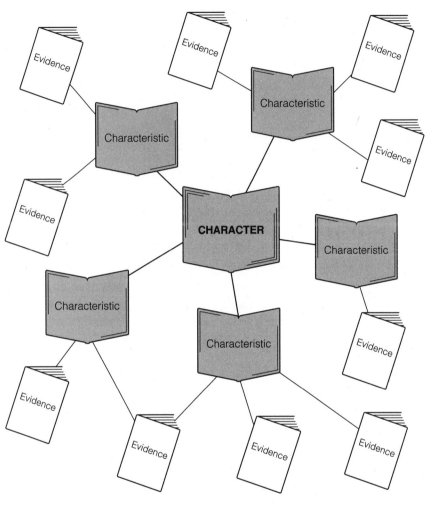

Figure 11.7   A Character Map

In this approach, students begin by identifying a conflict that plays a significant part in the book. Once they have chosen a conflict, they need to analyze and identify the cause of the conflict or identify the issue behind the conflict. At this point, it is important to help students realize that causes and issues may be more complex than they appear on the surface. The next step is to identify the participants—the protagonist and the antagonist. Students then identify the sources of support that each of these characters has. It is important to help students see that these sources might not be limited only to other characters; the support might come from the situation that spawned the conflict, the

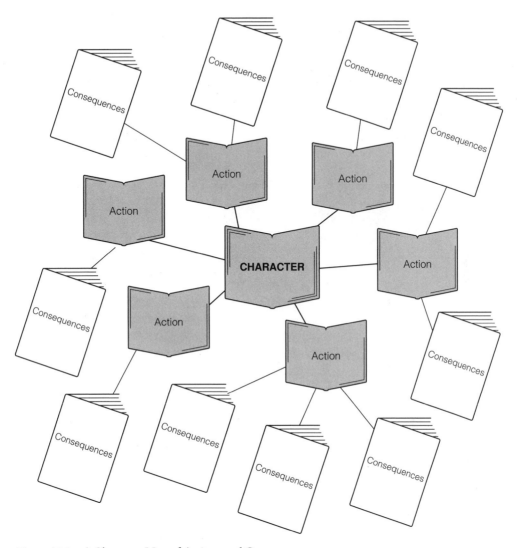

Figure 11.8 A Character Map of Actions and Consequences

ethical views or beliefs characters hold, the influence of the times, or any number of other internal and external factors. Once these elements have been mapped, the resolution of the conflict is added. Figure 11.9 shows how a conflict map can be organized.

This tool is an effective focusing technique that can be used with any type of instructional format. We have found, however, that it works particularly well with Learning Partners, because each is able to assume the role of the

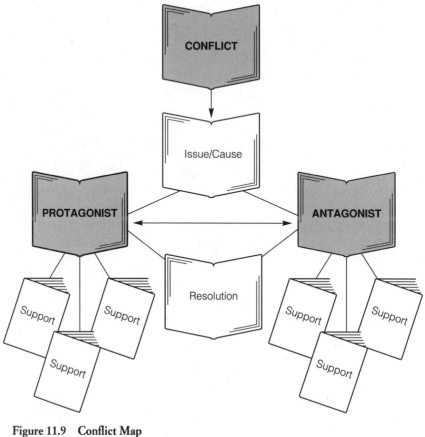

Figure 11.9   Conflict Map

protagonist or the antagonist and compare reactions to the conflict and its resolution. As each student focuses on one character in the conflict, he or she will
gain interesting insights about the conflict and the sources of support for the
characters.

Ideal/Value Mapping   Christopher Collier (1982) admits that he and his brother,
James Lincoln Collier, write historical fiction "with a didactic purpose—to
teach about the ideals and values that have been important in shaping the
course of American history" (p. 33). Based on that admission, we began to
look at historical fiction from the perspective of the ideals and values inherent
in the work. As a result, we developed a strategy to explore the ideals or values
in literature, especially in historical fiction. In this process, students identify an
ideal or value that is significantly explored in the work and place it in a circle

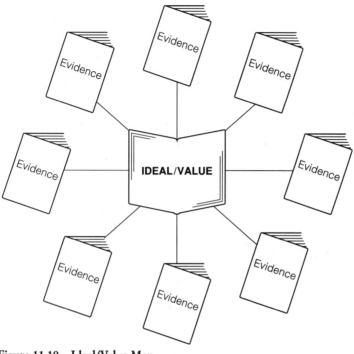

Figure 11.10 Ideal/Value Map

at the center of the map. Supporting evidence is then placed in circles and connected to the center, as shown in Figure 11.10. Figure 11.11 is a value map developed by Deborah L. Gleissner, a classroom teacher.

Comparison/Contrast Diagrams A graphic organizer that is useful in conceptualizing similarities and differences between characters, settings, themes, or any other predominant element is the comparison/contrast diagram, which is based on a Venn diagram. The map uses two or more overlapping circles containing elements being compared and contrasted. Figure 11.12 is a comparison/contrast diagram that we use in *Toward Literacy: Theory and Applications for Teaching Writing in the Content Areas* to illustrate the relationship between novels and short stories. In one circle, some of the unique characteristics of the novel are listed, and some of the unique characteristics of the short story are listed in the other circle. The overlapping area in the center represents the characteristics that novels and short stories have in common.

Comparison/contrast diagrams are useful structures for helping students when they are writing papers examining the similarities and differences in two works of literature. For example, students might be asked to write a paper

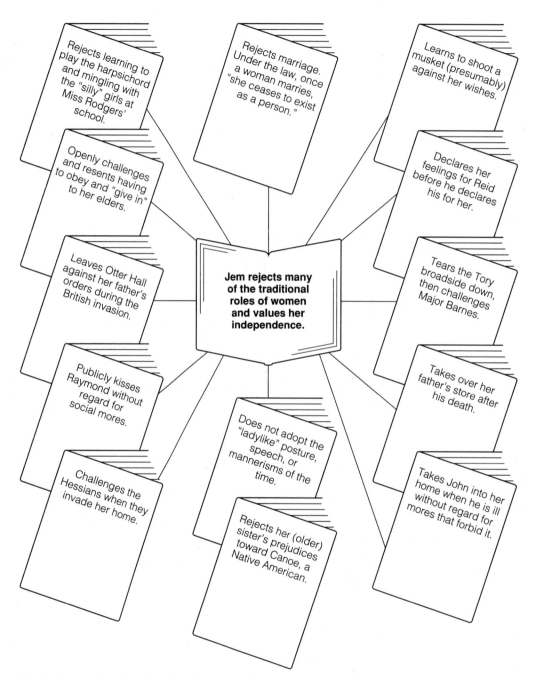

Figure 11.11 Value Map for *Time Enough for Drums*, by Ann Rinaldi.
Used by permission of Deborah L. Gleissner.

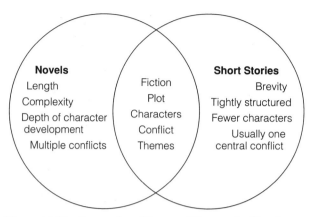

Figure 11.12   Comparison/Contrast Diagram for Novels and Short Stories

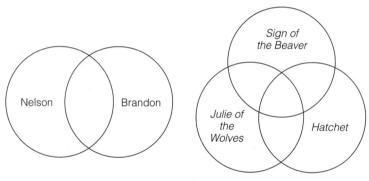

Figure 11.13   Sample Comparison/Contrast Diagrams

looking at similarities and differences between Nelson Sam, a character in Paul Pitts's *The Shadowman's Way* and Brandon Rogers, a character in another of Pitts's books, *Racing the Sun* (see Figure 11.13). The differences between these characters will be obvious to many students, but the subtle similarities will be more difficult. A structure like the comparison/contrast diagram will be useful in this case. Three books such as *Hatchet, Julie of the Wolves,* and *Sign of the Beaver,* which share some major characteristics, can be compared and contrasted using three overlapping circles. Figure 10.3 in Chapter 10 shows a similar type of diagram comparing characters in *The Cay* and *Sign of the Beaver.* Another variation might be to look at changes in characters that appear in more than one book. For example, readers might examine both Philip and Timothy in Theodore Taylor's *The Cay* and in its prequel/sequel *Timothy of*

The Versatility of Virginia Euwer Wolff

Title	Qualities of Main Character	Setting	Conflict	Theme	Style
Probably Still Nick Swansen					
The Mozart Season					
Make Lemonade					

Figure 11.14   Relationship Chart with Three Books

the Cay. Another example might be to look at the character of Janie in Caroline Cooney's *The Face on the Milk Carton* and its companion book, *Whatever Happened to Janie?*

Relationship Charts   Relationship charts provide students with an opportunity to see how several elements are related to each other. They also provide students with a framework for recording and organizing information. Relationship charts can be developed in S³ Groups, with Learning Partners, or during Individual Learning. They can then be used as a data source for discussions, writing activities, or creative projects. Revised and used over a period of time, relationship charts help students internalize themes and concepts.

Relationship charts can be organized in a variety of ways, including

1. Comparison of characters within one novel or across several novels; relationship of characters to each other

2. Comparison of a common theme in several different selections

3. Comparison of several books or several authors

4. Comparison of books within a genre or comparison of characteristics of different genres

	Food/ Dining	Housing/ Sleeping	Clothes	Medicine	Music	Relation- ships
Life in the scientific community						
Life with the Ekoes						

Figure 11.15   Relationship Chart with One Book

5. Comparison of how literary elements are used within one novel or across several novels
6. Relationship of elements such as setting or events to actions or feelings in plot structure

In Figure 11.14, three novels are examined using five criteria. In Figure 11.15, the same strategy based on Monica Hughes's *Ring-Rise, Ring-Set* (1982), is used.

Opinion Guide

Opinion guides help students identify their beliefs about important issues and compare them with the beliefs of the characters in a selection. Beliefs give rise to motives, which in turn give rise to actions. Conflict can arise from a number of circumstances including a character's internal confusion over beliefs, opposing beliefs between two or more characters, or opposing beliefs between the characters and the reader. Figure 11.16 is an opinion guide for *Stepping on the Cracks* by Mary Dowling Hahn. It was developed by Deborah L. Gleissner.

	You		Margaret		Margaret's parents	
Serving in war is our duty; no one is exempt.	☐ Agree	☐ Disagree Why?	☐ Agree	☐ Disagree Why?	☐ Agree	☐ Disagree Why?
It's OK to help someone who refuses to serve in a war.	☐ Agree	☐ Disagree Why?	☐ Agree	☐ Disagree Why?	☐ Agree	☐ Disagree Why?
How family members treat each other is no one else's business.	☐ Agree	☐ Disagree Why?	☐ Agree	☐ Disagree Why?	☐ Agree	☐ Disagree Why?

Figure 11.16 Opinion Guide.
Used by permission of Deborah L. Gleissner.

Polar Opposites

Yopp and Yopp (1992) describe how to use polar opposites to help students analyze the attributes and qualities of characters by rating them along a continuum with a scale of three to seven points. More important than the ratings, however, is the thinking that students must do in order to justify their ratings. They must also learn to use examples from the text to support their conclusions. Usually this justification involves inferential and evaluative thinking. Polar opposites can be used in S³ Groups, with Learning Partners, or during Individual Learning. They are a good source of information for discussions, writing activities, and creative projects, and students can learn to create their own polar opposites. Polar opposites can be used more than once while reading a work to show character growth and development. They are also a useful device when comparing the complexity of well-developed characters with stereotypes. Figure 11.17 is based on *Celine* by Brock Cole.

I think Celine is . . .

mature for her age. _____ _____ _____ _____ _____ immature for her age.
Rationale:

thoughtful and   self-centered
considerate of others. _____ _____ _____ _____ _____   and selfish.
Rationale:

creative and   messy, lazy, and
artistic.   _____ _____ _____ _____ _____   disorganized.
Rationale:

sociable.   _____ _____ _____ _____ _____   a loner.
Rationale:

funny and witty.   _____ _____ _____ _____ _____ serious and introspective.
Rationale:

Figure 11.17   Example of Polar Opposites

It's All Relative

Students select a family member (preferably from a different generation, such as parent, grandparent, aunt, or uncle) to whom they write a letter telling about a book they like and discussing the reasons for their reactions. This should be an authentic writing experience, and the letter should be sent to the family member in an attempt to encourage an ongoing dialogue.

Strategies for Internalization—Fiction

Creative Projects

Teachers frequently limit their post-reading instructional strategies with literature to discussion and writing activities. Although these are valuable avenues for exploring literature, activities that allow more options to meet diverse learning styles and to encourage greater creativity should be developed. By using creative projects for students, teachers enhance ongoing student involvement with their reading. Providing students with opportunities to stretch their imaginations by doing creative projects also provides them with opportunities for authentic interactions with books. Such creative projects lend themselves well to S³ Groups, Learning Partners, and Individual Learning and usually create a

Bridging

Use of Humor

Many people have the misconception that young adult novels are serious and deal only with difficult issues of growing up. Each of the following books uses humor even when addressing serious subjects: Book of the Banshee by Anne Fine, Celine by Brock Cole, Dinky Hocker Shoots Smack by M. E. Kerr, Won't Know Till I Get There by Walter Dean Myers, Reluctantly Alice by Phyllis Reynolds Naylor, and SQUASHED by Joan Bauer. The bridging experience explores how humor is used in two or more of these books.

depth of involvement, understanding, and aesthetic pleasure that is contagious and highly gratifying. Literature connections can be expressed through art, drama, music, media, and other content areas. These projects also offer a tangible way for students to see the interrelationships among their school subjects and their relationship to "real life."

The following are a few ideas that are used successfully by teachers:

1. Create a collage that illustrates the book as a whole or one of characters in the book.

2. Create a script dramatizing a scene from the book; then prepare the production.

3. Create a publicity campaign for a book or an author. Consider posters, videos, newspaper or magazine reviews, and radio or print ads.

4. Design a cover jacket for the book.

5. Write a song based on the conflict in the book or on one of the characters.

6. Design a mural based on the action in the book.

7. Prepare and conduct a talk show based on the issues in one or more books.

8. Make artistic representations of the characters in the book as you think they look.

9. Create a picture book, pop-up book, wordless picture book, or comic strip series based on the book.

10. Design a sweatshirt, T-shirt, scarf, or tie based on the book.

Character Crests

A strategy that challenges students to demonstrate an understanding of characterization is to develop a character crest, or coat of arms. In this strategy, students must create a graphic with four major sections in which they explore aspects of a character's life. In the first major section, students portray characteristics, such as courage, honesty, or deceitfulness; in the second, they depict what the character does, including work and hobbies; the third captures a sense of the setting or environment in which the character lives; and the fourth is open for any other notable aspects of the character's life. The remaining diagonal section is for a motto that captures the essence of the character. See Figure 11.18.

Fiction as Social Conscience

This strategy asks students to focus on the social issues behind a work, such as the control of human behavior in Lowry's *The Giver* or Sleator's *House of Stairs* or the ethical treatment of the environment, people, and animals in Dickenson's *Eva* and Hughes's *Ring-Rise, Ring-Set.* Students identify the significant social issues and present them in chart form. See Figure 11.19 on page 258.

Dilemma Resolution

The dilemma resolution strategy focuses on what is exciting in books, such as instances of conflict or disharmony. We have found that when students ask other students to tell them what happens

Bridging

Bridging a Play with a Historical Novel

Suggested by Char Palmer

Ann Rinaldi's novel A Break with Charity serves as an appropriate bridge to Arthur Miller's play The Crucible. Both of these works deal with the Salem witch trials during colonial days.

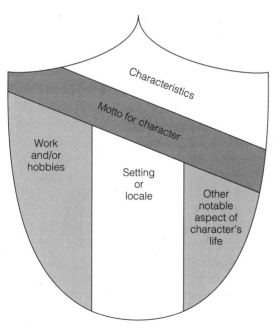

Figure 11.18 Character Crest

Issue	Roots in today's society	Evidence in book	Implications

Figure 11.19   Social Issue Chart

next in a book, they are asking about the action in the story. They want to know what has happened to propel the plot. For example, when Harry is caught by the security guard, one of the key events in James Lincoln Collier's *When the Stars Begin to Fall*, the question becomes, How can Harry handle this situation and how will he then proceed?

Using a dilemma as the focal point, student discussion can be directed to examine resolutions to the dilemma, posing alternatives to the resolution, or making judgments about the resolution. The exploration that students do during this process increases their critical thinking abilities. Using the example of Harry, questions for discussion might focus on how he might have extricated himself from suspicion. Then the situation lends itself to the discussion of a number of related issues. Was there justification in his spying? In his lying? What was his motivation? Does his motive justify the lying and spying? What will Harry do after he has been caught?

In Their Shoes

This strategy is a form of role playing that helps students identify with and understand characters. The teacher develops a series of situations—some serious, some silly, and some challenging. For example, teachers could pose the following questions: When leaving an expensive restaurant, your pants or dress are caught in an electronic door, and you are left in your underwear.

What do you do? and All alone, you find a briefcase with $5,000 in cash and negotiable bonds. What do you do? In groups, students select a character (positive or negative image) from their reading, and they assume the role of the character in responding to the situation. It is important that they stay in character. The group analyzes the character's actions and authenticity.

Strategies for Initiating—Nonfiction

Many of the strategies for initiating fiction are also appropriate for nonfiction. Additionally, we present the following strategies.

Pleased to Meet You

This strategy is designed to involve students with reading biographies and autobiographies. Work with a librarian to develop a master list of available biographies and autobiographies, including those written in series. Make copies of the list in the form of a checklist in which students determine which subjects of the biographies are familiar, which are not, and which they want to know more about. For example, see Figure 11.20.

Strategies for Connecting—Nonfiction

Many of the strategies for connecting with fiction are also appropriate for nonfiction. Additionally, we present the following strategies.

Memorable Scene

Students identify an incident in the life of a character whose biography or autobiography they have read. They then rewrite the incident into a scene that they and members of the S³ Groups present to the rest of the class.

Presenting . . .

After reading a biography of a famous individual, students continue their research to find pictures, videotapes, recordings, or audiotapes of the person and any others that will help make an introduction of this person more realistic. They write a short introduction about the person to be presented to the class along with the results of the research. Students and teachers can determine any number of formats for the introductions.

	Very Familiar	Familiar	Not Familiar	Want to Know More
Hillary Clinton				
Bill Clinton				
Roger Clemens				
Monica Hughes				
Sandra Day O'Connor				
Mo Vaughn				
Gary Paulsen				
Chris Evert				
Larry Bird				
Rosa Parks				
Nancy Lopez				
Walter Dean Myers				
Jackson Pollock				
Cesar Chavez				
Robert Cormier				
Magic Johnson				
Arthur Ashe				
Anita Hill				
Georgia O'Keeffe				
Marva Collins				
Katherine Paterson				
Amy Tan				

Figure 11.20   Biography Checklist

Strategies for Internalization—Nonfiction

Many of the strategies for internalizing fiction are also appropriate for nonfiction. Additionally, we present the following strategies.

Concept Collecting

Concept collecting is a strategy used primarily with nonfiction to help students develop a conceptual understanding of what they are reading. An additional advantage to this approach is that it can be used as a direct link to the students' own expository writing by asking them to focus on the concepts that they are presenting. We have found that students have a difficult time seeing the big picture in either their reading or writing. This strategy is designed to help them develop a framework for generalizing about ideas to gain a more in-depth understanding of the underlying concepts. Initially, this strategy is best done with the whole class or a group as the teacher models the process. Once students have had practice with this process and understand what concepts are, the following adaptation of the strategy may be presented to them. It applies concept collection as an individual note-taking process. The purpose of this activity is to help students focus on major concepts prior to and during reading. These directions may be given to the students:

1. Divide your paper into three columns.

2. Label the columns as follows: Concepts I think I know; Evidence; New Concepts I've learned.

3. As you preview the work, begin filling in the columns by listing the major concepts that you already understand about the subject.

4. Next, read the work. As you read, record any evidence that supports what you already know about the major concepts.

5. After completing the work, identify and list what you consider to be the major concepts of it.

6. Check the concepts listed with the text of the work.

7. In your S³ Groups, compare your lists for each column. Make a group master list, checking with the text as necessary. Be prepared to discuss the concepts from the work with the class.

Helping students to identify concepts is a valuable tool that they can then use in any discipline. Conceptual learning is essential to understanding any academic field. An additional advantage to concept collecting is that students can use the concepts they identify as the basis for expository writing activities.

Sharing the Connection

After the Rain
Norma Fox Mazer

A Newbery Honor Book, this is one of the most moving books I've read in a long time. I cried as I finished reading it and I was in public on a airplane at the time! Rachel, fifteen, learns to love her gruff, distant grandfather as he is dying. It is a realistic portrayal of an adolescent learning to understand and accept her family and herself. I also liked the warm, caring teenage friendships it presented. Both the boys and girls in my class liked this book and could relate to it. It generated a lot of discussion about families, death and dying, and what life is all about.

Maria Garcia, secondary English teacher

Summary

A variety of teaching strategies serve as a starting point for teachers and students as they read young adult literature. These strategies are organized according to the principles of the Reader Involvement Model—that is initiating, connecting, internalizing, and sharing. They are based on the theories of reading as a interactive process and literature as a transactional, aesthetic experience.

Suggested Activities

1. In your journal, reflect on which instructional strategies described in this chapter you like best and why.

2. Use one of the strategies from this chapter with a selection from young adult literature that you have recently read. If you are a teacher, use it with your students.

3. Prepare and give a Booktalk on one of your favorite young adult literature works.

4. Research an author of young adult literature. Look for any major recurring themes in his or her work.

References

Aker, D. 1992. From runned to ran: One journey toward a critical literacy. *Journal of Reading* 36 (2):104–12.

Alvermann, D. E., D. R. Dillon, and D. G. O'Brien. 1987. *Using discussion to promote reading comprehension.* Newark, Del.: International Reading Association.

Applebee, A. 1989. *A study of book-length works taught in high school English courses.* Albany: State University of New York.

———. 1992. Background for reform. In *Literature instruction,* edited by J. Langer. Urbana, Ill.: National Council of Teachers of English.

———. 1993. *Literature in the secondary schools.* Urbana, Ill.: National Council of Teachers of English.

Appleyard, J. A. 1990. *Becoming a reader: The experiences of fiction from childhood to adulthood.* Cambridge, Eng.: Cambridge University Press.

Asher, S. 1992. What about now? What about here? What about me? In *Reading their world,* edited by V. R. Monseau and G. M. Salvner. Portsmouth, N.H.: Boynton/Cook; Heinemann. Chapter 4 opening quote p. 82.

Atwell, N. 1987. *In the middle: Writing, reading, and learning with adolescents.* Upper Montclair, N.J.: Boynton/Cook.

———. 1993. Foreword to *Teachers as researchers: Reflection and action,* edited by L. Patterson et al. Newark, Del.: International Reading Association. Chapter 7 opening quote p. vii.

Au, K. H. 1993. *Literacy instruction in multicultural settings.* Fort Worth, Tex.: Harcourt Brace Jovanovich.

Bagnall, N. 1981. Literature isn't supposed to be realistic. *English Journal* 70 (1):9, 11–12.

Bauer, J. 1993. Interview. Pittsburgh, Penn.: National Council of Teachers of English.

Bauer, Joan. 1992. *SQUASHED.* New York: Delacorte. Chapter 11 opening quote p. 135.

Bauer, M. D. 1993. Interview. Pittsburgh, Penn.: National Council of Teachers of English.

Beach, R. 1993. *A teacher's introduction to reader-response theories.* Urbana, Ill.: National Council of Teachers of English.

Bintz, W. P. 1993. Resistant readers in secondary education: Some insights and implications. *Journal of Reading* 36 (8):604–15.

Bishop, R. S. 1991. Walter Dean Myers. In *Getting to know you,* edited by B. Kiefer. Urbana, Ill.: National Council of Teachers of English.

Bodart, J. 1980. *Booktalk!* N.Y.: H.W. Wilson.

———. 1985. *Booktalk! 2.* N.Y.: H.W. Wilson.

———. 1988. *Booktalk! 3.* N.Y.: H.W. Wilson.

———. 1992. *Booktalk! 4.* N.Y.: H.W. Wilson.

———. 1993. *Booktalk! 5.* N.Y.: H.W. Wilson.

Bridgers, S. E. 1992. Creating a bond between writer and reader. In *Reading their world,* edited by V. R. Monseau and G. M. Salvner. Portsmouth, N.H.: Boyton/Cook; Heinemann.

Brooks, B. 1993. Speech at the ALAN Workshop at the National Council of Teachers of English Fall Convention, Pittsburgh, Pennsylvania.

Brown, J. E. 1975. Reading preferences: What Utah secondary students are reading. Unpublished manuscript.

———. 1980. Adolescent preferences in reading: Teacher-student choices. Paper presented at Fall Conference of the Maine Council of English Language Arts. Bangor, Maine.

———. 1981. Reading preferences: What Mississippi secondary students are reading. Paper presented at Mississippi Reading Association Conference. Biloxi, Miss.

———. 1985a. Implications of student reading preferences for teacher educators. Paper presented at National Council of Teachers of English Spring Conference. Houston, Tex.

———. 1985b. Listening to students: The results of a survey of reading habits and preferences. Paper presented at MSU/MCTE Spring Conference. East Lansing, Mich.

———. 1985c. Reading preferences of Michigan high school students. *The Michigan English Teacher* 35 (5):12–13.

———. 1985d. A typology of critical approaches to literature. In *From Seeds to Harvest,* edited by K. B. Whale and T. J. Gambell. Canada: Canadian Council of Teachers of English.

———. 1990. Reading preferences: What Michigan secondary students are reading. Unpublished manuscript.

———. 1992a. Fighting censorship in Michigan. *SLATE Newsletter* (Spring).

———. 1992b. Reading preferences of Michigan high school students. Unpublished manuscript.

———. 1994, in press. *Preserving intellectual freedom: Fighting censorship in the schools.* Urbana, Ill.: National Council of Teachers of English.

Brown, J. E., et al. 1982. Revitalizing American history: Literature in the classroom. *The Social Studies* 73 (6):279–83.

Brown, J., L. Phillips, and E. Stephens. 1993. *Toward literacy: Theory and applications for teaching writing in the content areas.* Belmont, Calif.: Wadsworth.

Brown, J., B. Quirk, and E. Stephens, eds. 1988a. *A two-way street: Integrating reading and writing in the middle school.* Rochester, Mich.: Michigan Council of Teachers of English.

———. 1988b. *A two-way street: Integrating reading and writing in the secondary school.* Rochester, Mich.: Michigan Council of Teachers of English.

Brown, J .E., and E. Stephens, 1994. Being proactive, not waiting for the censor. In *Preserving intellectual freedom: Fighting censorship in the schools,* edited by J. E. Brown. Urbana, Ill.: National Council of Teachers of English.

Burress, L. and E. Jenkinson. The students' right to know. Urbana, Ill.: National Council of Teachers of English.

Carlsen, G. R. 1981. Literature isn't supposed to be realistic. *English Journal* 70 (1):8–12.

Carlsen, G. R., and N. Bagnall. 1981. Bait/Rebait column. *English Journal* January, 11–12.

Carlsen, G. R., and A. Sherrill. 1988. *Voices of readers: How we come to love books.* Urbana, Ill.: National Council of Teachers of English.

Carter, B., and R. F. Abrahamson. 1990. *Nonfiction for young adults from delight to wisdom.* Phoenix, Ariz.: Oryx Press.

Carter, B., and Young Adult Library Services Association. 1994. *Best books for young adults: The selection, the history, and the romance.* Chicago: American Library Association.

Censorship: Don't let it become an issue in your schools. 1978. Reprinted from *Language Arts.* Urbana, Ill.: National Council of Teachers of English.

Chambers, A. 1985. *Booktalk: Occasional writing on literature and children.* London: Bodley.

Cianciolo, P., and B. Quirk. 1993. *Teaching and learning: critical aesthetic response to literature.* E. Lansing, Mich.: Institute for Research on Teaching, Michigan State University.

Cline, D. M. 1993. A year with reading workshop. In *Teachers as researchers: reflection and action,* edited by L. Patterson et al. Newark, Del.: International Reading Association.

Cole, Brock. 1989. *Celine.* New York: Farrar, Straus & Giroux. Chapter 10 opening quote p. 42.

Collier, C. 1982. Criteria for historical fiction. *School Library Journal,* August, 32–33.

Crawford, L. 1993. *Language and literacy learning in multicultural classrooms.* Boston: Allyn & Bacon.

Crutcher, C. 1992. Healing through literature. In *Authors' Insights,* edited by D. R. Gallo. Portsmouth, N.H.: Boynton/Cook; Heinemann. Chapter 3 opening quote p. 39.

———. 1993. Interview. Pittsburgh, Penn.: National Council of Teachers of English.

Davis, J. E. 1986. Dare a teacher disturb the universe? Or even eat a peach? Closet censorship: Its prevention and cure. *ALAN Review* (Fall).

Devine, T. G. 1987. *Teaching study skills.* 2d ed. Newton, Mass.: Allyn & Bacon.

Donelson, K. 1972. The students' right to read. Revised ed. Urbana, Ill.: National Council of Teachers of English.

Donelson, K., and A. Nilsen. 1989. *Literature for today's young adults.* 3d ed. Glenview, Ill.: Scott, Foresman.

Elliott, G. R., and S. S. Feldman, 1990. Capturing the adolescent experience. In *At the threshold, The developing adolescent,* edited by S. S. Feldman and G. R. Elliott. Cambridge, Mass.: Harvard University Press.

The fight against censorship. 1990. *SLATE Newsletter* 15 (1):2.

Fish, S. 1980. *Is there a text in this class? The authority of interpretive communities.* Cambridge, Mass.: Harvard University Press.

Fitzgerald, J. 1992. Reading and writing stories. In *Reading/Writing connections: Learning from research,* edited by J. W. Irwin and M.A. Doyle. Newark, Del.: International Reading Association.

Fox, P. 1990. Paula Fox. In *Speaking for ourselves,* edited by D. R. Gallo. Urbana, Ill.: National Council of Teachers of English. Chapter 2 opening quote p. 70.

Frager, A. M. 1993. Affective dimensions of content area reading. *Journal of Reading* 36 (8):616–22.

Freedman, R. 1987. *Lincoln: A photobiography.* New York: Ticknor & Fields. Chapter 8 opening quote p. 59.

———. 1993. Interview. Pittsburgh, Penn.: National Council of Teachers of English.

Gallo, D. 1992. Listening to readers: Attitudes toward the young adult novel. In *Reading their world,* edited by V. R. Monseau and G. M. Salvner. Portsmouth, N.H.: Heinemann.

Gallo, D. R. 1984. Reactions to required reading: Some implications from a study of Connecticut students. *Connecticut English Journal* 15 (2):7–11.

———, ed. 1989. Who are the most important YA authors? *ALAN Review* 16 (3):18–20.

———, ed. 1990. *Speaking for ourselves.* Urbana, Ill.: National Council of Teachers of English.

———, ed. 1993a. *Literature for teenagers: New books, new approaches.* Connecticut Council of Teachers of English: Connecticut English Journal.

———, ed. 1993b. *Speaking for ourselves, too.* Urbana, Ill.: National Council of Teachers of English.

Gerlach, J. M. 1992. The young adult novel across the curriculum. In *Reading their world,* edited by V. R. Monseau and G. Salvner. Portsmouth N.H.: Boynton/Cook; Heineman.

Guidelines for the preparation of teachers of English language arts. 1986. National Council of Teachers of English Standing Committee on Teacher Preparation and Certification, Denny Wolfe, Chair. Urbana, Ill.: National Council of Teachers of English.

Hall, G. S. 1905. *Adolescence: Its psychology and its relations to physiology, anthropology, sociology, sex, crime, religion and education.* New York: D. Appleton.

Hamilton, V. 1990. Virginia Hamilton. In *Speaking for ourselves,* edited by D. R. Gallo. Urbana, Ill.: National Council of Teachers of English.

Hancock, M. R. 1992. Literature response journals: Insights beyond the printed page. *Language Arts* 69 (January): 36–42.

Hansen, J. 1993. Interview. Pittsburgh, Penn.: National Council of Teachers of English.

Harmon, M. 1993. *A study of sociolinguistic texts and subtexts as found in five high school American literature anthologies.* Ph.D. diss., Michigan State University.

Hipple, T. 1989. Have you read . . . ? Parts 2 and 3. *English Journal* 78 (8):79.

———. 1992. The universality of the young adult novel. In *Reading their world,* edited by V. Monseau and G. Salvner. Portsmouth, N.H.: Boynton/Cook; Heinemann. Chapter 1 opening quote pp. 13–14.

Hirtle, J. S. 1993. Connecting to the classics. In *Teachers as researchers: Reflection and action,* edited by L. Patterson et al. Newark, Del.: International Reading Association.

Holman, C. H. 1975. *A handbook to literature,* 3d ed. Indianapolis: Bobbs-Merrill.

Howard, E. 1988. *America as story: Historical fiction for secondary schools.* Chicago: American Library Association.

Hughes, M. 1993. Interview. Pittsburgh, Penn.: National Council of Teachers of English.

Jongsma, K. S. 1993. What students' written reflections reveal about literacy. In *Teachers as researchers: Reflection and action,* edited by L. Patterson, et al. Newark, Del.: International Reading Association.

Keating, D. P. 1990. Adolescent thinking. In *At the threshold: The developing adolescent,* edited by S. S. Feldman and G. R. Elliott. Cambridge, Mass: Harvard University Press.

Kerr, M. E. 1990. M. E. Kerr. In *Speaking for ourselves,* edited by D. Gallo. Urbana, Ill.: National Council of Teachers of English.

———. 1991. *M. E. Kerr.* New York: HarperCollins.

Langer, J., ed. 1992. *Literature instruction.* Urbana, Ill.: National Council of Teachers of English.

———. 1994. A response-based approach to reading literature. *Language Arts* 71 (3):203–11.

Latrobe, K. and M. Laughlin. 1989. *Readers theatre for young adults: Scripts and script development.* Englewood, Colo.: Teacher Ideas Press.

Lee, Marie G. 1992. *Finding my voice.* Boston, Mass.: Houghton Mifflin. Chapter 9 opening quote pp. 7–8.

Lukens, R. 1986. *A critical handbook of children's literature.* Glenview, Ill.: Scott, Foresman.

Mazer, H. 1992. Big books, sex, and the classics: Some thoughts on teaching literature. In *Authors' insights,* edited by D. R. Gallo. Portsmouth, N.H.: Boynton/Cook; Heinemann.

Mazer, N. F. 1990a. Letters to me. *ALAN Review* 17 (3):8–11.

———. 1990b. Norma Fox Mazer. In *Speaking for ourselves,* edited by D. Gallo. Urbana, Ill.: National Council of Teachers of English.

———. 1992. The ice-cream syndrome (aka promoting good reading habits). In *Authors' insights,* edited by D. R. Gallo. Portsmouth, N.H.: Boynton/Cook; Heinemann.

McMahon, S. 1994. Student-led book clubs: Traversing a river of interpretation. *The New Advocate* 7 (2):109–25.

Moffett, J. 1986. *Teaching the universe of discourse.* Boston: Houghton Mifflin.

Mohr, N. 1990. Nicholasa Mohr. In *Speaking for ourselves,* edited by D. R. Gallo. Urbana, Ill.: National Council of Teachers of English.

Monseau, V. R. 1992. Students and teachers as community of readers. In *Reading their world,* edited by V. R. Monseau and G. M. Salvner. Portsmouth, N.H: Boynton/Cook; Heinemann.

Monseau, V. R. and G. M. Salvner, eds. 1992. *Reading their world.* Portsmouth, N.H: Boyton/Cook; Heinemann.

Most frequently challenged books. 1990. *SLATE Newsletter* 15 (1):2.

Myers, W. D. 1990. In *Speaking for ourselves,* edited by D. Gallo. Urbana, Ill.: National Council of Teachers of English.

———. 1992. Speech at the ALAN Workshop at the National Council of Teachers of English Fall Convention, Louisville, Kentucky.

Nelms, E. D., and B. F. Nelms. 1992. Gary Paulsen: The storyteller's legacy. *English Journal* 81 (1):85–88.

Norton, D. 1983. *Through the eyes of a child: An introduction to children's literature.* Columbus, Oh.: Merrill.

Patterson, L., and P. Shannon. 1993. Reflection, inquiry, action. In *Teachers are researchers: Reflection and action,* edited by L. Patterson et al. Newark, Del.: International Reading Association.

Patton, L. 1993. Into the woods: The impact of prereading activities. In *Teachers as researchers: Reflection and action,* edited by L. Patterson et al. Newark, Del.: International Reading Association.

Paulsen, G. 1990. Trumpet Club authors on tape. Holmes, Penn.: The Trumpet Club.

———. 1991. Literature and adolescence. Speech given at the ALAN breakfast at the National Council of Teachers of English Fall Conference, Seattle, Washington

Peck, D. R. 1989. *Novels of initiation.* New York: Teachers College Press, Columbia University.

Peck, R. 1992a. Nobody but a reader ever became a writer. In *Authors' insights,* edited by D. R. Gallo. Portsmouth, N.H.: Heinemann.

———. 1992b. Problem novels for readers without any. In *Reading their world,* edited by V. Monseau & G. Salvner.

Portsmouth, N.H.: Boynton/Cook; Heinemann.

Purves, A. C. 1984. Teaching literature as an intellectual activity. ADE *Bulletin* 78 (Summer): 17–19.

———. 1992. Testing literature. In *Literature instruction,* edited by J. A. Langer. Urbana, Ill.: National Council of Teachers of English.

Purves, A. C., T. Rogers, and A. O. Soter. 1990. *How porcupines make love II: Teaching a response-centered literature curriculum.* New York: Longman.

Rinsky, L., and R. Schweiker. 1977. In defense of the 'new realism' for children and adolescents. *Kappan* 58 (6):472–75.

Rochman, H. 1993. *Against borders: Promoting books for a multicultural world.* Chicago: American Library Association. Chapter 5 opening quote p. 15.

Rosenblatt, L. 1978. *The reader, the text, the poem.* Carbondale: Southern Illinois University.

———. 1983. *Literature as exploration.* 4th ed. New York: Modern Language Association of America.

———. 1985. Language, literature, and value. In *Language, schooling, and society,* edited by Stephen N. Tchudi. Upper Montclair, N.J.: Boynton/Cook.

———. 1991. Literature—S.O.S.! *Language Arts* 68 (Oct.) 444–48.

Rylant, C. 1993. Cynthia Rylant. In *Speaking for ourselves, too,* edited by D. R. Gallo. Urbana, Ill.: National Council of Teachers of English.

Sacco, M. 1993. Defending books: A title index. *ALAN Review* 39–41.

Salisbury, G. 1993. Interview. Pittsburgh, Penn.: National Council of Teachers of English.

Samway, K. D., et al. 1991. Reading the skeleton, the heart, and the brain of a book: Students' perspectives on literature study circles. *The Reading Teacher* 45 (3):196–205.

Sasse, M. H. 1988. Literature in a multi-ethnic culture. In *Literature in the classroom: Readers, texts, and contexts,* edited by B. F. Nelms. Urbana, Ill.: National Council of Teachers of English.

Simmons, J. S., and H. E. Deluzain. 1992. *Teaching literature in middle and secondary grades.* Boston: Allyn & Bacon.

Sleator, W. 1992. Chaos, strange attractors, and other peculiarities in the English classroom. In *Authors' insights,* edited by D. R. Gallo. Portsmouth, N.H.: Boynton/Cook.

Smith, F. 1986. *Insult to intelligence.* New York: Arbor House.

Solzhenitsyn, A. 1972. *Nobel lecture.* New York: Farrar, Straus and Giroux.

Soto, G. 1993. Gary Soto. In *Speaking for ourselves, too,* edited by D. R. Gallo. Urbana, Ill.: National Council of Teachers of English.

Speaker, R. B., Jr., and P. R. Speaker. 1991. Sentence collecting: Authentic literacy events in the classroom. *Journal of Reading* 5 (2): 92–95.

Stephens, E. and J. Brown. 1994a. Making classroom connections: learning partners. *Notes Plus.: A Quarterly of Practical Teaching Ideas.* Urbana, Ill.: National Council of Teachers of English. 2–3.

Stover, L. 1991. Exploring and celebrating cultural diversity and similarity through young adult novels. *ALAN Review* 18 (3):12–15.

Stover, L. T. and E. Tway. 1992. Cultural diversity and the young adult novel. In *Reading their world,* edited by V R. Monseau and G. M. Salvner. Portsmouth, N.H.: Boynton/Cook; Heinemann.

Teachers as readers: Forming book groups for professionals. n.d. New York: Association of American Publishers.

Thomson, J. 1987.*Understanding teenagers' reading: Reading processes and the teaching of literature.* Norwood, South Australia: Australian Association for the Teaching of English.

Trelease, J., ed. 1989. *The new read-aloud handbook.* New York: Penguin.

———, ed. 1992. *Hey! Listen to this.* New York: Penguin.

———, ed. 1993. *Read all about it! Great read-aloud stories, poems, and newspaper pieces for preteens and teens.* New York: Penguin.

Vacca, R., and W. Linek. 1992. Writing to learn. In *Reading/writing connections: learning from research,* edited by J. W. Irwin and M. A. Doyle. Newark, Del.: International Reading Association.

Vacca, R., and J. Vacca. 1989. *Content area reading,* 3d ed. Glenview, Ill.: Scott, Foresman.

Vygotsky, Lev. 1978. *Mind in society.* Cambridge, Mass: Harvard University Press.

Webb, C. A. 1990. Reading and testing versus MTV. *Illinois English Bulletin* 79 (1):79–82.

Wolff, V. E. 1993. Interview. Pittsburgh, Penn.: National Council of Teachers of English.

Yep, L. 1993. Interview. Pittsburgh, Penn.: National Council of Teachers of English.

———. 1993. *Dragon's Gate.* New York: HarperCollins Children's Books. Chapter 6 opening quote p. 218.

Yopp, R. H. and H. K. Yopp. 1992. *Literature-based reading activities.* Boston: Allyn & Bacon.

Literature for Young Adults

The titles and authors included here are representative of the breadth of quality works that are available for classrooms as well as individuals. Certainly, we have not included all of the books or all of the authors whom we could recommend; however, this list is designed as a beginning for teachers and students. We recommend you update it regularly from your own reading. This list includes many of the titles that have been mentioned in this book, including some classics, some poetry collections, and some works of nonfiction; however, most of the books are fiction written for young adults.

Adoff, A. *I Am the Darker Brother* (editor).
——. *Malcolm X.*
Alcott, L. M. *Little Women.*
Anaya, R. A. *Bless Me, Ultima.*
Angelou, M. *Gather Together in My Name.*
——. *I Know Why the Caged Bird Sings.*
——. *Singin' and Swingin' and Gettin' Merry Like Christmas.*
Arrick, F. *Chernowitz!*
——. *What You Don't Know Can Kill You.*
——. *Where'd You Get the Gun, Billy?*
Austen, J. *Pride and Prejudice.*
Avi. *The Fighting Ground.*
——. *The Man Who Was Poe.*
——. *Nothing But the Truth.*
——. *The True Confessions of Charlotte Doyle.*
——. *Windcatcher.*
Babbitt, N. *The Eyes of the Amaryllis.*
——. *Tuck Everlasting.*
Baker, J. *Window.*
Bauer, J. *SQUASHED.*
——. *Sticks.*
——. *THWONK.*
Bauer, M. D. *Am I Blue? Coming Out from the Silence* (editor).
——. *A Dream of Queens and Castles.*
——. *Face to Face.*

——. *Foster Child.*

——. *Like Mother, Like Daughter.*

——. *On My Honor.*

——. *A Question of Trust.*

——. *Rain of Fire.*

——. *Shelter from the Wind.*

——. *Tangled Butterfly.*

——. *A Taste of Smoke.*

——. *What's Your Story? A Young Person's Guide to Writing Fiction.*

Bennett, J. *The Dark Corridor.*

——. *The Hooded Man.*

——. *Sing Me a Death Song.*

——. *Skinhead.*

Blos, Joan W. *Brothers of the Heart.*

——. *A Gathering of Days: A New England Girl's Journal, 1830–32.*

Bode, J. *Beating the Odds: Stories of Unexpected Achievers.*

——. *New Kids in Town: Stories of Immigrant Youths.*

——. *Voices of Rape.*

Bograd, L. *The Kolokol Papers.*

Bradbury, R. *Fahrenheit 451.*

Brancato, R. *Winning.*

Bridgers, S. E. *All Together Now.*

——. *Notes for Another Life.*

——. *Permanent Connections.*

Brontë, C. *Jane Eyre.*

Brooks, B. *The Moves Make the Man.*

——. *No Kidding.*

Brooks, M. *Paradise Cafe and Other Stories.*

Bunting, E. *Fly Away Home.*

——. *The Hideout.*

——. *Jumping the Nail.*

——. *The Wall.*

Burns, O. *Cold Sassy Tree.*

Cannon, A. E. *The Shadow Brothers.*

Carter, A. R. *Up Country.*

Childress, A. *A Hero Ain't Nothing But a Sandwich.*

——. *Rainbow Jordan.*

Choi, S. N. *Echoes of the White Giraffe.*

——. *Year of Impossible Goodbyes.*

Cisneros, S. *House on Mango Street.*

——. *Woman Hollering Creek.*

Clayton, E. *Martin Luther King: The Peaceful Warrior.*

Cole, B. *Celine.*

——. *The Goats.*

Collier, J. L., and C. Collier. *The Bloody Country.*

——. *Jump Ship to Freedom.*

——. *My Brother Sam Is Dead.*

——. *Who Is Carrie?*

Collier, J. L. *Outside Looking In.*

——. *When the Stars Begin to Fall.*

Coman, C. *Tell Me Everything.*

Conlon-McKenna, M. *Under the Hawthorn Tree.*

Cooney, C. *The Face on the Milk Carton.*

——. *Operation: Homefront.*

——. *The Party's Over.*

——. *Whatever Happened to Janie?*

Cormier, R. *After the Chocolate War.*

——. *After the First Death.*

——. *The Bumblebee Flies Anyway.*

——. *The Chocolate War.*

——. *8 Plus 1.*

——. *I Am the Cheese.*

——. *Other Bells for Us to Ring.*

——. *Tunes for Bears to Dance To.*

Crew, L. *Children of the River.*

Crutcher, C. *Athletic Shorts: Six Short Stories.*

——. *Chinese Handcuffs.*

——. *The Crazy Horse Electric Game.*

——. *Running Loose.*

——. *Staying Fat for Sarah Byrnes.*

——. *Stotan!*

Danziger, P. *Can You Sue Your Parents for Malpractice?*
——.*The Cat Ate My Gym Suit.*

Davis, J. *Checking on the Moon.*
——. *Sex Education.*

Dickinson, P. *Eva.*

Duncan, L. *Daughters of Eve.*
——. *Killing Mr. Griffin.*
——. *Summer of Fear.*

Dunning, S. et al. *Reflections on the Gift of WaterMelon Pickle* (editors).
——. *Some Haystacks Don't Have Any Needles.*

Durant, P. R. *When Heroes Die.*

Dygard, T. J. *The Rookie Arrives.*
——. *Wilderness Peril.*

Fine, A. *Alias Madame Doubtfire.*
——. *The Book of the Banshee.*
——. *My War with Goggle-Eyes.*

Fox, P. *One-Eyed Cat.*
——. *The Slave Dancer.*

Frank, A. *The Diary of a Young Girl.*
——. *Tales from the Secret Annex.*

Freedman, R. *Children of the Wild West.*
——. *Cowboys of the Wild West.*
——. *Eleanor Roosevelt: A Life of Discovery.*
——. *Franklin Delano Roosevelt.*
——. *Immigrant Kids.*
——. *Lincoln: A Photobiography.*
——. *The Wright Brothers: How They Invented the Airplane.*

Gallo, D. (editor).*Center Stage.*
——. *Connection: Short Stories by Outstanding Writers for Young Adults.*
——. *Join In: Multiethnic Short Stories by Outstanding Writers for Young Adults.*
——. *Short Circuits: Thirteen Shocking Stories by Outstanding Writers for Young Adults.*

——. *Sixteen Short Stories by Outstanding Writers for Young Adults.*
——. *Visions: Nineteen Short Stories by Outstanding Writers for Young Adults.*
——. *Within Reach.*

Garland, S. *The Lotus Seed.*
——. *The Shadow of the Dragon.*

George, J. C. *Julie of the Wolves.*
——. *Water Sky.*

Giden, M. *The Planet of Amazement.*

Glenn, M. *Back to Class.*
——. *Class Dismissed: High School Poems.*
——. *Class Dismissed II: More High School Poems.*
——. *My Friend's Got This Problem, Mr. Chandler.*

Golding, W. *Lord of the Flies.*

Gordon, S. *The Middle of Somewhere.*
——. *Waiting for the Rain.*

Greene, B. *The Drowning of Stephan Jones.*
——. *Summer of My German Soldier.*
——. *Them That Glitter and Them That Don't.*

Greene, S. *The Boy Who Drank Too Much.*

Guest, J. *Ordinary People.*

Guy, R. *Ruby.*

Hahn, M. D. *The Dead Man in Indian Creek.*
——. *December Stillness.*
——. *Stepping on the Cracks.*
——. *The Wind Blows Backwards.*

Hamilton, V. *Anthony Burns: The Defeat and Triumph of a Fugitive Slave.*
——. *Dustland.*
——. *The Gathering.*
——. *The House of Dies Drear.*
——. *Justice and Her Brothers.*
——. *Plain City.*
——. *A White Romance.*
——. *Zeely.*

Hansen, J. *Between Two Fires.*
——. *The Captive.*
——. *The Gift-Giver.*
——. *Home Boy.*
——. *Out from This Place.*
——. *Which Way Freedom?*
——. *Yellow Bird and Me.*

Hayes, D. *The Trouble with Lemons.*

Hemingway, E. *The Old Man and the Sea.*

Hentoff, N. *The Day They Came to Arrest the Book.*

Hersom, K. *Half Child.*

Hicyilmaz, G. *Against the Storm.*

Highwater, J. *Anpao.*

Hinton, S. E. *The Outsiders.*
——. *That Was Then, This Is Now.*

Hobbs, W. *Beardance.*
——. *Bearstone.*
——. *Change in Altitudes.*
——. *Down River.*

Holland, I. *The Man Without a Face.*
——. *The Unfrightened Dark.*

Honeycutt, N. *Ask Me Something Easy.*
——. *Juliet Fisher and the Foolproof Plan.*

Houston, J. W., and J. D. Houston. *Farewell to Manzanar.*

Hughes, M. *Beyond the Dark River.*
——. *Crisis on Conshelf Ten.*
——. *The Crystal Drop.*
——. *Devil on My Back.*
——. *The Dream Catcher.*
——. *The Guardian of Isis.*
——. *Hunter in the Dark.*
——. *Invitation to the Game.*
——. *The Isis Pedlar.*
——. *Keeper of the Isis Light.*
——. *The Promise.*
——. *Ring-Rise, Ring-Set.*
——. *Sandwriter.*

Hunt, I. *Across Five Aprils.*

Innocenti, R. *Rose Blanche.*

Janeczko, P. *Don't Forget to Fly.*
——. *The Place My Words Are Looking For.*
——. *Poetspeak: In Their Work, About Their Work.*
——. *Postcard Poems: A Collection of Poetry for Sharing.*
——. *Strings: A Gathering of Family Poems.*

Joyce, J. *A Portrait of the Artist as a Young Man.*

Kaye, M. *Real Heroes.*

Keehn, S. M. *I Am Regina.*

Kerr, M. E. *Dinky Hocker Shoots Smack.*
——. *Fell.*
——. *Fell Back.*
——. *Fell Down.*
——. *Gentlehands.*
——. *I'll Love You When You're More Like Me.*
——. *Is That You, Miss Blue?*
——. *Linger.*
——. *Little Little.*
——. *Me Me Me Me Me Not a Novel.*
——. *Night Kites.*

Knowles, J. *A Separate Peace.*

Koertge, R. *Mariposa Blues.*

Korman, G. *Don't Care High.*

Kuklin, S. *Speaking Out: Teenagers Take On Race, Sex, and Identity.*

Laird, E. *Kiss the Dust.*

Lamb, W. (editor). *The Ground Zero Club and Other Prize-winning Plays from the 1985–86 Young Playwrights Festival.*
——. *Hey Little Walter and Other Prize-winning Plays from the 1989–90 Young Playwrights Festival.*

———. *Meeting the Winter Bike Rider and Other Prize-winning Plays from the 1983–84 Young Playwrights Festival.*

———. *Sparks in the Park and Other Prize-winning Plays from the 1987–88 Young Playwrights Festival.*

Lee, H. *To Kill a Mockingbird.*

Lee, M. *Finding My Voice.*

———. *If It Hadn't Been for Yoon Jun.*

LeMieux, A. C. *The TV Guidance Counselor.*

Lester, J. *To Be a Slave.*

Lewis, S. *Elmer Gantry.*

Lipsyte, R. *The Contender.*

———. *One Fat Summer.*

Lord, B .B. *In the Year of the Boar and Jackie Robinson.*

Lowry, L. *Find a Stranger, Say Goodbye.*

———. *The Giver.*

———. *Number the Stars.*

———. *A Summer to Die.*

Lyons, M. E. *Letters from a Slave Girl: The Story of Harriet Jacobs.*

MacLachlan, P. *Journey* .

Malmgren, D. *The Ninth Issue.*

Mazer, H. *The Island Keeper.*

———. *The Last Mission.*

———. *When the Phone Rang.*

Mazer, N. F. *After the Rain.*

———. *Babyface.*

———. *Dear Bill, Remember Me? and Other Stories.*

———. *A Figure of Speech.*

———. *Mrs. Fish, Ape, and Me, the Dump Queen.*

———. *Saturday, the Twelfth of October.*

———. *Silver.*

———. *Summer Girls, Love Boys and Other Stories.*

———. *Taking Terri Mueller.*

———. *Up in Seth's Room.*

———. *Waltzing on Water: Poems by Women* (edited with Marjorie Lewis).

Mazer, H., and N. F. Mazer. *Bright Days, Stupid Nights.*

———. *The Solid Gold Kid.*

McCullers, C. *The Heart is a Lonely Hunter.*

McKissack, P. C., and F. McKissack. *Sojourner Truth: Ain't I a Woman?*

Meltzer, M. *All Times, All People: A World History of Slavery.*

———. *Rescue: The Story of How Gentiles Saved Jews in the Holocaust.*

———. *Starting from Home: A Writer's Beginnings.*

Mori, K. *Shizuko's Daughter.*

Murphy, J. *The Boys' War: Confederate and Union Soldiers Talk About the Civil War.*

Myers, W. D. *Fallen Angels.*

———. *Fast Sam, Cool Clyde, and Stuff.*

———. *Hoops.*

———. *Malcolm X: By Any Means Necessary.*

———. *Mop, Moondance, and the Nagasaki Knights.*

———. *Motown and Didi.*

———. *The Outside Shot.*

———. *Scorpions.*

———. *Somewhere in the Darkness.*

———. *Won't Know Till I Get There.*

Naidou, B. *Chain of Fire.*

———. *Journey to Jo'burg.*

Naylor, P. R. *Reluctantly Alice.*

———. *Shiloh.*

———. *To Walk the Sky Path.*

Nhong, H. Q. *The Land I Lost.*

Nye, N. S. *Different Ways to Pray.*

———. *Hugging the Jukebox.*

——. *This Same Sky: A Collection of Poems from Around the World* (editor).
——. *Yellow Glove.*

O'Brien, R. *Z for Zachariah.*

O'Dell, S. *Island of the Blue Dolphins.*

O'Dell, S., and E. Hall. *Thunder Rolling in the Mountains.*

Okimoto, J. D. *Molly by Any Other Name.*

Oneal, Z. *A Formal Feeling.*
——. *The Language of Goldfish.*
——. *In Summer Light.*

Paterson, K. *Bridge to Terabithia.*
——. *Jacob Have I Loved.*
——. *Park's Quest.*

Paulsen, G. *Canyons.*
——. *The Cookcamp.*
——. *The Crossing.*
——. *Dancing Carl.*
——. *Dogsong.*
——. *Eastern Sun, Winter Moon: An Autobiography.*
——. *The Foxman.*
——. *Hatchet.*
——. *The Haymeadow.*
——. *The Island.*
——. *The Monument.*
——. *NightJohn.*
——. *The Night the White Deer Died.*
——. *Popcorn Days and Buttermilk Nights.*
——. *The River.*
——. *Sentries.*
——. *Tiltawhirl John.*
——. *Tracker.*
——. *Winterkill.*
——. *The Winter Room.*
——. *Woodsong.*
——. *The Voyage of the Frog.*

Peck, R.. *Anonymously Yours* (An autobiography).
——. *Are You in the House Alone?*
——. *Bel-Air Bambi and the Mall Rats.*

——. *Close Enough to Touch.*
——. *Don't Look and It Won't Hurt.*
——. *Dreamland Lake.*
——. *Father Figure.*
——. *Ghosts I Have Been.*
——. *Princess Ashley.*
——. *Remembering the Good Times.*
——. *Secrets of the Shopping Mall.*
——. *Those Summer Girls I Never Met.*
——. *Through a Brief Darkness.*
——. *Unfinished Portrait of Jessica.*
——. *Voices After Midnight.*

Peck, R. N. *A Day No Pigs Would Die.*

Pfeffer, S. B. *A Matter of Principle.*

Pike, C. *Remember Me.*

Pitts, P. *Racing the Sun.*
——. *The Shadowman's Way.*

Pullman, P. *Ruby in the Smoke.*
——. *Shadow in the North.*
——. *The Tiger in the Well.*
——. *The White Mercedes.*

Rana, I. *The Roller Birds of Rampur.*

Rankin, L. *Daughter of the Mountains.*

Remarque, E. M. *All Quiet on the Western Front.*

Rinaldi, A. *A Break with Charity.*
——. *The Last Silk Dress.*
——. *Time Enough for Drums.*
——. *Wolf by the Ears.*

Rostkowski, M. *After the Dancing Days.*

Roth-Hano, R. *Touch Wood: A Girlhood in Occupied France.*

Rylant, C. *A Fine White Dust.*
——. *Missing May.*

Salinger, J. D. *The Catcher in the Rye.*

Salisbury, G. *Blue Skin of the Sea.*
——. *Under the Blood-Red Sun.*

Sebestyen, O. *The Girl in the Box.*
——. *Words by Heart.*

Semel, N. *Becoming Gershona.*

Sender, R. M. *The Cage.*

Sleator, W. *The Boy Who Reversed Himself.*
———. *House of Stairs.*

Soto, G. *Baseball in April and Other Stories.*
———. *Living Up the Street.*
———. *Local News.*
———. *Pacific Crossing.*
———. *The Skirt.*
———. *Small Faces.*
———. *Taking Sides.*

Speare, E. *Sign of the Beaver.*

Spinka, P. K. *White Hare's Horses.*

Stanley, D., and P. Vennema. *Bard of Avon: The Story of William Shakespeare.*

Staples, S. F. *Haveli.*
———. *Shabanu, Daughter of the Wind.*

Steinbeck, J. *The Red Pony.*

Strasser, T. *A Very Touchy Subject.*

Strickland, M. R. *Poems That Sing to You* (editor).

Taylor, M. *Let the Circle Be Unbroken.*
———. *The Road to Memphis.*
———. *Roll of Thunder, Hear My Cry.*

Taylor, T. *The Cay.*
———. *The Sniper.*
———. *Timothy of the Cay.*
———. *The Weirdo.*

Thomas, J. C. (editor). *A Gathering of Flowers: Stories About Being Young in America.* (editor).

Thompson, J. *Goofbang Value Daze.*
———. *The Grounding of Group Six.*
———. *Shepard.*

Twain, Mark. *The Adventures of Huckleberry Finn.*

Uchida, Y. *The Best Bad Thing.*
———. *A Jar Of Dreams.*

———. *Journey Home.*
———. *Journey to Topaz.*

Voigt, C. *Building Blocks.*
———. *The Callender Papers.*
———. *David and Jonathan.*
———. *Dicey's Song.*
———. *Homecoming.*
———. *Izzy, Willy-Nilly.*
———. *Jackaroo.*
———. *Orfe.*
———. *A Solitary Blue.*

Vos, I. *Anna Is Still Here.*
———. *Hide and Seek.*

Vuong, L. D. *The Brocaded Slippers and Other Vietnamese Tales.*

Walker, K. *Peter.*

Westall, R. *Fathom Five.*
———. *Ghost Abbey.*
———. *The Machine Gunners.*
———. *The Watch House.*

Wharton, E. *Ethan Frome.*

Whelan, G. *Goodbye Viet Nam.*
———. *The Secret Keeper.*
———. *A Time to be Silent.*

White, E. E. *Friends for Life.*
———. *Long Live the Queen.*
———. *The President's Daughter.*
———. *White House Autumn.*

Wier, E. *The Loner.*

Williams-Garcia, R. *Fast Talk on a Slow Track.*

Windsor, P. *The Christmas Killer.*
———. *The Sandman's Eyes.*

Wolff, V. E. *Make Lemonade.*
———. *Mozart Season.*
———. *Probably Still Nick Swansen.*

Wrede, P. *Dealing with Dragons.*
———. *Searching for Dragons.*
———. *Talking to Dragons.*

X, Malcom, and A. Haley. *The Autobiography of Malcolm X.*

Yates, E. *Amos Fortune, Free Man.*

Yep, L. *Child of the Owl.*

———. *Dragon's Gate.*

———. *Dragonwings.*

———. *The Rainbow People.*

———. *The Star Fisher.*

Yolen, J. *The Devil's Arithmetic.*

Zindel, P. *The Effects of Gamma Rays on Man-in-the-Moon Marigolds.*

———. *Pigman.*

———. *Pigman and Me.*

Award-Winning Books for Young Adults

Jane Addams Children's Book Award

Sponsored by the Women's International League for Peace and Freedom and the Jane Addams Peace Association, this award is for the children's book which best promotes peace, equality and social justice.

1994 *Freedom's Children: Young Civil Rights Activists Tell Their Own Stories.* Ellen Levine.

1993 *A Taste of Salt: A Story of Modern Haiti.* Frances Temple.

1992 *Journey of the Sparrows.* Fran Buss.

1991 *Big Book for Peace.* Ann Durrell and Marilyn Sachs.

1990 *Long Hard Journey: The Story of the Pullman Porter.* Patricia and Frederick McKissack.

1989 *Anthony Burns: The Defeat and Triumph of a Fugitive Slave.* Virginia Hamilton.
Looking Out. Victoria Boutis.

1988 *Waiting for the Rain: A Novel of South Africa.* Shelia Gordon.

1987 *Nobody Wants a Nuclear War.* Judith Vigna.

1986 *Ain't Gonna Study War No More: The Story of America's Peace Seekers.* Milton Meltzer.

1985 *Short Life of Sophie Scholl.* Herman Vinke.

1984 *Rain of Fire.* Marion Dane Bauer.

1983 *Hiroshima No Pika.* Toshi Maruki.

1982 *Spirit to Ride the Whirlwind.* Athena V. Lord.

Boston Globe-Horn Book Award

The Boston Globe-Horn Book Award has been presented annually since 1967 by the *Boston Globe* and the Horn Book magazine.

1993 Fiction: *Ajeemah and His Son.* James Berry.
Honor Book: *The Giver.* Lois Lowry.

Nonfiction: *Sojourner Truth: Ain't I a Woman?* Patricia C. and Frederick McKissack.
Illustration: *Fortune Teller.* Lloyd Alexander.

1992 Fiction: *Missing May.* Cynthia Rylant.
Nonfiction: *Talking with Artists.* Pat Cummings.
Illustration: *Seven Blind Mice.* Ed Young.

1991 Fiction: *The True Confessions of Charlotte Doyle.* Avi.
Nonfiction: *Appalachia: The Voices of Sleeping Birds.* Cynthia Rylant.
Illustration: *The Tale of the Mandarin Duck.* Katherine Paterson.

1990 Fiction: *Maniac Magee.* Jerry Spinelli.
Nonfiction: *The Great Little Madison.* Jean Fritz.
Illustration: *Lon Po Po.* Ed Young.

1989 Fiction: *The Village by the Sea.* Paula Fox.
Nonfiction: *The Way Things Work.* David Macaulay.
Illustration: *Shy Charles.* Rosemary Wells.

1988 Fiction: *The Friendship.* Mildred Taylor.
Nonfiction: *Anthony Burns: The Defeat and Triumph of a Fugitive Slave.* Virginia Hamilton.
Illustration: *The Boy of the Three-Year Nap.* Dianne Snyder, illustrated by Allen Say.

1987 Fiction: *Rabble Starkey.* Lois Lowry.
Nonfiction: *Pilgrims of Plimoth.* Marcia Sewall.
Illustration: *Mufaro's Beautiful Daughter.* John Streptoe.

1986 Fiction: *In Summer Light.* Zibby Oneal.
Nonfiction: *Auks, Rocks, and the Odd Dinosaur: Inside Stories from the Smithsonian's Museum of Natural History.* Peggy Thomson.
Illustration: *The Paper Crane.* Molly Bang.

1985 Fiction: *The Moves Make the Man.* Bruce Brooks.
Nonfiction: *Commodore Perry in the Land of the Shogun.* Rhoda Blumberg.
Illustration: *Mama Don't Allow.* Thacher Hurd.

1984 Fiction: *A Little Fear.* Patricia Wrightson.
Nonfiction: *The Double Life of Pocahontas.* Jean Fritz.
Illustration: *Jonah and the Great Fish.* Retold and illustrated by Warwick Hutton.

1983 Fiction: *Sweet Whispers, Brother Rush.* Virginia Hamilton.
Nonfiction: *Behind Barbed Wire: The Imprisonment of Japanese Americans During World War II.* Daniel S. Davis.
Illustration: *A Chair for My Mother.* Vera B. Williams.

1982 Fiction: *Playing Beatie Bow.* Ruth Park.
Nonfiction: *Upon the Head of the Goat: A Childhood in Hungary, 1939–1944.* Aranka Siegal.

1981 Fiction: *The Leaving.* Lynn Hall.
Nonfiction: *The Weaver's Gift.* Kathryn Lasky.
Illustration: *Outside Over There.* Maurice Sendak.

1980 Fiction: *Conrad's War*. Andrew Davies.
Nonfiction: *Building: The Fight Against Gravity*. Mario Salvadori.
Illustration: *The Garden of Abdul Gasazi*. Chris Van Allsburg.

Margaret A. Edwards Award Authors

The Margaret A. Edwards Award honors an author's lifetime achievement for writing books that have been popular with teenagers over a period of time. . . . Established in 1987, the annual award honors Margaret A. Edwards, a pioneer in young adult library services. The award is administered by the Young Adult Library Services Association of the American Library Association and sponsored by *School Library Journal.*

1994 Walter Dean Myers

1993 M. E. Kerr

1992 Lois Duncan

1991 Robert Cormier

1990 Richard Peck

1989 No award

1988 S. E. Hinton

Golden Kite Awards

This award was established in 1973 by the Society of Children's Book Writers. It is presented annually to those who "best exhibit excellence in writing or illustration and genuinely appeal to the interests and concerns of children."

1993 Fiction: *Make Lemonade*. Virginia Euwer Wolff.

Nonfiction: *Eleanor Roosevelt: A Life of Discovery*. Russell Freedman.
Picture-Illustration: *By the Light of the Halloween Moon*. Kevin Hawkes.

1992 Fiction: *Letters from a Slave Girl: The Harriet Jacobs Story*. Mary E. Lyons.
Nonfiction: *The Long Road to Gettysburg*. Jim Murphy.
Picture-Illustration: *Chicken Sunday*. Patricia Polacco.

1991 Fiction: *The Raincatchers*. Jean Thesman.
Nonfiction: *The Wright Brothers: How They Invented the Airplane*. Russell Freedman.
Picture-Illustration: *Mama, Do You Love Me?* Barbara M. Joose, illustrated by Barbara Lavellee.

1990 Fiction: *The True Confessions of Charlotte Doyle*. Avi.
Nonfiction: *The Boys' War: Confederate and Union Soldiers Talk About the Civil War*. Jim Murphy.
Picture-Illustration: *Home Place*. Crescent Dragonwagon, illustrated by Jerry Pinkney.

1989 Fiction: *Jenny of the Tetons*. Kristiana Gregory.
Nonfiction: *Panama Canal: Gateway to the World*. Judith St. George.
Picture-Illustration: *Tom Thumb*. Richard Jesse Watson.

1988 Fiction: *Borrowed Children*. George Ella Lyon.
Nonfiction: *Let There Be Light: A Book About Windows*. James Cross Giblin.
Picture-Illustration: *Forest of Dreams*. Rosemary Wells, illustrated by Susan Jeffers.

1987   Fiction: *Rabble Starkey*. Lois Lowry.
Nonfiction: *The Incredible Journey of Lewis and Clark*. Rhoda Blumberg.
Picture-Illustration: *The Devil & Mother Crump*. Valerie Scho Carey, illustrated by Arnold Lobel.

1986   Fiction: *After the Dancing Days*. Margaret I. Rostkowski.
Nonfiction: *Poverty in America*. Milton Meltzer.
Picture-Illustration: *Alphabatics*. Suse MacDonald.

1985   Fiction: *Sarah, Plain and Tall*. Patricia MacLachlan.
Nonfiction: *Commodore Perry in the Land of the Shogun*. Rhoda Blumberg.
Picture-Illustration: *The Donkey's Dream*. Barbara Helen Berger.

1984   Fiction: *Tancy*. Belinda Hurmence.
Nonfiction: *Walls: Defenses Throughout History*. James Cross Giblin.
Picture-Illustration: *The Napping House*. Audrey Wood, illustrated by Don Wood.

1983   Fiction: *The Tempering*. Gloria Skurzynski.
Nonfiction: *The Illustrated Dinosaur Dictionary*. Helen Roney Sattler.
Picture-Illustration: *The Little Red Riding Hood*. Trina Schart Hyman.

1982   Fiction: *Ralph S. Mouse*. Beverly Cleary.
Nonfiction: *Chimney Sweeps*. James Cross Giblin.
Picture-Illustration: *Giorgio's Village*. Tomie de Paola.

IRA Children's Book Award Winners

Since 1987, the International Reading Association has recognized a book in a young adult or older reader category.

1993   *Letters from Rifka*. Karen Hesse.

1992   *Rescue Josh McGuire*. Ben Mikaelsen.

1991   *Under the Hawthorn Tree*. Marita Conlon-McKenna.

1990   *Children of the River*. Linda Crew.

1989   *Probably Still Nick Swansen*. Virginia Euwer Wolff.

1988   *Ruby in the Smoke*. Philip Pullman.

1987   *After the Dancing Days*. Margaret I. Rostkowski.

National Jewish Book Awards

This award was begun in 1952 to "encourage and award the author of an original, English publication for children, which embraces a Jewish theme, or to recognize the cumulative work of an author's contribution to Jewish juvenile literature. The Children's Illustrated Book category (ILLUS) was begun in 1982 to award the illustrations that are intrinsic to the text."

1993   No award was given. It will be combined with the 1994 award.

1992   *The Man from the Other Side*. Uri Orlev, translated by Hillel Halkin. *Chicken Man*. Michelle Edwards.

1991   *Becoming Gershona*. Nava Semel. *Hanukkah*. Roni Schotter.

1990   *Number the Stars*. Lois Lowry. *Berchick, My Mother's Horse*. Esther Silverstein Blanc.

1989   *Devil's Arithmetic*. Jane Yolen.

Just Enough Is Plenty: A Hanukkah Tale. Barbara Goldin.

1988 *The Return.* Sonia Levitin.
Exodus. Adapted from the Bible by Miriam Chaikin.

1987 *Monday in Odessa.* Eileen Bluestone Sherman.
Poems for Jewish Holidays. Selected by Myra Cohen Livingston.

1986 *In Kindling Flame: The Story of Hannah Senesch, 1921–1944.* Linda Atkinson.
Brothers. Retold by Florence B. Freedman.

1985 *Good If It Goes.* Gail Provost and Gail Levine-Freidus.
Mrs. Moskowitz and the Sabbath Candlesticks. Amy Schwartz.

1984 *The Jewish Kids Catalog.* Chaya Burstein.

1983 *King of the Seventh Grade.* Barbara Cohen.
Yussel's Prayer: A Yom Kippur Story. Barbara Cohen.

1982 *The Night Journey.* Kathryn Lasky.

Coretta Scott King Award

Begun in 1969, this award honors Mrs. King for "her courage and determination to continue the work for peace and world brotherhood." The award also commemorates the life of Dr. Martin Luther King. The award is presented by the American Library Association.

1994 *Toning the Sweep.* Angela Johnson.
Soul Looks Back in Wonder. Tom Feelings.

Honor Books: *Malcolm X: By Any Means Necessary.* Walter Dean Myers.

Brown Honey in Broomwheat Tea. Joyce Carol Thomas.

1993 *The Dark-Thirty: Southern Tales of the Supernatural.* Patricia McKissack.
Honor Books: *Somewhere in the Darkness.* Walter Dean Myers.
Mississippi Challenge. Mildred Pitts Walter.
Sojourner Truth: Ain't I a Woman? Patricia McKissack and Frederick McKissack.

1992 *Now Is Your Time: The African American Struggle for Freedom.* Walter Dean Myers.
Tar Beach. Faith Ringold.

1991 *Road to Memphis.* Mildred Taylor.
Aida. Told by Leontyne Price.

1990 *Long Hard Journey.* Patricia McKissack and Frederick McKissack.
Nathaniel Talking. Eloise Greenfield.

1989 *Fallen Angels.* Walter Dean Myers.
Mirandy and Brother Wind. Patricia McKissack.

1988 *Friendship.* Mildred Taylor.
Mufaro's Beautiful Daughter: An African Tale. Edited by John Steptoe.

1987 *Justin and the Best Biscuits in the World.* Mildred Walter.

1986 *Patchwork Quilt.* Valerie Flournoy.
The People Could Fly: Black American Folktales. Retold by Virginia Hamilton.

1985 *Motown and Didi: A Love Story.* Walter Dean Myers.

1984 *Everett Anderson's Goodbye.* Lucille Clifton.
My Mama Needs Me. Mildred Pitts Walter.

Newbery Medal Books

The Newbery Award was established in 1922 in honor of the English publisher and bookseller, John Newbery. It is presented annually by the American Library Association to "the author of the most distinguished contribution to American literature for children" published in the preceding year. The winning book is awarded the Newbery Medal and one or more runners-up are designated as Honor Books.

1994 *The Giver.* Lois Lowry.
Honor Books: *Crazy Lady.* Jane Leslie Conly.
Dragon's Gate. Laurence Yep.
Eleanor Roosevelt: A Life of Discovery. Russell Freedman.

1993 *Missing May.* Cynthia Rylant.
Honor Books: *The Dark-Thirty: Southern Tales of the Supernatural.* Patricia McKissack.
Somewhere in the Darkness. Walter Dean Myers.
What Hearts. Bruce Brooks.

1992 *Shiloh.* Phyllis Reynolds Naylor.
Honor Books: *Nothing But the Truth.* Avi.
The Wright Brothers: How They Invented the Airplane. Russell Freedman.

1991 *Maniac Magee.* Jerry Spinelli.
Honor Book: *The True Confessions of Charlotte Doyle.* Avi.

1990 *Number the Stars.* Lois Lowry.
Honor Books: *Afternoon of the Elves.* Janet Taylor Lisel.
Shabanu, Daughter of the Wind. Susan Fisher Staples.
The Winter Room. Gary Paulsen.

1989 *Joyful Noise: Poems for Two Voices.* Paul Fleishman.
Honor Books: *In the Beginning.* Virginia Hamilton.
Scorpions. Walter Dean Myers.

1988 *Lincoln: A Photobiography.* Russell Freedman.
Honor Books: *After the Rain.* Norma Fox Mazer.
Hatchet. Gary Paulsen.

1987 *The Whipping Boy.* Sid Fleischman.
Honor Books: *A Fine White Dust.* Cynthia Rylant.
On My Honor. Marion Dane Bauer.
Volcano: The Eruption and Healing of Mount St. Helens. Patricia Lauber.

1986 *Sarah, Plain and Tall.* Patricia MacLachlan.
Honor Books: *Commodore Perry in the Land of the Shogun.* Rhoda Blumberg.
Dogsong. Gary Paulsen.

1985 *The Hero and the Crown.* Robin McKinley.
Honor Books: *Like Jake and Me.* Mavis Jukes.
The Moves Make the Man. Bruce Brooks.
One-Eyed Cat. Paula Fox.

1984 *Dear Mr Henshaw.* Beverly Cleary.
Honor Books: *The Sign of the Beaver.* Elizabeth George Speare.
A Solitary Blue. Cynthia Voigt.
Sugaring Time. Kathryn Lasky.
The Wish Giver. Bill Brittain.

1983 *Dicey's Song.* Cynthia Voigt.
Honor Books: *The Blue Sword.* Robin McKinley.
Doctor DeSoto. William Steig.
Graven Images. Paul Fleischman.
Homesick: My Own Story. Jean Fitz.

Sweet Whispers, Brother Rush.
Virginia Hamilton.

1982 *A Visit to William Blake's Inn: Poems for Innocent and Experienced Travelers.* Nancy Willard.
Honor Books: *Ramona Quimby, Age 8.* Beverly Cleary.
Upon the Head of the Goat: A Childhood in Hungary, 1939–1944. Aranka Siegal.

1981 *Jacob Have I Loved.* Katherine Paterson.
Honor Books: *The Fledgling.* Jane Langton.
A Ring of Endless Light. Madeleine L'Engle.

1980 *A Gathering of Days: A New England Girl's Journal, 1830–32.* Joan Blos.
Honor Book: *The Road from Home: The Story of an Armenian Girl.* David Kerdian.

Scott O'Dell Award for Historical Fiction

This award was established in 1981 by Scott O'Dell and is administered by the Bulletin of the Center for Children's Books. "The book content must be historical fiction set in the new world and have literary merit."

1993 *Bull Run.* Paul Fleishman.

1992 *Stepping on the Cracks.* Mary Hahn.

1991 *Time of Troubles.* Pieter Van Raven.

1990 *Shades of Gray.* Carolyn Reeder.

1989 *Honorable Prison.* Lylle DeJenkins.

1988 *Charley Skeddle.* Patricia Beatty.

1987 *Streams to the River, River to the Sea: A Novel of Sacagawea.* Scott O'Dell.

1986 *Sarah, Plain and Tall.* Patricia MacLachlan.

1985 *Fighting Ground.* Avi.

1984 *Sign of the Beaver.* Elizabeth Speare.

Orbis Pictus

Given annually since 1990 by the National Council of Teachers of English, the award honors distinction in nonfiction for children. It commemorates *Orbis Pictus* by Johannes Amos Commenius, which is considered to be the first work of nonfiction exclusively for young readers.

1994 *Crossing America on an Immigrant Train.* Jim Murphy.
Honor Books: *To the Top of the World: Adventures with Arctic Wolves.* Jim Brandenburg.
Making Sense: Animal Perception and Communication. Bruce Brooks.

1993 *Children of the Dust Bowl: The True Story of the School at Weed Patch Camp.* Jerry Stanley.
Honor Books: *Talking with Artists.* Pat Cummings.
Come Back Salmon. Molly Cone.

1992 *Flight: The Journey of Charles Lindbergh.* Robert Burleigh, illustrated by Mike Wimmer.
Honor Books: *Now Is Your Time: The African American Struggle for Freedom.* Walter Dean Myers.
Prairie Vision: The Life and Times of Solomon Butcher. Pam Conrad.

1991 *Franklin Delano Roosevelt.* Russell Freedman.
Honor Books: *Arctic Memories.* by Normee Ekoomiak.
Seeing the Earth from Space. Patricia Lauber.

1990 *The Great Little Madison.* Jean Fritz.
Honor Books:
The Great American Gold Rush.
Rhoda Blumberg.
The News About Dinosaurs. Patricia
Lauber.

Edgar Allan Poe Awards

The Mystery Writers of America annually
honor the best work in mystery, crime,
suspense, and intrigue. The following
information lists the books recognized
from 1980–1993, awarded in the Young
Adult category.

1993 *The Name of the Game with Murder.*
Joan Lowery Nixon.

1992 *A Little Bit Dead.* Chap Reaver.

1991 *Mote.* Chap Reaver.

1990 *Show Me the Evidence.* Alane
Ferguson.

1989 *Incident at Loring Groves.* Sonia
Levitin.

1988 *Lucy Forever and Miss Rosetree,
Shrinks.* Susan Shreve.

1987 *The Other Side of the Dark.* Joan
Lowery Nixon.

1986 *The Sandman's Eyes.* Patricia
Windsor.

1985 *Night Cry.* Phyllis Reynolds Naylor.

1984 *The Callender Papers.* Cynthia Voigt.

1983 *The Murder of Hound Dog Bates.*
Robbie Branscum.

1982 *Taking Terri Mueller.* Norma Fox
Mazer.

1981 *The Seance.* Joan Lowery Nixon.

1980 *The Kidnapping of Christina
Lattimore.* Joan Lowery Nixon.

Carter G. Woodson Book Award

This award was established in 1973 by the
National Council for the Social Studies in
honor of Harvard University professor
Carter G. Woodson. Woodson is known by
many as the father of American black history. The award recognizes trade books
that provide a "multicultural or multiethnic perspective." From 1989, awards
have been given on both an elementary
and secondary level. These are indicated
with an E or S following the author's name.

1993 *Madame C. J. Walker.* Patricia and
Fredrick McKissack. E

Mississippi Challenge. Mildred Pitts
Walter. S

1992 *The Last Princess: The Story of
Ka'iolani of Hawai'i.* Fay Stanley. E
*Native American Doctor: The Story of
Susan LaFlesche Picotte.* Jeri Ferris. S

1991 *Shirley Chisholm: Teacher and Con-
gresswoman.* Catherine Scheader. E
Sorrow's Kitchen: Zora Hurston.
Mary Lyon. S

1990 *In Two Worlds: A Yup'ik Eskimo
Family.* Aylette Jenness and Alice
Rivers. E
Paul Robeson: Hero Before His Time.
Rebecca Larsen. S

1989 *Walking the Road to Freedom: A
Story About Sojourner Truth.* Jeri
Ferris. E
Marian Anderson. Charles Patterson.
S

1988 *Black Music in America: A History
Through Its People.* James Haskins.

1987 *Happily May I Walk.* Arlene
Hirschfelder.

1986 *Dark Harvest: Migrant Farmworkers in America.* Brent Ashabranner.

1985 *To Live in Two Worlds: American Indian Youth Today.* Brent Ashabranner.

1984 *Mexico and the United States: Their Linked Destines.* E. B. Fincher.

1983 *Morning Star, Black Sun: The Cheyenne Indians and America's Energy Crisis.* Brent Ashabranner.

Other Awards

School Library Journal "Best Books of the Year" is presented annually in the December issue. The criteria for recognition include "clarity, [and] excellence in text and illustrations" and a book's "potential to attract readership among children and young adults."

International Reading Association "Young Adult Choices" is presented annually in the November issue of *The Journal of Reading.*

"Booklist Editors' Choices" is published annually in the January issue of *Booklist.*

ALA Best Books for Young Adults

ALA Recommended Books for the Reluctant Young Adult Reader

A P P E N D I X   C

Resources for Teachers

The following periodicals provide reviews and in some cases informative articles about books for young adults. These sources can help teachers with the selection of books. They may also suggest ways to implement books into the curriculum.

The ALAN Review
The National Council of Teachers of English
1111 Kenyon Road
Urbana, IL 61801

Booklinks
50 East Huron Street
Chicago, IL 60611

Booklist
ALA
50 East Huron Street
Chicago, IL 60611

Books for the Teen Ager
Office of Young Adult Services
New York Public Library
Fifth Avenue and 42nd Street
New York, NY 10018

Bulletin of the Center for Children's Books
P.O. Box 37005
Chicago, IL 60637

Children's Book Council
568 Broadway
New York, NY 10012

The English Journal
The National Council of Teachers of English
1111 Kenyon Road
Urbana, IL 61801

Horn Book
14 Beacon Street
Boston, MA 02108

Horn Book Guide
14 Beacon Street
Boston, MA 02108

Interracial Books for Children Bulletin
1841 Broadway
New York, NY 10023

Journal of Reading
The International Reading Association
800 Barksdale Road
P.O. Box 8139
Newark, DE 19714-8139

Journal in Youth Services in Libraries
ALA
50 East Huron Street
Chicago, IL 60611

Kirkus Reviews
200 Park Avenue South
Suite 1118
New York, NY 10003

Kliatt Young Adult Paperback Book Guide
425 Watertown Street
Newton, MA 02062

Language Arts
The National Council of Teachers of English
1111 Kenyon Road
Urbana, IL 61801

The New Advocate
Christopher Gordon Publishers
480 Washington Street
Norwood, MA 02062

Reading Teacher
The International Reading Association
800 Barksdale Road
P.O. Box 8139
Newark, DE 19714-8139

The School Library Journal
P.O. Box 1978
Marion, OH 43305

Signal Newsletter
IRA
P.O. Box 8139
Newark, DE 19714-8139

Voice of Youth Advocates (VOYA)
52 Liberty Street
Metuchen, NJ 08840

A P P E N D I X D

Organizations Providing Information on Censorship

American Civil Liberties Union
ACLU Washington Office
122 Maryland Avenue, NE
Washington, DC 20002
202-737-5900

The American Library Association
50 East Huron Street
Chicago, IL 60611
800-545-2433

Association for Supervision and
Curriculum Development
1250 North Pitt Street
Alexandria, VA 22314-1403
703-549-9110

Association of American Publishers, Inc.
2005 Massachusetts Avenue, NW
Washington, DC 20036
202-232-3335

The International Reading Association
800 Barksdale Road
P.O. Box 8139
Newark, DE 19714-8139
302-731-1600

National Coalition Against Censorship
2 West 64th Street
New York, NY 10023
212-724-1500

The National Council of Teachers of
English
1111 Kenyon Road
Urbana, IL 61801
800-369-6283

Office of Intellectual Freedom
(*Newsletter on Intellectual Freedom*)
Freedom to Read Foundation
50 East Huron Street
Chicago, IL 60611

People for the American Way
2000 M Street, NW
Suite 400
Washington, DC 20036

The National Council of Teachers of
English publishes several pamphlets that
should be available in every school. They
include *The Students' Right to Know, The*

Students' Right to Read, and *Censorship: Don't Let It Become an Issue in Your Schools. Common Ground,* a joint publication of the National Council of Teachers of English and the International Reading Association, is a source of many helpful suggestions for schools facing censorship.

Essential Elements of Educational Resource Selection Policies and Reevaluation Procedures

A decision must be made about what the Selection Policy and Reevaluation procedures will cover—classroom resources, library/media center resources or all resources used in the school or school district. (Whatever the decision, it should be noted that school districts must have policies covering all resources used, whether they are inclusive or separate.)

Selection Policy

1. Statement of the philosophy of resource selection for the school or district.

2. Statement of the objectives of resource selection.

3. Statement about intellectual freedom and the teachers' and students' constitutional rights to read, view and listen citing documents such as *Library Bill of Rights, Students' Right to Read, Freedom to View.*

4. Statement of the legal responsibility of the governing board and the delegation of authority to teachers and media people.

Selection Procedures

1. Description of resources covered by the policy.

2. Outline of the process used in the selection of resources.

3. Listing of criteria for the selection of all resources including gifts.

4. Statement that all resources selected will meet established criteria.

5. Procedures for selection including: consulting reputable selection sources, curriculum guides, preview and professional judgment.

6. Statement that recommendations for selection may be made by anyone but that final decisions for purchase are made by professional media personnel and teachers.

Reevaluation Procedures

1. Statement that the procedure applies to all requests for reevaluation including those originating from school personnel and School Board members.

2. Person to whom the request for reevaluation is directed.

3. Statement of procedure for informal meeting with the teacher or media person involved.

4. Explanation of the selection and reevaluation procedures and the use of the Statement of Concern about Library/Media Center Resources form.

5. Reevaluation committee—the members, how and when chosen or elected, length of term. Teachers and media personnel must be included on the committee, others may be included.

6. Outline of the process used by the reevaluation committee and a timeline.

7. Statement indicating open hearings including provision for testimony from appropriate individuals and open records.

8. Statement about the status of the resource during the reevaluation process.

9. Criteria for the reevaluation of resources.

10. Statement that the decision about the disposition of the resource be based on the established criteria.

11. Statement indicating to whom the decision of the reevaluation committee is communicated.

12. Statement of whether the decision relates to one grade level, one school or the entire district.

13. Statement of whether the same resources will be reevaluated more than once during a specified time period.

14. Provision for appeal to the School Board.

Supporting Documents

Library Bill of Rights (American Library Association)

Freedom to Read Statement (American Association of Publishers)

Freedom to View (Educational Film Library Association)

Students' Right to Read (National Council of Teachers of English)

Policy on the Freedom to Teach, to Learn, and to Express Ideas in the Public Schools (Minnesota State Board of Education)

Other documents mentioned in the policy

Scource: Minnesota Coalition Against Censorship
628 Central Avenue
Minneapolis, MN 55414
Adopted 5/22/1980
Revised 2/14/1985

A P P E N D I X   F

SLATE Starter Sheet: Developing Rationales

The purpose of this Starter Sheet is to help teachers and English language arts departments to develop rationales for the literature they use in their classrooms and to provide a list of rationales that are currently available through SLATE. It is organized into four areas: What is a rationale? Why develop them? How do we develop rationales? Where do we get more assistance?

What Is a Rationale?

We frequently hear the term *rationale* defined as a justification for doing something. Certainly that perspective is a vital one as we explore the need for developing rationales for books or other instructional material. Both Diane Shugert (1979) and Margaret Sacco (1993) advocate writing and keeping a file of rationales in advance as a defense against potential censorship. We will frame the discussion in a broader context, describing the overriding role of rationales in classroom planning. Teachers must make decisions about what they will teach and how they will then teach it, decisions that will achieve their purposes and address their students' needs. The value of developing a rationale is that it provides a framework for this planning.

Source: Jean E. Brown and Elaine C. Stephens. April 1994. In *SLATE Starter Sheet*. Urbana, Ill.: National Council of Teachers of English.

A rationale is the articulation of the reasons for using a particular literary work, film, or teaching method. Minimally, a rationale should include:

- a bibliographic citation and the intended audience
- a brief summary of the work and its educational significance
- the purposes of using the work and how it will be used
- potential problems with the work and how these can be handled
- alternative works an individual student might read or view

Shugert (1979) identifies criteria for assessing rationales. Among these guidelines are that they are well thought out, avoid specialized technical jargon, are specific and thorough, and are written so that they will be readily understood by teachers who use the work. These and other components of rationales will be explored in the section on Guidelines for Writing a Rationale.

Why Develop a Rationale?

Rationale development should be a part of thoughtful planning for classroom instruction. If we have not reflected on the *whys* of what we teach, we will be unprepared to meet the needs and challenges of our students and to respond to potential complaints, either from parents or from others in the community who seek to influence the curriculum.

While rationales are important in every aspect of teaching, we will focus here on the need for well-developed rationales for books used in the classroom—whether in whole-class instruction, small-group work, or classroom libraries. Teachers who make curricular decisions based upon mere expediency leave themselves vulnerable. Problems can be averted by carefully analyzing the audience (the students), the school, and the community and taking into full account the most effective means for meeting students' interests and educational needs.

How Do We Develop Rationales?

Teachers are frequently advised to have a written rationale for every book that they use. Realistically, this issue might be better addressed in a less absolute way by exploring four levels of rationale development. In an ideal situation, teachers would automatically write a rationale for every book that they teach, assign, include on a reading list, or keep in their classroom libraries. But mandating teachers to take on such a task when they are already overburdened is unrealistic and unreasonable. If teachers were required to write rationales for every book, many might simply stick to their literature anthologies and even avoid potentially controversial selections in those books. So while Shugert (1979, pp. 190–91) rightly cautions about using shortcuts to rationales, we do suggest options in the belief that the circumstances and conditions will determine what the teachers will do at any time.

1. A brief written statement of purpose for using a particular book—the *why* for using it and *where it will fit in the curriculum.* This is prepared by individual teachers based on the students, school, and community noted above and on curricular and instructional objectives and needs. At this level of rationale writing it is essential for teachers to have a *written* statement. Just thinking about the reason is not enough to demonstrate thoughtful planning, if a protest should arise, nor does it provide teachers with opportunities to be reflective about their decisions.

2. The second level involves a more detailed accounting through use of forms. Figures 1 and 2 show sample forms from the Connecticut Council of Teachers of English (Shugert, 1979, pp. 192–93). These samples provide two approaches—the first for an individual teacher to complete and the second for department members to fill out together. Of course, both forms can be modified to meet the needs of particular school situations.

3. The third level provides for the development of fully constituted rationales by individual teachers, departmental or district-wide committees, or the district English language arts coordinator or supervisor in cooperation with teachers. These rationales include many of the elements discussed above and will be explored further in the next section.

4. The fourth level calls for the collection of existing rationales that have been developed by other teachers or by professional organizations. By their nature these rationales are often comprehensive because they are developed as a service for schools that have challenges.

Guidelines for Writing a Rationale

The guidelines below will promote consistency as well as provide direction and support for writing rationales individually, in small collegial groups, or in departments. Sacco, in a paper prepared for the Assembly on Literature for Adolescents (ALAN) Intellectual Freedom Committee, and Shugert (1979) are among those who have presented systematic views of *how* to put together a rationale. Sacco uses a highly structured format in developing rationales with

Completion Form

Teacher's Rationale

School: Teacher:

Title:

Grade or Course:

Approximate date(s) a book will be used:

This book will be (check one or more):

☐   Studied by the whole class.

☐   Studied by small groups.

☐   Placed on a reading list.

☐   Placed in a classroom library.

☐   Recommended to individual students.

☐   Part of a larger study of (explain):

☐   Other (explain):

Ways in which the book is especially appropriate for students in this class:

Ways in which the book is especially pertinent to the objectives of this course or unit:

Special problems that might arise in relation to the book and some planned activities which handle this problem:

Some other appropriate books an individual student might read in place of this book:

Figure 1   Individual Teacher's Form

her undergraduate students; Shugert provides a more open ended approach based on the following questions posed by Donelson (1979, p. 166):

1. For what classes is this book especially appropriate?
2. To what particular objectives, literary or psychological or pedagogical, does this book lend itself?
3. In what ways will the book be used to meet those objectives?
4. What problems of style, tone, or theme or possible grounds for censorship exist in the book?

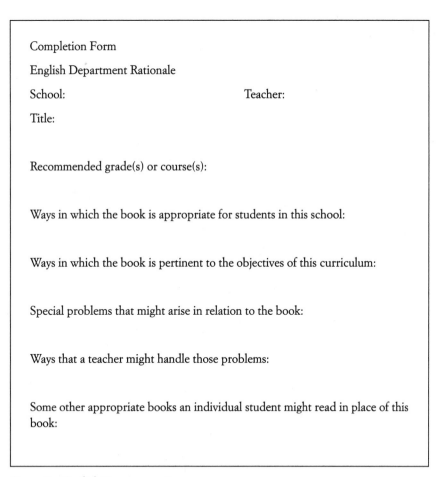

Completion Form

English Department Rationale

School: Teacher:

Title:

Recommended grade(s) or course(s):

Ways in which the book is appropriate for students in this school:

Ways in which the book is pertinent to the objectives of this curriculum:

Special problems that might arise in relation to the book:

Ways that a teacher might handle those problems:

Some other appropriate books an individual student might read in place of this book:

Figure 2   English Department Form

5. How does the teacher plan to meet those problems?

6. Assuming that the objectives are met, how would students be different because of their reading of this book? (p. 166)

Fundamentally, Sacco, Shugert, and Donelson concur that the role of the rationale is to provide a written statement of teachers' best professional perspective on their curriculum. The following guidelines for preparing rationales draw upon and synthesize their ideas.

1. *The bibliographic citation.* A rationale should begin with a complete bibliographic citation including author's name, complete book title, publisher, publication date, and edition.

2. *The intended audience.* The rationale should articulate the type of class and the range of grade levels at which the book will be used. The rationale should indicate whether the book is going to be used for individual study, small-group work, or whole-class study, along with an explanation of reasons for why the book is being used.

3. *A brief summary of the work.* There are a number of reasons for summarizing a book in the rationale. Writing a summary requires an in-depth look at the book. The summary provides an overview of the book for anyone who chooses to read it, and it can also reflect aspects of a work that the teacher considers most important and aspects that relate to its educational significance.

4. *The relationship of the book to the program.* Reading a book is not an isolated educational experience; as a part of the total program, the book should be consistent with the ongoing objectives of the class. Regardless of the quality of a book, if it does not make sense within the broad goals of the program, it is an inappropriate choice in that particular classroom. Any discussion of objectives should also include an examination of *how* a book will be used, including the teaching methodology and methods of assessment.

5. *The impact of the book.* One of the significant arguments for any work is the ways in which it will open new perspectives to its readers. In determining the reasons for using a book, teachers should also consider the potential impact it will have on students' behavior or attitudes.

6. *Potential problems with the work.* Teachers and districts are often blindsided by complaints that they never anticipated. The reflective process of developing a rationale is an opportunity for anticipating uses of language, actions, and situations in a work that might be the source of challenges. Additionally, as teachers examine potential problems, they have the

opportunity to make decisions about how to address the problems, establishing a framework that supports the book's quality and strengths. For example, a teacher might anticipate an objection to the language in Walter Dean Myers's *Fallen Angels*. The issue can be addressed within the context of the realistic portrayal of young men fighting in Vietnam; the language, while inappropriate in many settings, helps build the portrait of the war's horrors. The language quite simply adds to the book's credibility.

7. *Collection of information about the book.* It is useful to collect references about the book, especially published book reviews. Professional journals and booklists from various associations (e.g., NCTE, the International Reading Association, American Library Association, journals like *ALAN Review, Horn Book,* and *New Advocate,* as well as non-school sources like the *New York Times Book Review* and *Time* magazine, are rich resources that can be searched via various databases for reviews of particular books. Reviews that address any controversial issues in the book are particularly helpful. These materials should be kept in a file with the rationale.

8. *Collection of supplementary information.* Teachers should collect additional materials, such as biographical information about the author, especially if it includes any critical assessment of the author's work.

9. *Collection of books of rationales.* Books of rationales such as *Rationales for Commonly Challenged/Taught Books (Connecticut English Journal, Vol. 15,* 1983), *Celebrating Censored Books!* (Wisconsin Council of Teachers of English, Ed. Nicholas J. Karolides), and *Hit List* (Intellectual Freedom Committee, American Library Association, 1989) are valuable as part of the teacher's individual library or as part of the English department's professional library.

10. *Alternative works an individual student might read.* For each book they use, teachers should have a list of related titles that might serve either as an alternative or as a supplement to the book. The list of alternatives is useful when parents exercise their right to choose what their child will read. Additionally, the list may be used when students are choosing books from several options, or when they want to read related works. In other words, the listing can be useful in a number of ways, not just in response to a challenge.

What to Do Once There Is a Challenge

The widely used NCTE booklet entitled "The Students' Right to Read" (1977) provides a model for establishing an orderly process of review when books or other instructional materials are challenged. Rationales are dynamic documents that can play an important part in that process because they provide a perspective about the quality and value of a work.

When there is a challenge, the arena for the discussion becomes public, with many people involved. Too often, administrators are asked to respond to parental or public complaints about a work that they may never have read. School board members often are also involved. A rationale provides an orderly perspective about the quality and value of a work. It provides a summary, objectives for using the book, and potential problems in using it, as well as the background materials and opinions of the critics, all compiled in a folder for examination by those who will be involved in discussion of the challenge. Rationales are often used to refute the individual or collective charges that are made against a work. Additionally, the reviews and supplementary materials provide a framework of support from educators and critics.

Having a rationale can be equated to being prepared. Many groups that are organized to control the curriculum depend upon the schools to be unprepared when they mount a challenge. Being prepared can help schools to short-circuit highly organized challenges in some cases. Also, rationales can provide information that parents are seeking when they raise questions about curriculum materials.

Where to Get More Assistance—SLATE at Work

Rationales for works taught in English and language arts, K–12, are available through SLATE when particular book protests arise. The NCTE/SLATE program for responding to challenges to instructional materials is coordinated through the office of the Deputy Executive Director. SLATE has become an informal clearinghouse for rationales for works that are often taught (or included on booklists) in English and language arts, K–12, classrooms. Listed at the end of this SLATE Starter Sheet are the works for which rationales have already been prepared.

NCTE frequently receives calls for assistance from teachers in the field who are involved in book challenges. If the subject of protest is one of the books listed below, SLATE sends rationales to the teacher at no cost. In response to calls for assistance, SLATE also sends, at no cost, a Censorship Packet that includes "The Students' Right to Read," "Guidelines for Dealing with Censorship of Nonprint Materials," and other useful documents. Frequently, representatives of SLATE also write letters in defense of challenged books to appropriate administrators or school board members. This is done in cooperation with local and regional SLATE representatives and sometimes with additional support from organizations such as the American Library

Association, National Education Association, American Federation of Teachers, International Reading Association, or the National Coalition Against Censorship. The Council sometimes signs on to *amicus* briefs when censorship cases go to court.

You are urged to save the list at the end of this Starter Sheet and refer to it in the event of book challenges in your school, district, or state. The list, which presently contains rationales for over 200 titles, will continue to grow as SLATE learns about new book challenges. If you think a particular work should be included, and it is not on the list, please send the title and author to SLATE, c/o NCTE, 1111 W. Kenyon Road, Urbana, IL 61801-1096. Better yet, you can volunteer to write a rationale for the book in accordance with the guidelines for rationales described here.

The rationales at NCTE are drawn from several sources, including the previously mentioned resources: *Rationales for Commonly Taught Books, Celebrating Censored Books!* and *Hit List.* Some of the rationales were written by teachers, others by supervisors, and others by teacher educators. By far the most prolific contributor has been Margaret Sacco, who with the students in her adolescent literature and media course at Miami University, Ohio, has written dozens of rationales for young adult novels in cooperation with ALAN. SLATE is grateful for her continuing contributions and for the pioneering work done by the Connecticut and Wisconsin affiliates in the aforementioned publications.

SLATE emphasizes that the books listed below and the rationales for them in no way constitute an "approved" NCTE reading list. Selection of instructional materials and development of appropriate criteria for inclusion in K–12 programs should be geared toward local situations and should range more widely than any particular list can suggest. Similarly, the existence of a rationale for a particular book does not imply that the book is endorsed for teaching in any grade and under all conditions. For example, teachers might judge some books to be more appropriate for inclusion on an optional reading list than for whole-class study. Other books might be seen as particularly appropriate for certain grade levels or student populations. Again, such decisions are in the realm of the professional judgment of teachers in the field. The primary use of rationales is to provide additional support and documentation for the thoughtful educational choices that are made by teachers.

References

American Library Association. Young Adult Services Division's Intellectual Freedom Committee (1989). *Hit List: Frequently Challenged Young Adult Titles: References to Defend Them.* Chicago: ALA.

Donelson, K. (1979). "Censorship in the 1970s: Some Ways to Handle It When It Comes (And It Will)" in *Dealing with Censorship,* edited by James Davis. Urbana, IL: NCTE.

Karolides, N. J., and L. Burress, editors. (1985). *Celebrating Censored Books!* Racine: Wisconsin Council of Teachers of English.

NCTE Committee on the Right to Read. (1982). "The Students' Right to Read." Urbana, IL: NCTE.

NCTE Task Force on Guidelines for Dealing with Censorship of Nonprint Materials. (1993). "Guidelines for Dealing with Censorship of Nonprint Materials." Urbana, IL: NCTE.

Sacco, M. T. "Writing Rationales for Using Young Adult Literature in the Classroom," unpublished manuscript.

Shugert, D., editor. (1983). *Rationales for Commonly Challenged/Taught Books* in *Connecticut English Journal,* Vol. 15, 1983.

Shugert, D. (1979). "How to Write a Rationale in Defense of a Book," in *Dealing with Censorship,* edited by James Davis. Urbana, IL: NCTE.

Books for Which Rationales Are Available in Censorship Cases

About David, Susan Beth Pfeffer
After the First Death,
    Robert Cormier
After the First Love,
    Isabelle Holland
All Together Now,
    Sue Ellen Bridgers
Animal Farm, George Orwell
Annie on My Mind, Nancy Garden
Are You in the House Alone?
    Richard Peck
Arizona Kid, Ron Koertge
The Autobiography of Miss Jane
    Pittman, Ernest Gaines
A Band of Angels, Julian Thompson
Being There, Jerzy Kosinski
Benjamin Franklin, Ingri d'Aulaire
The Best Christmas Pageant Ever,
    Barbara Robinson
Beyond the Chocolate War,
    Robert Cormier

The Bible
Black Boy, Richard Wright
Black Like Me, John Griffin
Bless the Beasts and Children,
    Glendon Swarthout
Blood Red Ochre, Kevin Major
Blubber, Judy Blume
Brave New World, Aldous Huxley
Bridge to Terabithia,
    Katherine Paterson
Building Blocks, Cynthia Voigt
The Bumblebee Flies Anyway,
    Robert Cormier
The Cage, Ruth Minsky Spender
Call it Courage, Sperry Armstrong
The Canterbury Tales,
    Geoffrey Chaucer
The Cay, Theodore Taylor
Catch 22, Joseph Heller
Catcher in the Rye, J. D. Salinger
Charlotte's Web, E. B. White

The Chocolate War, Robert Cormier
A Clockwork Orange,
    Anthony Burgess
Cold Sassy Tree, Olive Ann Burns
The Color Purple, Alice Walker
Commander Toad in Space,
    Jane Yolen
The Contender, Robert Lipsyte
Crow Boy, Taro Yashima
The Crucible, Arthur Miller
Cry, The Beloved Country,
    Alan Paton
Cujo, Stephen King
Daddy's Roommate,
    Michael Willhoite
A Day No Pigs Would Die,
    Robert Peck
*The Day They Came to Arrest the
    Book,* Nat Hentoff
Death Be Not Proud, John Gunther
Death of a Salesman,
    Arthur Miller
Deenie, Judy Blume
Deliverance, James Dickey
Diary of a Young Girl, Anne Frank
Dicey's Song, Cynthia Voigt
Dinky Hocker Shoots Smack,
    M. E. Kerr
The Divorce Express,
    Paula Danziger
Don't Look Behind You,
    Lois Duncan
Duplicate, William Sleator
The Electric Kool-Aid Acid Test,
    Tom Wolfe
"Enoch," Robert Bloch
Ethan Frome, Edith Wharton
The Executioner, Jay Bennett
Fade, Robert Cormier
Fallen Angels, Walter Dean Myers

Famous All Over Town,
    Danny Santiago
Far from Shore, Kevin Major
A Farewell to Arms,
    Ernest Hemingway
Fell, M. E. Kerr
Flowers for Algernon, Daniel Keyes
Forever, Judy Blume
*From the Mixed Up Files of Mrs.
    Basil E. Frankweiler,*
    E. L. Konigsburg
A Gathering of Old Men,
    Ernest J. Gaines
The Giver, Lynn Hall
Go Ask Alice, Anonymous
The Goats, Brock Cole
Going for the Big One,
    P. J. Petersen
The Good Earth, Pearl Buck
Good-bye and Keep Cold, J. Davis
Good-bye Tomorrow,
    Gloria D. Miklowitz
The Grapes of Wrath,
    John Steinbeck
The Great Gatsby,
    F. Scott Fitzgerald
The Great Gilly Hopkins,
    Katherine Paterson
Grendel, John Gardner
The Grounding of Group 6,
    Julian Thompson
Hamlet, William Shakespeare
Happy Endings Are All Alike,
    Sandra Scoppettone
Harriet the Spy, Louise Fitzhugh
Healer, Peter Dickinson
The Heart Is a Lonely Hunter,
    Carson McCullers
*A Hero Ain't Nothin' but a
    Sandwich,* Alice Childress

Hiroshima, John Hersey
The Hobbit, J. R. R. Tolkien
Home before Dark,
    Sue Ellen Bridgers
House of Stairs, William Sleator
Huckleberry Finn, Mark Twain
I Am the Cheese, Robert Cormier
I Know Why the Caged Bird Sings,
    Maya Angelou
I Never Promised You a Rose
    Garden, Joanne Greenberg
If Beale Street Could Talk,
    James Baldwin
I'll Get There, It Better Be Worth
    the Trip, John Donovan
In Country, Bobbie Mason
In the Night Kitchen, Maurice
    Sendak
Interstellar Pig, William Sleator
It's OK If You Don't Love Me,
    Norma Klein
Izzy, Willy-Nilly, Cynthia Voigt
Jacob Have I Loved,
    Katherine Paterson
James and the Giant Peach,
    Roald Dahl
Jane Eyre, Charlotte Brontë
Johnny Got His Gun,
    Dalton Trumbo
Journey to Topaz, Yoshiko Uchida
Jubilee, Margaret Walker
Julie of the Wolves,
    Jean Craighead George
Killing Mr. Griffin, Lois Duncan
King of the Wind, Marguerite Henry
The Last Mission, Harry Mazer
The Late Great Me,
    Sandra Scoppettone
Learning How to Fall, Norma Klein
The Learning Tree, Gordon Parks

A Light in the Attic, Shel Silverstein
The Little House on the Prairie,
    Laura Wilder
Little Women, Louisa Alcott
Lord of the Flies, William Golding
The Lords of Discipline, Pat Conroy
"The Lottery," Shirley Jackson
Love Is Not Enough, Marilyn Levy
Love Story, Eric Segal
The Man without a Face,
    Isabelle Holland
Manchild in the Promised Land,
    Claude Brown
Maniac Magee, Jerry Spinelli
May I Cross Your Golden River,
    Paige Dixon
Memory, Margaret Mahy
Merchant of Venice,
    William Shakespeare
Midnight Hour Encores,
    Bruce Brooks
Mr. & Mrs. Bo Jo Jones, Ann Head
Mr. Popper's Penguins,
    Richard Atwater
The Moffats, Eleanor Estes
Mom, the Wolfman and Me,
    Norma Klein
Moonlight Man, Paula Fox
Morris, the Moose, B. Wiseman
The Moves Make the Man,
    Bruce Brooks
My Brother Sam Is Dead,
    James Lincoln and
    Christopher Collier
My Darling, My Hamburger,
    Paul Zindel
Never Cry Wolf, Farley Mowat
Night Kites, M. E. Kerr
Nineteen Eighty-Four,
    George Orwell

No More Saturday Nights,
Norma Klein
Of Mice and Men, John Steinbeck
The Old Man and the Sea,
Ernest Hemingway
On Fire, Ouida Sebestyen
On the Beach, Nevil Shute
*One Day in the Life of Ivan
Denisovich,*
Aleksander Solzhenitsyn
One Fat Summer, Robert Lipsyte
One Fine Day, Nonny Hogrogran
One Flew over the Cuckoo's Nest,
Ken Kesey
Ordinary People, Judith Guest
Other Bells for Us to Ring,
Robert Cormier
The Other Way to Listen,
Byrd Baylor
*Our Bodies, Ourselves: A Book by
and for Women,* Boston
Women's Health Book
Collective Staff
The Outsiders, S. E. Hinton
The Pearl, John Steinbeck
Permanent Connections, Sue
Ellen Bridgers
Pet Semetary, Stephen King
The Pigman, Paul Zindel
Prank, Kathryn Lasky
Princess Ashley, Richard Peck
Rage, Richard Bachman
(aka Stephen King)
Ragtime, E. L. Doctorow
Remembering the Good Times,
Richard Peck
Robodad, Alden Carter
Roll of Thunder, Hear My Cry,
Mildred Taylor

Romeo & Juliet,
William Shakespeare
Run, Shelley, Run!,
Gertrude Samuels
Running Loose, Chris Crutcher
The Scarlet Letter,
Nathaniel Hawthorne
Secrets Not Meant to Be Kept,
Gloria Miklowitz
A Separate Peace, John Knowles
Seventeen against the Dealer,
Cynthia Voigt
Sex Education, Jenny Davis
Sheila's Dying, Alden Carter
The Silver Kiss, Annette Klause
Simon Pure, Julian F. Thompson
Singularity, William Sleator
Slaughterhouse Five, Kurt Vonnegut
The Slave Dancer, Paula Fox
Snow Treasure, Marie McSwigan
*Starring Sally J. Freedman as
Herself,* Judy Blume
Steffie Can't Come Out to Play,
Fran Arrick
Stotan!, Chris Crutcher
Stranger with My Face,
Lois Duncan
Strega Nona, Thomas
Anthony de Paola
Summer of Fear, Lois Duncan
Summer of My German Soldier,
Bette Greene
Summer Rules, Robert Lipsyte
Sweet Bells Jangled Out of Tune,
Robin Brancato
Sweet Whispers, Brother Rush,
Virginia Hamilton
The Tale of Peter Rabbit,
Beatrix Potter

Tales of a Fourth-Grade Nothing,
    Judy Blume
Taming the Star Runner,
    S. E. Hinton
A Taste of Blackberries, Doris Smith
Tell Us Your Secret, Barbara Cohen
That's My Baby, Norma Klein
Their Eyes Were Watching God,
    Zora Neale Hurston
Then Again Maybe I Won't,
    Judy Blume
Thirty-Six Exposures, Kevin Major
Tiger Eyes, Judy Blume
To Kill a Mockingbird, Harper Lee
Tom Sawyer, Mark Twain
A Tree Grows in Brooklyn,
    Betty Smith
Trouble River, Betsy Byars
The Truth Trap, Francis A. Miller
Trying Hard to Hear You,
    Sandra Scoppettone
Tunnel Vision, Fran Arrick
Up a Road Slowly, Irene Hunt
Up Country, Alden Carter
Up in Seth's Room, Norma Mazer
The Very Hungry Caterpillar,
    Eric Carle
Wart, Son of Toad, Alden Carter

*A Way of Love, A Way of Life: A
    Young Person's Guide to What It
    Means to Be Gay,*
    Frances Hanckel and
    John Cunningham
We All Fall Down, Robert Cormier
Weetzie Bat, Francesca Lia Block
The Westing Game, Ellen Raskin
When the Phone Rang,
    Harry Mazer
Where It Stops, Nobody Knows,
    Amy Ehrlich
Where the Red Fern Grows,
    Wilson Rawls
Where the Sidewalk Ends,
    Shel Silverstein
Where the Wild Things Are,
    Maurice Sendak
A White Romance,
    Virginia Hamilton
Winnie the Pooh, A. A. Milne
Winning, Robin Brancato
Words by Heart, Ouida Sebestyen
A Wrinkle in Time,
    Madeleine L'Engle
Wuthering Heights, Emily Brontë
The Year of the Gopher,
    Phyllis Naylor

Author and Title Index

Subject Index